Unmasking the Angel

Unmasking the Angel

Revealing the Spiritual Identity of a Local Congregation

BY Stephen Langford

FOREWORD BY
Ruth Gouldbourne

WIPF & STOCK · Eugene, Oregon

UNMASKING THE ANGEL
Revealing the Spiritual Identity of a Local Congregation

Copyright © 2025 Stephen Langford. All rights reserved. Except for brief quotations in critical publications or reviews, no part of this book may be reproduced in any manner without prior written permission from the publisher. Write: Permissions, Wipf and Stock Publishers, 199 W. 8th Ave., Suite 3, Eugene, OR 97401.

Wipf & Stock
An Imprint of Wipf and Stock Publishers
199 W. 8th Ave., Suite 3
Eugene, OR 97401

www.wipfandstock.com

PAPERBACK ISBN: 978-1-6667-4301-2
HARDCOVER ISBN: 978-1-6667-4302-9
EBOOK ISBN: 978-1-6667-4303-6

VERSION NUMBER 04/28/25

Steinke, Peter L. *Healthy Congregations: A Systems Approach.* Herndon, VA: The Alban Institute, 1996. Published by Rowman and Litterfield Publishing Group Inc. Reproduced with permission by The Licensor through PLSclear Ref No: 104061

Lucie-Smith, Alexander. *Narrative Theology and Moral Theology.* Aldershot: Ashgate Publishing Ltd, 2007. Published by Informa UK Limited. Reproduced with permission by The Licensor through PLSclear Ref No: 88796

Scriptures taken from the Holy Bible, New International Version®, NIV®. Copyright © 1973, 1978, 1984, 2011 by Biblica, Inc.™ Used by permission of Zondervan. All rights reserved worldwide. www.zondervan.com The "NIV" and "New International Version" are trademarks registered in the United States Patent and Trademark Office by Biblica, Inc.™

To Elaine Langford and Brian Haymes
without whom this book would never have been written

Contents

Foreword by Ruth Gouldbourne | ix
Preface | xi
Acknowledgments | xiii

Introduction | 1
1 What is the angel of the church? | 24
2 Architecture and Ambience | 37
3 Demographics | 61
4 Authority, Ministry, and Power | 100
5 Handling Conflict | 130
6 Denominational Rubrics, Theology, and Worship | 156
7 Self-Understanding | 194
8 Transforming the Angel and Drawing Conclusions | 216

Bibliography | 233
Index | 243

Foreword

ALTHOUGH WE NUMBER OVER two thousand churches in our denomination, we do not have the capacity to provide a large number of those who are purely devoted to scholarship among us, and so we are deeply indebted to those who combine roles. We have a long and distinguished tradition of scholar pastors; those who as well as serving our local churches also do serious academic work and also the work needed to make it available beyond the academy.

We count Steve Langford among this number. Having taken time out to write his doctoral thesis, he has now found time as part of his ministerial service to edit it for a wider readership in this volume.

As a community of two thousand or so churches, we are wide-ranging and diverse, each congregation having its own story and setting. In this work, Langford offers a creative approach to understanding individual church communities and, particularly for ministers, of serving them effectively. Interacting with the work of Walter Wink in particular, and considering issues raised by his writings on "the angel of the church," he examines the life story of three different congregations with the intention of exploring how records and memories, buildings and settings can aid the understanding of the identity of the "angel." He then develops the ideas in ways that offer possibilities for enabling congregations to live in harmony with their vocation and explore their identities as communities of the people of God for their particular places and times with imagination and faithfulness.

By investigating history, Langford enables us to see how patterns and assumptions are expressed as identity, and he explores how these might be developed, questioned, challenged, or renewed, and thus offers insights for congregations seeking to be faithful and appropriate in a world that is different from that in which they started up.

In addition to his engagement with Wink's writings, Langford also draws on a wide range of scholars to explore further the dynamic of congregational life, and he offers these insights in a coherent whole, offering to those who serve churches to draw on and explore material that would otherwise often be hidden away.

Langford has a rich personal ministry of enabling congregations to understand their stories and take steps into fruitful futures. In this presentation of his thesis, he offers these riches to a wider community. This is a gift indeed.

Rev. Dr. Ruth Gouldbourne

Preface

Rev. David Runcorn could not possibly have known what he had started when, in 1999, he addressed a class of mixed Anglican and Baptist students at Trinity College in Bristol. As part of a series of lectures on pastoral theology, Runcorn introduced his students to the work of Walter Wink and the concept of the angel of the church.

Developing the idea that there was a spiritual dimension of the earthly church encapsulated within a transcendent being called "the angel of the church," Runcorn was captivating. He spoke from his own experience in ministry and urged his students to read through the records of the churches where they served. He argued that in the stories told and the actions taken by a congregation, the key lay to understanding the nature of the angel of a church. Twenty-five years later, I have finally settled down to write this book.

The book itself is based on the thesis that I submitted to the University of Bristol and Bristol Baptist College in 2017 and formed the basis of my PhD. It is, therefore, an academic text and reads as such. Although my passion for the spiritual nature of the church has developed over the past twenty years, it continues to owe its beginning to the enthusiasm expressed by Runcorn during his lecture on Walter Wink and the angels of churches.

At this point, I should probably say that I am a Baptist by conviction, and therefore, the stories that I will tell to illustrate and explore Wink's concept of the angel of the church will come from local Baptist congregations. Despite this, many of the illustrations will be applicable across different church traditions. Indeed, Runcorn is an Anglican priest, and before he died in 2012, Wink was a Methodist. Having said this, I recognize that there are parts of this book where as I explore areas of ecclesiology the stories will not necessarily translate into another tradition. For this, I seek your forbearance.

The book itself follows a pattern set out by Wink in his chapter "The Angel of the Church" in *Unmasking the Powers*. Here, he considers an eclectic collection of subjects relating to church life. These include the physical architecture of the building within which the church gathers for worship, their demographic makeup, and their approach to authority, ministry, and power. Taking each aspect of Wink's concept in turn, I seek to examine, critique, and justify them through the stories told in the minute books of the Baptist churches in Budleigh Salterton, Newton Abbot, and South Street in Exeter. The stories themselves are interesting in their own right; however, when put together, they form a mosaic of impressions that reveal the spiritual nature, and thus the angel, of each of the congregations.

In many ways, the work started in this book is unfinished, and with that in mind, my quest to understand the angels of the churches within which I serve continues. What is more, I hope that in publishing my research, someone might take up the baton and explore further what it means to understand and engage with the angel of the church.

Acknowledgments

As I have mentioned above, this book is based on my PhD thesis. Undertaking this, I spent three happy years at Bristol Baptist College under the supervision of Stuart Murray Williams. It was under his gentle guidance that my thesis emerged.

By its very nature, original research requires source material, and in this respect, I am eternally grateful to the staff at the Devon Heritage Centre in Exeter, as much of the material for this book came from the records that they hold. I am also grateful for the leaders, past and present, from the Baptist churches in Bovey Tracey, Budleigh Salterton, Kilmington and South Street Exeter and the now-closed church in Newton Abbot, who have permitted me to publish their stories. Any errors in the telling of these stories are my own.

As for the secondary material used in the original thesis and the book, I was fortunate to have access to the full range of libraries at Bristol University as well as the theological libraries at Bristol Baptist College and Trinity College. For this, I am grateful. I am particularly thankful to Mike Brealey, the librarian during my time at Bristol Baptist College, whose willingness and ability to obtain some of the more obscure reference books used in the original research was invaluable.

In addition to material, research also requires funding and, in this respect, therefore, I am deeply thankful to the trustees of the Lacy Ashton Trust, the Caleb Bailey Trust, and the Bristol Baptist Fund for providing financial assistance during my period of study. I am also grateful to my mum, Joyce Langford, who released a legacy from my late father, Michael Gerald Langford, which went a long way toward paying my college fees.

Inevitably, transforming a PhD thesis into a book takes time. In this respect, I am thankful to the congregations at St. Andrew's Street Baptist

Church Cambridge and Bromley Baptist Church for allowing me the time to undertake the necessary transformation.

Finally, I am indebted to the boundless love, encouragement, and belief in me and my work given to me by my wife, Elaine Langford. I am also grateful for the gentle persuasion to publish from my late friend and mentor, Brian Haymes. Without the help of these two, my PhD would remain gathering dust on the shelves of Bristol University and Bristol Baptist College.

Introduction

BORN IN 1935, WALTER Wink studied for his undergraduate degree at Southern Methodist University in Dallas, where he majored in history and minored in philosophy and English. His postgraduate education took place at Union Theological Seminary, New York City, where he was awarded an MDiv in 1959 and a PhD in 1963. From 1976 until he died in 2012, he was professor of biblical interpretation at Auburn Theological Seminary in New York City.[1] During his academic career, Wink published works on biblical interpretation and addressing spiritual powers. However, his most prolific work was in the field of non-violent responses to conflict and injustice. In this arena, his research combines a biblical understanding of spiritual power with an appreciation of the underlying earthly power structures at work in the governance of nations. He uses this appreciation of the spiritual nature of earthly power structures in his reflection on the end of apartheid in South Africa.[2] As an appreciation of his work "The Effectiveness of Nonviolent Strategies for Social Change and the Biblical Roots of Nonviolent Philosophy," Wink was awarded the 1989–90 Peace Fellowship by the United States Institute of Peace.[3] In addition to being a renowned advocate of non-violence, Wink is also well known for his trilogy of works on spiritual power: *Naming the Powers*, *Unmasking the Powers*, and *Engaging the Powers*.

---

1. This information was originally available from Walter Wink's online curriculum vitae. However, the information was taken down shortly after his death in 2012 and is now available at Wikipedia, Walter Wink."
2. Wink, *Violence and Nonviolence in South Africa*.
3. United States Institute of Peace, "Former Senior Fellows."

The Powers Trilogy

As its title suggests, the focus of his first book on this subject, *Naming the Powers*, is an exercise in naming and defining the roles of power in a society. It is primarily an explanation of the offices and exercise of power described in the New Testament. These powers are not necessarily spiritual. Throughout *Naming the Powers*, Wink is careful to differentiate between the power exercised by earthly authorities and spiritual entities. As he names the powers, Wink cross-references biblical texts with passages from Jewish intertestamental literature. This adds an additional dimension to his explanation and introduces the reader to the influence of the intertestamental theology on New Testament literature. It is not until his second book, *Unmasking the Powers*, that he explores some well-known titles of spiritual entities in detail. *Unmasking the Powers* contains chapters exploring how Satan and demons might be understood as well as an exploration of three types of angels.[4] Wink's third work, *Engaging the Powers*, moves away from these spiritual archetypes and focuses on a nonviolent engagement with the prevailing domination system.[5] While the term "domination system" might be interpreted as a form of spiritual power, Wink uses the term in confluence with "the myth of redemptive violence."[6] Thus, *Engaging the Powers* is primarily a polemic against a worldview that justifies the use of good or justifiable violence to combat the intrusion of bad or unjustified violence. In addition to his Powers Trilogy, Wink explores the nature of spiritual power in two other key publications: *When the Powers Fall: Reconciliation in the Healing of Nations* and *The Powers That Be: Theology for a New Millennium*. *When The Powers Fall* was written for the Life and Peace Institute and acts as an introduction to a series of works entitled *Reconciliation and the Church in Transition to Democracy*.[7] His work *The Powers That Be* is a digest of the earlier Powers Trilogy with some additional material from *Violence and Nonviolence in South Africa*.[8] Neither of these significantly

---

4. Wink, *Unmasking the Powers*, vii–viii.

5. Wink uses the term "domination system" in the title for each of the first five chapters of *Engaging the Powers*.

6. Wink, *Engaging the Powers*.

7. Wink, *When the Powers Fall*, vii. This book was originally published under the title *Healing a Nation's Wounds: Reconciliation on the Road to Democracy* (1997) by the Life and Peace Institute.

8. Wink, *Powers That Be*, ix.

adds to his description of spiritual entities. This means that the majority of Wink's work on the gods, angels, and demons is found in *Unmasking the Powers*. However, even here, Wink only dedicates a single chapter to the angel of the church.[9]

Wink's exploration of spiritual power appears to divide opinion, with Andrew Lincoln describing the trilogy as "brilliant" and Clinton Arnold offering a substantial critique.[10] The foundation of Arnold's critique is that Wink's work is based on a belief that spiritual powers are a myth and, therefore, do not exist in reality.[11] Although this is Wink's starting point, Arnold's critique does not account for how Wink's theology develops.

The Angel of the Church

A developing theology may explain why Wink's definition of the angel of the church is imprecise. Initially, he describes the angel as a spiritual guide, implying that it is a transcendent entity that exists separately and yet is inseparable from the church.[12] However, he also uses the term as a collective noun, suggesting that the concept encapsulates the social dynamics, aspirations, and vocation of the church. If this second position were to represent the totality of his belief, there would be a strong argument that his description of the angel of the church is purely sociological. In this respect, some aspects of Wink's work clearly resonate with a sociological approach; however, this does not do justice to the compass of his position. The description of the angel of the church is, for Wink, part of a journey of faith that takes him from a form of theology that seeks to deconstruct and rationalize the mystical aspects of Christian faith to a position that embraces them.[13]

Wink first noticed the significance of the angel of the church in 1964 when, as a result of his teaching on the book of Revelation, he was struck by how the letters to the seven churches in chapters 2 and 3 are addressed to the angel and not to a leader or a faith community.[14] In view of this, he begins his chapter by considering how the term "angel of the church"

9. Wink, *Unmasking the Powers*, 69–86.

10. Lincoln, "Liberation from the Powers," 335; Arnold, *Powers of Darkness*, 198–201.

11. Arnold, *Powers of Darkness*, 199.

12. Wink, *Unmasking the Powers*, 70.

13. Wink, *Naming the Powers*, 5.

14. Wink, *Unmasking the Powers*, 69.

might be understood. As with the quest to define Wink's concept, defining the angel of the church is not a straightforward task. While the Greek word *angelos is* widely translated as "messenger," strictly how the messenger to the church is interpreted is complex. This is particularly true in the book of Revelation where angels appear to fulfill a multiplicity of roles. Although this complexity will be explored in the next chapter, in summary, Wink takes the view that the angel of the church is a development of the idea that individual nations each have their own guardian angel.[15]

Is the angel an entity?

Although Wink explores the concepts of angels of nations and churches in *Unmasking the Powers*, he will not be drawn on whether the angel of the church has a metaphysical status. However, he is willing to describe the angel of the church as a collective entity. What is more, Wink is willing to concede that the angel of the church has an inner spirit that reveals itself in the personality and vocation of the earthly church. He also argues that this viewpoint correlates with how the ancients understood angels.[16]

Adopting this position, Wink reveals a tension within his theological stance. While his trilogy of publications on spiritual power represents a journey into mystical theology, his training in rational thought moves him away from accepting that angels are an entity. Furthermore, by correlating an ancient understanding of angels with an organization's inner spirit, Wink does not do himself justice with respect to his later description of the interaction between the transcendent and earthly realms. This is particularly evident in his discussion with a minister named Melinda over the nature of the angel of one of the churches she pastors. Although the story of Melinda will be explored toward the end of this book, at this point, it is important to note that, as part of Wink's discussion with Melinda, he asked her to construct a representation of the angel of her church.[17] While asking Melinda to construct the angel of her congregation does not necessarily mean that the spirit of the church takes the form of an entity, Wink is suggesting that she construct a physical representation of something that exists.

---

15. Wink, *Unmasking the Powers*, 69–70.
16. Wink, *Unmasking the Powers*, 71.
17. Wink, *Unmasking the Powers*, 84.

Vocation

Exploring the nature of the church and its angel, Wink begins with a review of letters to the seven churches in the book of Revelation. Here, he notes the similarity in structure, with each of the letters being divided into three sections:

i. An introduction affirming that these are the words of Christ;

ii. The body of the letter where the issues facing the church are highlighted and a prescription offered;

iii. The conclusion that contains an appeal to listen to the challenge being presented and the promise of a reward for participating in the transformation.[18]

Although each of the seven letters follows a similar format, each is tailored to address the specific situation of each congregation. This suggests that if a congregation is represented by its own particular angel, the nature of each angel will differ. Wink's work supports this position, arguing that the nature of the angel of the church is formed out of two co-existing attributes: the current nature of the church and its vocation.[19]

As will become evident in the lives of the congregations explored in this thesis, the nature of the church is a complex mix of positive and negative attributes. Wink makes a similar observation with respect to the angels of the churches addressed in Revelation. However, he suggests that, such is the dysfunctional nature of these churches, their continued existence is not linked to their earthly acumen. Instead, Wink argues, the churches addressed in the opening chapters of Revelation continue to exist because of their role in proclaiming Christ to their locality. Although significant in differentiating the church from other organizations, the proclamation of Christ forms part of a congregation's vocation. For Wink, a church's vocation also encompasses the possibility of what the church might become in Christ. Reflecting on the letters to the seven churches, Wink notes that each letter contains an appeal to be transformed. It is these exhortations that provide an eschatological dimension to a congregation's vocation. Furthermore, it is this potential of what a church might become in Christ that sets a congregation's vocation apart from all other organizations.

---

18. Wink, *Unmasking the Powers*, 72.
19. Wink, *Unmasking the Powers*, 72–73.

According to Wink, the coexistence of the current personality of a church and the possibility of what it might become in Christ provides a rich source of material by which the spiritual nature of a congregation can be studied.[20] Traditionally, congregational analysis has been carried out using a variety of disciplines that together have become known as congregational studies. However, while Wink might consider his work to be a form of congregational analysis, the eschatological dimension of a congregation's life is one of the features that sets his work apart from the traditional forms of congregational studies.

As its title suggests, congregational studies is the study of faith communities. While the discipline has received a high profile in the USA, it has an equally long history in the United Kingdom.[21] Traditionally, as scholars have observed and reflected on the way congregations function, they have drawn upon one or more of four academic disciplines, anthropology, sociology, organizational systems, and theology, to describe their findings.[22] In addition to using these tools, congregational studies are usually divided into two types: "extrinsic" and "intrinsic" studies.[23] "Extrinsic studies" evaluates the church on a broad canvas, such as its role within society[24] or the characteristics of church growth,[25] whereas "intrinsic studies" considers the life of the congregation, either in relation to itself or other congregations.[26] The transcendent element of Wink's concept of the angel of the church extends both the traditional intrinsic and extrinsic forms of congregational studies by including the influence of the heavenly realms.

A Polemic Against a Materialistic Mindset

In addition to using the concept of an angel of the church as a form of congregational studies, Wink also uses the term "angel" as a polemic against a materialistic mindset. He argues for rediscovering the way early

---

20. Wink, *Unmasking the Powers*, 73.
21. Guest et al., *Congregational Studies in the UK*, xi.
22. Cameron et al., *Studying Local Churches*, 12–18.
23. Guest et al., *Congregational Studies in the UK*, 1.
24. Guest et al., *Congregational Studies in the UK*, 2.
25. Guest et al., *Congregational Studies in the UK*, 5–6.
26. Guest et al., *Congregational Studies in the UK*, 2.

faith communities understood angels, demons, and spiritual powers.[27] According to Wink, this requires a mythical reading of *Archon*, the Greek word for power.[28] The argument for a mystical or, perhaps more specifically, a transcendent understanding of spiritual powers is not without its supporters. In *The Future of Man*, Teilhard de Chardin argues along similar lines.[29] Writing in 1959, de Chardin is aware of a growing rejection of religious faith.[30] He suggests that this is due to the expansion of the enlightenment which has, in turn, led to the belief that the socialization process that human beings are involved in will eventually result in the birth of an ultra-human.[31] Concluding his exploration of this process, de Chardin argues that the choice between Marxism and a form of Christianity has lost its zest, and human beings will eventually struggle to find a spiritual home.[32] By offering the choice of Marxism or lukewarm Christianity, de Chardin's work is placed within a distinct historical context. However, his argument for a resurgence of authentic faith continues to resonate well beyond the fall of Communism and its attendant critique of Marxism.[33] In view of de Chardin's concerns, Wink's desire to reintroduce a theological language that encompasses angels, demons, and spiritual powers creates a significantly new paradigm for congregational studies. This is not to say that traditional forms of congregational studies do not have a theological dimension. However, Wink's introduction of the concept of a transcendent entity reflecting the earthly church differentiates his work from other commentators on church life.[34]

Corporate Angels

One of the questions arising from Wink's work on the angel of church is, "Do all organizations have an angel?" This question arises from Wink's use of the motor manufacturer General Motors to illustrate the spiritual

---

27. Wink, *Unmasking the Powers*, 3.
28. Wink, *Cracking the Gnostic Code*, 5.
29. Wink cites de Chardin in this respect in *Unmasking the Powers*, 3.
30. Chardin, *Future of Man*, 272.
31. Chardin, *Future of Man*, 273–74.
32. Chardin, *Future of Man*, 281.
33. Chardin, *Future of Man*, 281.
34. Cameron et al., *Studying Local Churches*, provides an example of theology being used as a tool for congregational studies.

resilience intrinsic to the angel of the church.[35] Within Wink's work, the question of angels of organizations other than the church is not clearly defined. While he advocates that the church is unique due to its role in presenting Christ to its locality, he also suggests that all corporations have an inner reality. However, he caveats this with the contention that this inner reality would have been called an angel in the ancient world.[36] Though this could imply that Wink is simply using the term "angel" to describe what might be called a system by psychologists or an institutional structure by sociologists, his commitment to rediscovering the transcendent nature of the church suggests otherwise.

The question of corporate angels is complicated still further when placed within the matrix of Wink's exploration of the angels of nations. For, there is a strong argument for the angels of churches being different from other organizations due to their role in proclaiming Christ. However, this may not be so in the case of nations. Unfortunately, although Wink is committed to rediscovering a spiritual language to encompass the way churches and nations function within *Unmasking the Powers*, he does not extend his work to exploring the angels of organizations. This may be because although the Scriptures and intertestamental literature refer to angels of nations and churches, they do not mention organizations. Of course, this may be due to organizations and corporations not being known or experienced by the ancient world as they are today.

However, as the concept of the angel of the church is developed from the addressees of the letters to the seven churches in Revelation, extending it to other forms of corporate organization might be possible. In this respect, Wink's belief that one aspect of the angel of the church is its intrinsic nature with all its strengths and weaknesses lends itself to attributing the term to a secular corporation. Anglican priest and broadcaster Angela Tilby takes this position. Describing the nature of BBC North during the time that she worked there, Tilby uses adjectives such as "friendly," "prickly," "anxious," "defensive," and "vain." She also suggests that while the character of the organization might come across as somewhat intimidating, it could, if treated well, also be kind.[37]

---

35. Wink's use of General Motors as an illustration of how the angel of the church can be observed will be explored more fully in chapter 7.

36. Wink, *Unmasking the Powers*, 71.

37. From an unpublished address given in the Durham dioceses in 1998, cited in Warren, *Healthy Churches Handbook*, 97.

The difficulty with Tilby's assessment is that it appears to presume that churches and secular organizations function in the same way. Wink believes this is not the case. Prior to using the General Motors illustration, he contends that the angel of the church is formed from a confluence of personality and vocation.[38] The suggestion here is that the vocation the church has in Christ separates the church from other forms of organization. This is particularly evident among Baptists when they gather to discuss the day-to-day business of the church. Although a Baptist church meeting contains all the elements of a business meeting, it is usually framed within the context of a spiritual encounter. Commenting on this, Ernest Payne describes the church meeting as a place where the church submits itself to the guidance of the Holy Spirit, in the hope that they might discover the mind of Christ.[39]

This desire to know the mind of Christ in respect of the day-to-day business of the church is illustrated in the records of church meetings, by the way acts of prayer and worship are included in the minutes. Thus, references to the pastor opening the meeting in prayer or with a short devotional reflection on a passage of scripture are commonplace. Having stated this, it should be noted that just because secular business meetings might not be framed in this way, it does not preclude them from having a transcendent entity. However, with its earthly mission and eschatological possibility in Christ, the church is different.

Literature Review

As part of the research process for producing this book, a review of the current literature was carried out. In this respect, very little has been written that offers more than a passing comment on Wink's work on the angel of the church. However, his references to spiritual power have been explored by a number of theologians. It has formed part of academic works, such as Stephen Finamore's *God, Order and Chaos* and Robert Moses' *Practices of Power: Revisiting the Principalities and Powers in the Pauline Letters*. Despite referencing Wink with respect to the use of spiritual power, neither Finamore nor Moses develop the concept of the angel of the church. In Finamore's publication, Wink's work is used in conversation with that of René Girard in a discussion of the myth of redemptive

---

38. Wink, *Unmasking the Powers*, 73.
39. Payne, *Fellowship of Believers*, 156.

violence.⁴⁰ As for Moses, he cites Wink's work on defining the language of spiritual power as a model for understanding the way such language is used within the Pauline epistles. Moses considers the strength of Wink's work to be his move away from demythologizing the concept of spiritual power, but its weakness is his assumption that New Testament authors could not separate the spiritual and physical realms.⁴¹ By arguing that organizations have a spiritual as well as physical dimension, Wink's work provides a critique of the forms of social study that seek to demythologize the nature and functions of the church.

In 2008, a collection of essays in honor of Wink's contribution to the Auburn Theological Seminary was edited by D. Seiple and Frederick Weidmann.⁴² As the sphere of Wink's work is large, this publication was unable to examine every aspect. Therefore, while there is a short essay titled "Engaging Walter Wink's Powers," there is not a specific exploration of the angel of the church.⁴³

Susan Beaumont refers to Wink's work in *How to Lead When You Don't Know Where You Are Going: Leading in a Liminal Season*. In chapter 3, "Tending the Soul of an Institution," Beaumont compares Wink's concept of the angel of the church with the soul of an organization.⁴⁴ However, beyond noting the similarities and that Wink does not use the term "soul," she does not develop the concept of the angel of the church.

The only work directly related to this concept is by Robert Warren in *The Healthy Churches Handbook*.⁴⁵ Describing his work, Warren points out that he aims to provide a practical guide for churches wishing to discover their strengths and weaknesses.⁴⁶ As such, his work is written in a how-to style that is more practical than Wink's experiential exploration of the angel of the church. Unsurprisingly, Warren's work does not develop the concepts underpinning the facets of church life that Wink considers important. In the chapter devoted to the angel of the church, Warren first offers a digest of the spiritual context that forms the heart of Wink's work. He then considers how the angel of the church might be addressed and transformed. Neither of these narratives adds to Wink's

---

40. Finamore, *God, Order and Chaos*, 110, 17–18.
41. Moses, *Practices of Power*, 31–37.
42. Seiple and Weidmann, *Enigmas and Powers*.
43. McIntosh, "Engaging Walter Wink's Powers."
44. Beaumont, *How to Lead*, 51–52.
45. Warren, *Healthy Churches Handbook*, appendix 6.
46. Warren, *Healthy Churches Handbook*, vii.

description of the angel. The only part of Warren's work that is unique is the worksheet that he includes among his appendices.

In appendix 6, Warren describes a number of exercises that might help a congregation identify its angel. Some of these exercise questions seem, at first glance, to be removed from the central task of unmasking the angel. However, when developed further, Warren demonstrates how asking the congregation to describe their church using a color or as an animal can encourage a group of people to think creatively and thus envisage how their angel might appear. Warren then progresses the discussion by asking questions regarding the church's personality and vocation.[47] Together, these questions help the group to see how their corporate personality might affect the way they function. This, in turn, enables them to both understand and articulate their congregation's and, thus, their angel's distinctive features.

Having provided resources to assist in revealing the nature of the angel, Warren offers suggestions as to how a congregation might discern its vocation.[48] This is important, as it resonates with Wink's belief that it is a church's vocation that sets apart an exploration of the angel of the church from a sociological or anthropological study.[49] However, after introducing his process for identifying the angel, Warren begins to refer to an angel of vocation.[50] While this might simply represent poor syntax, it might also suggest that Warren holds a dualistic view of a congregation's angel. Suppose he intended the investigation into the nature and the vocation of the angel to be separate studies. In that case, he may understand the church to be represented in the heavenly realms by one angel holding its personality and a second affecting its vocation. If this is Warren's position, then it differs significantly from Wink's concept of an angel, which is defined by the confluence of personality and vocation.[51]

With the majority of academic reflection focusing on Wink's understanding of spiritual power, and Warren's failure to develop the foundations of the angel of the church, the way is open to explore and develop Wink's concept. In view of this, most of this book will focus on the facets that Wink suggests add to the nature of the angel of the

---

47. Warren, *Healthy Churches Handbook*, 133–37.
48. Warren, *Healthy Churches Handbook*, 137.
49. Wink, *Unmasking the Powers*, 73.
50. Warren, *Healthy Churches Handbook*, 137.
51. Wink, *Unmasking the Powers*, 71–73, 93.

church. In each case, his focus will be developed and illustrated with stories from Baptist congregations.

The reason for using stories from Baptist church records, rather than congregations from a different ecclesial tradition, is partly that it represents the author's church tradition but also that Baptist polity lends itself to individual congregations expressing their corporate faith differently from each other. Having stated this, it will become evident that the applicability of Wink's concept of an angel of the church is not restricted to Baptist congregations. Wink was an American Methodist and illustrates his work from his experiences within those traditions. With these connections to American Methodism and English Baptists, it is possible to surmise that the concepts explored within this thesis might be extrapolated to other forms of ecclesiology.

The Source Material

The stories used to illustrate Wink's concept of the angel of the church will come primarily from the records kept by the Baptist congregations in Budleigh Salterton and Newton Abbot, and to a lesser extent, from the church in South Street in Exeter. In addition to these primary sources, narratives recounted in journals such as *The Baptist Quarterly* and *Ministry Today* will also be used to illustrate the facets of church life raised by Wink's thesis.

The strength of using original records to illustrate the theoretical concepts arising from Wink's work is that they represent individual churches grappling with the ordinary issues relating to congregational life. Furthermore, extensive records of church meetings at Budleigh Salterton, Newton Abbot, and South Street in Exeter have been made publicly available through the Devon Heritage Centre. Most of these churches also have long histories, and while the records at Budleigh Salterton only date back as far as the nineteenth century, the records kept by the Baptists in South Street in Exeter date back to 1749. As for Newton Abbot, although the original records date from 1863, references in hand-written journals and published histories refer to some aspects of church life from as far back as 1697.

In addition to their long histories and availability of records, these churches were also chosen for their geographical proximity and diversity. All of these churches are situated in the South West of England and are, or have been, members of the same local Baptist Association. They are also located in different topographical locations. The church at Newton Abbot was in a small market town,[52] Budleigh Salterton is a seaside location, and the church in South Street in Exeter is situated in the city center.

Of course, the difficulty with using the records from these congregations as illustrative material is that they are often incomplete, and their descriptions of events are often brief. Commenting on the nature of church records, Malcolm Egner suggests that the amount of detail recorded in the minute books is dependent on the practice of the church and the minute taker.[53] Egner's research also highlights that the focus of church records changes over time. Whereas in the seventeenth century, church discipline formed the basis of church records, during the nineteenth century it was membership and procedural issues that dominated the accounts of meetings.[54]

The issue of brief descriptions is particularly relevant to some of the minutes kept by the Baptists at South Street in Exeter. The minute book for the period 1904 to 1936 is an excellent example of this as it is almost exclusively a record of individuals received into membership and transferred to other congregations. Furthermore, the earliest minute book from the Baptist church in South Street in Exeter was deliberately destroyed shortly after the restoration of the monarchy in 1660.[55] Where the records are present, they are sometimes incomplete due to lapses in administration; for example, the record of the church meeting held on July 6, 1904, at the Baptist church at South Street in Exeter opens with "Mr_____ in the chair."[56] In contrast, although the publicly available records from the Baptist church at Budleigh Salterton only cover the period between 1843 and 1975, they are in good order and contain a significant amount of useful detail.

The publicly available records for Newton Abbot Baptist Church are particularly interesting as they are virtually complete from the church's opening in 1863 and its closure in 2009. Furthermore, in addition to the usual minutes of deacons and church meetings, there are also a number of personal letters from church members to the minister

---

52. The Newton Abbot Baptist Church referred to in this thesis closed in 2009.
53. Egner, "Re-Imagining the Covenant Community," 4.
54. Egner, "Re-Imagining the Covenant Community," 22–23.
55. James, *History of the Dissenting Churches*, 169.
56. Church meeting minutes July 6, 1904, 75-9-1-4, South Street Baptist Church minute book May 18, 1904–Feb. 26, 1936, Devon Heritage Centre (hereafter DHC).

and church secretary that date from periods when the church is facing significant challenges. These letters provide an insight into the anxiety felt by the congregation as the church grapples with issues relating to ministry and difficulties with their premises.

Of the records examined for use in this publication, the minutes and correspondence kept and made public by the Baptists in Newton Abbot provide the richest source of illustrative material. For this reason, the Baptists at Newton Abbot, along with those at Budleigh Salterton, will provide the majority of the key stories examined in this thesis.

Although the records from the churches in Exeter, Budleigh Salterton, and Newton Abbot provide illustrations for most of the areas of church life that Wink suggests may reveal the nature of the angel of the church, they do not cover everything. Therefore, there are occasions when accounts from the life of Baptist congregations further afield will be included.

Published Church Histories

In addition to personal correspondence and the minutes of deacons and church meetings, there are published historical accounts of some of the churches used in this study. These publications differ immensely in length, focus, and quality. For example, the formation of the Baptist congregation in Budleigh Salterton is documented in two short pamphlets and two short books. The longest of these, at 102 pages, is *The Baptist Church in Budleigh Salterton 1843–2018*, and this provides the most comprehensive history of the church.

There is a similar lack of published resources in the case of the Baptist church in Newton Abbot. Arthur Gabb's "A Short History of the Baptist Cause in Newton Abbot" is only twenty pages in length.[57] A similar brevity is encountered when the existence of Baptist congregations is included in the general histories of a town or a city. The accounts describing Newton Abbot Baptist Church in D. M. Stirling's *A History of Newton Abbot and Newton Bushel*, published in 1830, and A. J. Rhodes's *Newton Abbot: Its History and Development*,[58] published in 1903, are limited to a single page out of 179 and 267 pages, respectively.

---

57. Arthur Gabb, "Short History of the Baptist Cause in Newton Abbot," in Extracts from the minutes of the Old Church, 6916D/68, Newton Abbot Baptist Church, n.d., DHC.

58. Rhodes, *Newton Abbot*, 97.

Commenting on the nature of published church histories, James Hopewell suggests that, in many cases, these documents are not written by historians but by members of that congregation. He argues that this restricts their interest as they focus on accomplishments and dates rather than the joys and sorrows associated with the struggle to maintain a vibrant faith community.[59] In addition to their brevity, Hopewell also argues that church histories are often limited by their focus or prejudice. H. E. Bickers's *A Brief History of the Baptist Church now meeting in South Street Chapel, Exeter, from the year 1656*, is an example of this, as it primarily concentrates on the ministers of the South Street Baptist Church in Exeter. However, there are exceptions, as Graham Wise's *The Baptist Church in Budleigh Salterton 1843–2018* provides a broad account of church life among the Baptists of Budleigh Salterton.

Despite the limitations voiced by Hopewell, published church histories can provide useful insights into the nature and vocation of the church not necessarily reported in the church minute books. For example, Alan Brockett's *Nonconformity in Exeter 1650–1875* explores the early history of the Baptists in Exeter in the context of the rise of other nonconformist groups such as the Presbyterians, Quakers, and Unitarians, whereas Gardner and Frost's *Faith in Exeter: The Story of the Palace Gate Project* deals with the involvement of the Baptists from the South Street Church with a social project in central Exeter.

A Methodology for Using Church Records

The records used throughout this publication were, at the time the research was conducted, freely available from the Devon Heritage Centre. However, although the material used is in the public domain it is also important to note that some of the records, particularly in respect of Newton Abbot Baptist Church, are sensitive. In view of this, a set of basic principles for using the available material has been outlined below.

Exploring the nature of social research, Martyn Hammersley suggests that there are a relatively small number of ethical principles commonly included in professional or international codes of practice. These include a concern to minimize harm, respecting anonymity, a desire to preserve privacy, and a commitment to acting equitably.[60] This

---

59. Hopewell, *Congregation*, 157.
60. Hammersley, "On Ethical Principles," 435.

commitment to minimizing harm is reflected in the Economic and Social Research Council (ESRC) list of expectations for ethical research.[61] It also forms part of the British Educational Research Association (BERA) guidelines.[62]

Although the records used are in the public domain, where possible, permission has been sought and granted by the leaders of the Baptist churches at South Street, Exeter, and Budleigh Salterton. What is more, even though the Baptist church in Newton Abbot is now closed, permission to use the records has been obtained from two former ministers. Even so, where quotations are made from documents that include names of persons who are likely to be still living the citations have been anonymized.[63] Of course, the replacement of these names, and in some cases, dates of events, does not preclude recognition by individuals reading this publication who know the church and the period being referenced. However, it does offer a level of anonymity in respect of a wider audience.

Possible Ways of Understanding Wink's Concept

The basis of this study is deducing the nature of a church from their records. It also relies on a specific hermeneutic for interpreting the records kept by a congregation. In view of this, it is important to note that there are other ways of reading the data. Aside from the traditional sociological and anthropological ways of understanding how human beings function within groups and organizations, the disciplines of congregational studies and practical theology also provide a way of understanding the nature of the church.

Practical Theology

Writing in 1961, James Gustafson suggests that, while theology has been used to interpret the life and function of the church, it has tended to be from a biblical studies or doctrinal perspective.[64] Gustafson argues that,

---

61. UK Research and Innovation, "Framework for Research Ethics."

62. British Educational Research Association, "Ethical Guidelines for Educational Research," 5.

63. The anonymizing will take the form of random letters being used in place of names.

64. Gustafson, *Treasures in Earthen Vessels*, 1.

although the church cannot be fully understood outside its belief systems, it must also be understood as a human community.[65] Gustafson is correct in asserting the value of the social sciences in interpreting church life. However, his contention that their influence has been absent is open to critique. From Wink's perspective, society's move toward secularism has made it increasingly difficult to speak of spiritual entities and power.[66] Likewise, the discipline of congregational studies has sought to integrate theology and the social sciences to form a holistic view of church life. Frances Ward highlights this as she charts the way pastoral theology has made the transition to practical theology.[67] For Ward, practical theology is interdisciplinary and draws not only on different aspects of theology but also the influences from contemporary issues and cultural contexts.[68] In this respect, Wink's angel of the church represents a form of practical theology, as it integrates biblical studies, doctrinal and organizational views of the church, as well as the sociological and anthropological facets of human experience. However, while the doctrinal views of the church will reference her relationship with the transcendent Christ and her eschatological hope, Wink's model also places the inner nature of the church in the heavenly realms within the angelic entity.

Wink's position represents a form of ethnography which, according to Peter Collins, provides a method for understanding the intrinsic nature of the church.[69] Collins suggests that the key to this is questioning the vocation of an organization along with its modus operandi.[70] For Wink, whatever the church does, its intrinsic nature links the earthly manifestations of a fellowship: the way human beings interact with each other and form a cohesive group in the pursuit of a common vocation. However, in Wink's opinion, a congregation's vocation is not quantified by its earthly mission but rather by what the church might become in Christ. Therefore, making sense of what the church does can only be achieved by accounting for the earthly, transcendent, and eschatological dimensions of a congregation's existence.[71]

---

65. Gustafson, *Treasures in Earthen Vessels*, 99–100.
66. Wink, *Unmasking the Powers*, 1.
67. Cameron et al., *Studying Local Churches*, 17.
68. Cameron et al., *Studying Local Churches*, 18.
69. Collins, "Congregations, Narratives and Identity," 99.
70. Collins, "Congregations, Narratives and Identity," 99.
71. Wink, *Unmasking the Powers*, 73.

Interiority and the Angel of the Church

It is this relationship between the earthly and the transcendent that makes Wink's work distinctive. This is particularly true of his conception of the interface between heaven and earth. In this respect, Wink's theory of interiority allows for the transcendent angel of the church not only to be formed by the corporate spirituality of the congregation but also to affect them from the inside. This, in turn, creates a spiritual nature that is resilient to drastic change and yet able to be influenced by external factors.

Wink explains his understanding of a spiritual interiority in *Engaging the Powers*. Introducing this work, he describes five ways that the relationship between heaven and earth might be understood. While he does not specifically use any of these descriptions in respect of the angel of the church, they are helpful in understanding the relationship between the church and its transcendent angel. Describing them as worldviews, Wink provides five different ways of understanding the relationship between the transcendent heavens and the physical earth. He gives these views the following titles: ancient, spiritualistic, materialistic, theological, and integral.[72]

The Ancient Worldview

According to Wink, an ancient view of heaven and earth is where the heavens are above, and there is a vertical connection between the two. Furthermore, in this ancient understanding, the actions of the earth are mirrored in heaven, and likewise, the actions of heaven are mirrored on earth.[73] In this scenario, it is easy to see how the early Christians might have understood the connection between the earthly church and its transcendent angel. It might also explain why the letters to the seven churches in the book of Revelation are addressed to the angel rather than the church, and this will be explained more fully in the next chapter.

---

72. Wink, *Engaging the Powers*, 3.
73. Wink, *Engaging the Powers*, 4.

The Spiritualistic Worldview

For Wink, the spiritualistic worldview represents the position adopted by the Gnostics. It is a viewpoint that considers the earth and anything related to it as evil and controlled by imperfect, evil powers. In contrast, the spirit, which originates in the heavenly realms, is considered to be perfect. When human beings procreate, an earthly body is created. This earthly body contains a heavenly spirit known as the soul. However, in the act of procreation, this spiritual soul is trapped within the earthly body and forgets its transcendent origins.[74] From this perspective, while the spirit originates in the heavenly realms, once it becomes part of the human nature, it no longer has any connection to the transcendent. In view of the permanent separation of the spiritual soul from the heavenly realms, this position is incongruent with Wink's concept of an angel of the church. Therefore, while a spiritualistic worldview might critique Wink's concept, it is unable to contribute to the development of this thesis.

The Materialistic Worldview

The materialistic worldview emerged during the Enlightenment and, in Wink's opinion, represents the rejection of a spiritual dimension.[75] The characteristics of this worldview are an emphasis on logical thinking and empirical measurement, and, as a result, the transcendent realm is rejected. As has been mentioned previously, this viewpoint plays a significant part in Wink's thinking as it formed the basis of his theological training. However, rather than embrace the rational and seek a logical explanation for the term "angel of the church," Wink's Powers Trilogy is a polemic against a materialistic worldview.

The Theological Worldview

Whereas the materialistic worldview rejects the existence of the spiritual realm, a theological interpretation of life has a place for the transcendent realms. However, in Wink's opinion, while the theological worldview acknowledges the existence of a heavenly realm, it fails to allow for a link between the heavenly and the earthly. He argues that

74. Wink, *Engaging the Powers*, 4.
75. Wink, *Engaging the Powers*, 5.

this separation of the heavenly realms has taken place to protect their existence from scientific inquiry.[76] Unfortunately, if Wink is correct, in this separation of the transcendent realms and the physical earth there is no room for inquiring into the nature of a transcendent angel that affects the nature of the earthly church. In view of this, this worldview will not be explored further in this thesis.

The Integral Worldview

In an integral worldview, heaven and earth exist together as an inner and outer aspect of a single reality. This is Wink's preferred viewpoint as he believes it represents a coming together of a number of facets, all of which point to every aspect of life having an outer and inner aspect.[77] Tom Wright offers a similar viewpoint, arguing that the images of worship portrayed in the fourth and fifth chapters of Revelation are a present reality existing in an alternative dimension rather than a promise fulfilled at the end of time.[78] Furthermore, by arguing for heaven as an inner aspect of an outer reality, Wink circumvents the criticism that his understanding of an angel of the church represents a form of dualism. For, if the earthly congregation equates to the outer expression of an inner, transcendent spirituality, the actions and decisions of the earthly church must reveal the nature of its angel.

The idea that the inner spirit can affect the outward function of an organization is not limited to theological discourse. The language of psychology recognizes the way external actions are a result of an inner tension. This aspect of Wink's theology is highlighted by his reference to the influence of Carl Jung and Elizabeth Boyden Howes.[79]

The Influence of Carl Jung and Elizabeth Boyden Howes

By noting the influence of Jung and Howes, Wink highlights his interest in psychological concepts and their integration with theological

---

76. Wink, *Engaging the Powers*, 5.
77. Wink, *Engaging the Powers*, 5.
78. Wright, *Surprised by Hope*, 26.
79. Wink, *Unmasking the Powers*, ix. Jung is a reputable writer on psychotherapy and Boyden Howes was a Jungian psychologist known for her integration of psychology and religion.

practice. This interest may provide the foundation for Wink's belief that the heavenly realms are a form of interiority within the earthly as opposed to an external dimension. Commenting on the relationship between the inner and outer aspects of human life, the organizational psychologist Manfred Kets de Vries contends that the primary purpose of psychoanalysis is to explain the role of the unconscious in the way human beings make decisions and act.[80] Although Wink does not advocate a psychological understanding of the inner and outer self as a method of understanding and addressing the angel, he freely admits that Jungian forms of psychology have influenced his work.[81]

The science of psychology and the art of Wink's spiritual form of theology both consider how a group functions from an inner and outer perspective. However, there is a question to be asked regarding the claim that the angel of the church is a transcendent entity rather than a construct of the human psyche. In this respect, Wink's integral worldview, which places that transcendence within the organization as opposed to above it, is helpful. If the angel represents the spiritual core of a congregation, it enables the transcendent to interact easily with the physical. This, in turn, allows for the spiritual nature of the church and how it functions to be affected by both its relationship with God and its physical locality. Thus, an integral worldview allows Wink to respect an ancient viewpoint where heaven and earth are connected, and each affects the other and provides a basis from which he can critique a materialistic worldview.

Gestalt

In addition to using the principles of interiority to understand the nature of the angel of the church, Wink also uses the term "Gestalt." The difficulty here is that while Wink uses the term "Gestalt" to describe a holistic view of the church that encompasses both its physical function and its spiritual interior, he does not use the term in all its fullness.

Critiquing a Western mindset, Wink suggests that a bias toward individualism creates difficulties when viewing the life of an organization in its entirety.[82] For Wink, viewing an organization's entirety involves its history and perception of vocation, as well as the characteristics of its

---

80. Kets de Vries, "Introduction: Exploding the Myth," 4.
81. Wink, *Unmasking the Powers*, ix.
82. Wink, *Unmasking the Powers*, 73.

human members.[83] Describing this, he uses the term "Gestalt," a German word often used in relation to a school of psychology developed by Fredrick Perls.

The philosophy underpinning Gestalt therapy is that, for human beings to exist, they must interact with and adapt to their environment.[84] Although he does not reference the full compass of Gestalt as expressed by Perls, Wink does view the church as being more than the gathering of its members and, to some extent, refers to how a church interacts with its environment. This is evident as he explores how the angel of the church might be observed. Here, Wink points the enquirer to consider everything from the architecture, the church's leadership, and power structure to the way it handles conflict.[85] What is more, he suggests that a congregation's history plays as much a part in the church's present nature as the physical attributes of architecture and its demographics. Furthermore, some of Wink's illustrations imply that unresolved adaptive cycles have an ongoing effect on the life of a church. Therefore, while Wink uses the term "Gestalt" and appears to do so in a very limited way, a deeper appreciation of his work reveals that the principles of Gestalt therapy have significantly influenced his concept of an angel of the church.

The Way Ahead

In view of all that has gone before, this publication will now explore Wink's concept of an angel of the church. Beginning with a brief exploration of the scriptural and intertestamental references to angels of churches, the rest of the book will focus on the facets of church life that Wink considers to be possible indicators of the nature of the angel of a church.

The following chapters aim to develop and critique Wink's work from different perspectives. They are also designed to expose the complexity involved in the spiritual nature of an organization. Throughout this study, the process of exploration and critique will be anchored in the theological nature and vocation of the church. This is important as it distinguishes churches from other forms of organizations. This premise is also significant in Wink's work. Although he relates his concept of the angel of the church

---

83. Wink, *Unmasking the Powers*, 73.
84. Philippson and Harris, *Gestalt*, loc. 442 of 2004.
85. Wink, *Unmasking the Powers*, 73–76.

to other organizations, he is clear that the angel of the church enables a theological understanding of how congregations function.[86]

Before exploring the facets of church life that Wink suggests offer a window through which the nature of the angel of the church can be observed, the next chapter will consider how the term *angelos* might be understood in respect of the opening stanza of the letters to the seven churches in Revelation. It will also review some of the concepts regarding angels of communities expressed in the intertestamental literature.

---

86. Wink, *Unmasking the Powers*, 73.

1

What is the angel of the church?

THE TERM "ANGEL OF the church" is taken from the opening lines of the letters to the seven churches in Revelation. In each case, Christ instructs John to write to the angel of the church in a specific city. As these letters are not addressed to a named person or, alternatively, "to the leaders of the church in . . ." the question of exactly who or what the angel is is open to speculation. Biblical commentators have approached the question in several ways. Some scholars have argued that the term "angel" should be translated as "messenger" and, therefore, should be seen either as local church leaders or human emissaries.[1] Others have adopted the opposite position, contending that an angel should be understood as a transcendent spiritual entity,[2] while two scholars consider the angel as a visionary construct within a visionary literary genre.[3]

The Angel of the Church as a Human Messenger

Exploring the possibility that the angel is a human messenger, David Aune reminds his readers that the Septuagint provides a precedent for using the term angel to describe a human messenger. He explains that, in Mal 2:7, the Jewish priest is described as "a messenger of the Lord

---

1. Hecataeus of Abdera. See Fee, *Revelation*, 255.
2. Boring, *Revelation*; Boxall, *Revelation of St John*.
3. Fiorenza, *Book of Revelation*; Enroth, "Hearing Formula in the Book of Revelation."

Sabaoth."[4] Margaret Barker also views the angel as a human messenger and cites Mal 2:7.[5] Barker suggests that the Qumran community understood the priest as an angel of the Lord. Supporting her argument, she points to a passage from the Qumran literature where the sons of Zadok are blessed with the wish that they may become known as an angel of God's presence.[6]

The Angel of the Church as a Prophetic Guild

Presenting an alternative view of the angels as human messengers, Aune speculates that they may be prophets or members of a prophetic guild. He supports this argument by referencing *Jewish Antiquities* by Josephus. Aune suggests that in *Ant.* 15:136, Josephus refers to the Jews receiving their laws "through messengers from God."[7] This is an ambiguous statement as it fails to define the messenger as a human or spiritual entity. However, commenting on his own translation of Josephus's works, Ralph Marcus explains that the scholarly consensus is that, in this context, the term "angel" means spiritual beings. Despite this, Marcus thinks that the text is more likely to refer to prophets or a priest than an angel.[8] David Hill agrees with Marcus's assumption, arguing that when Josephus uses the term angel in *Ant.* 15:136, he is probably describing human messengers fulfilling the role of prophet as they teach the Jews the laws and doctrines of their faith.[9]

The Angel of the Church as Local Church Leaders

In his commentary on Revelation, Philip Edgcumbe Hughes offers an alternative to the concept of a prophetic guild by suggesting that the angels are human emissaries sent to visit John on Patmos.[10] However, despite

---

4. Aune, *Revelation 1–5*, 111.
Writing in *The Harvard Theological Review*, Francis Walton explains that the early usage of the term "angel," meaning messenger, may predate the LXX. Walton, "Messenger of God," 255.
5. Barker, *Revelation of Jesus Christ*, 103.
6. Barker, *Revelation of Jesus Christ*, 103 (citing 1Qsb IV).
7. Aune, *Revelation 1–5*, 111.
8. Josephus, *Jewish Antiquities, Books XV–XVII*, 66 (translator's footnote).
9. Hill, *New Testament Prophecy*, 30.
10. Hughes, *Book of the Revelation*, 30.

allowing for the possibility that the angels of the seven churches could be spiritual entities, he is not convinced and considers it more likely that they are church leaders.[11] Aune also notes that, as the angels are recipients of the letters, it is logical to assume that they are present on earth.[12]

Although there is logic to Hughes's argument for viewing the angels of the seven churches as human messengers, it fails to recognize continuity in how angels are referred to throughout the book of Revelation. Aside from the seven angels of the churches, there are sixty other occasions when angels are referred to in the book of Revelation. On each of these occasions, angels take the form of heavenly beings.

Continuity Within the Book of Revelation

Reflecting on the argument of continuity, Aune adopts a contrary position. He suggests that this argument is flawed as it assumes each time the term "angel" is written, it is used in the same way. Aune's contention is given further weight if the angels of the seven churches are understood as a distinct angelic group, similar to how the angel trumpeters in Rev 8:2 and the angels tasked to distribute plagues in Rev 15:6 are defined. Despite this, Aune does not countenance the argument that angels should be understood as human beings. Pointing to the relationship between the seven stars and the angels in Rev 1:20, he considers it very unlikely these angels could act as exclusive representatives of the seven churches.[13]

The Angel of the Church as a Congregation's Alter Ego

An alternative to understanding the angels of the seven churches as spiritual beings could be to view them as each congregation's alter ego. Commenting on this, Aune doubts that a single person could embrace the strengths and weaknesses of each of the churches described in the seven letters.[14] Furthermore, the language used to describe the angels suggests that they are something other than single individuals. Aune points out that, within the seven letters, there are occasions when the author switches between using second person singular and second

11. Hughes, *Book of the Revelation*, 31.
12. Aune, *Revelation 1–5*, 112.
13. Aune, *Revelation 1–5*, 109.
14. Aune, *Revelation 1–5*, 109.

person plural to describe the angel and argues that this suggests that the angel is not simply an individual entity.[15] Wink also notes the use of both the singular and plural pronouns and contends that this points to the congregation being a physical embodiment of the spiritual angel.[16] Ian Boxall supports the argument for the relationship between heaven and earth on the basis of an apocalyptic tradition.[17] Furthermore, Boxall's comment supports Wink's argument that an alternative worldview is required when reading Revelation. In view of this, if, as Wink suggests, heaven and earth exist together as a single reality, there is no reason why the alter ego of a congregation might not exist simultaneously within the earthly and heavenly realms.

Aune adds further support to the notion that the angel is a heavenly manifestation of the nature of the earthly community by noting the way the message for the churches is given to the angel by the Spirit.[18] He also points out that the first chapter of Revelation equates the seven angels to seven stars and the churches to lampstands (Rev 1:19), highlighting them as distinct but linked entities.[19] Wink also notes this link between the heavenly angel and its earthly congregation by suggesting that the angel does not have an identity other than that which is found in the church.[20] This contention raises the question, Does the angel die when the church no longer exists? The simple answer is yes. What is more, it is worth noting that the angels of churches are subject to divine judgment in respect of their oversight of their churches. However, the justification for this comes from the biblical and intertestamental references to angels of nations rather than to angels of churches.

Angels in Jewish Intertestamental Literature

Countering the argument that the angel of the church is a representation of a human messenger, Gordon Fee notes that the references to angels in Revelation are influenced by Jewish apocalyptic language. Fee recognizes that, in this context, it is not easy to translate the term "angel" into English.

15. Aune, *Revelation 1–5*, 109.
16. Wink, *Unmasking the Powers*, 70–71.
17. Wink, *Unmasking the Powers*, 70.
18. Aune, *Revelation 1–5*, 109.
19. Aune, *Revelation 1–5*, 109.
20. Wink, "Our Stories, Cosmic Stories," 215.

However, he contends that it is usual within the Greek translation of the Old Testament (the Septuagint) for the term "angel" to be understood as a heavenly messenger.[21] M. Eugene Boring also argues against a human understanding of the term "angel." He also contends that the book of Revelation is written in a Jewish apocalyptic tradition that accepts that earthly realities have a transcendent counterpart.[22] The weight of Boring's appeal to the apocalyptic tradition should not be underestimated as, during the intertestamental period, a theology of angels developed within the apocalyptic literature. This is particularly true of the books of Enoch and Jubilees but is most evident in the Sabbath Shirot.[23]

A full exploration of the way angelology develops within the intertestamental apocalyptic literature and its influence on the book of Revelation is beyond the scope of this book. However, Carol Newsom's translation of the Sabbath Shirot and Maxwell Davidson's comparison between the angelic texts in the books of Enoch and the Qumran documents bear mentioning.

The Heavenly Temple

Chapter 4 of Newsom's *Songs of the Sabbath Sacrifice* considers the terms used in the Sabbath Shirot to describe the heavenly temple. Her work is a detailed and systematic comparison of the Hebraic terms used to describe heaven and the physical attributes of a temple within the Sabbath Shirot and the Old Testament. She concludes that within the Sabbath Shirot, the language used to describe the heavenly temple is technical and cultic in nature.[24] This use of technical language to describe the presence of a temple in heaven that echoes the structure of its earthly counterpart provides an important buttress to Wink's concept of an angel of the church. While sociologists, family systems specialists, and organizational psychologists observe and comment on the physical nature of the church, their work does not usually make provision for the possibility that the church has an additional transcendent nature that replicates that of the physical world. In this context, Wink's work adds an additional dimension, as he believes

---

21. Fee, *Revelation*, 20.
22. Boring, *Revelation*, 86.
23. See Davidson, *Angels at Qumran*; Newsom, *Songs of the Sabbath Sacrifice*.
24. Newsom, *Songs of the Sabbath Sacrifice*, 47.

that each earthly congregation has a spiritual entity that cannot exist without the presence of its earthly counterpart.[25]

The Heavenly Priesthood

In addition to arguing for a heavenly temple, Newsom also contends for an angelic priesthood. Her research suggests that within the intertestamental literature, the primary responsibility of the angelic priesthood was to keep the heavenly temple pure. They accomplish this by keeping the law, offering sacrifices, and revealing the truth contained in the law.[26] Of course, linking the concept of an angelic priesthood with the letters to the seven angels in Revelation is not without its difficulties. Although there is a clear argument to be made for the angels representing the churches in the heavenly realms, the letters addressed to them suggest that each angel carries with it the strengths and weaknesses of the church. Therefore, these angels introduce the impurities of church life to the heavenly temple. Furthermore, the letters to the seven angels also suggest that while the causes of God's displeasure and the possibility of judgment are revealed to the churches by the angel, the act of judgment is carried out by God.

An answer to this dilemma may be found within the differing contexts of the Sabbath Shirot and the letters to the church in Revelation. By speaking of the angels offering sacrifices of propitiation,[27] the Sabbath Shirot represents a pre-Christian era, whereas the instructions to address the strengths and weaknesses of the churches through the angels comes from the risen Christ, Rev 1:19. In this new era, the angel continues to fulfill a priestly role as it acts as an intermediary representing the church, with its strengths and weaknesses, to Christ without the need to offer sacrifices.

Maxwell Davidson and the Angels at Qumran

Of course, the concept of understanding the angels of the churches as spiritual intermediaries is not restricted to the New Testament. Although Maxwell Davidson's work *Angels at Qumran* concentrates on the links between

---

25. Wink, "Our Stories, Cosmic Stories," 215.
26. Newsom, *Songs of the Sabbath Sacrifice*, 30.
27. Newsom, *Songs of the Sabbath Sacrifice*, 30.

the existence and roles of angels in the books of Enoch and the Qumran documents, he does explore the role angels play as intermediaries.

Davidson points out that the Enoch books contain references to angels operating between human beings and God. He argues that 1 En 1:1–3 illustrates people praying to angels and asking them to bring their plight before God. Likewise, Davidson notes that the Book of Dreams records an angel interceding for Israel. He argues that the reason behind these accounts of angelic mediators arises from an emphasis on the inaccessibility of God within the theology of the Second Temple period. The exception to the concept of offering prayers through angelic intermediaries is found in the prayer of the sheep, also recorded in the Book of Dreams. Here, the text records intercessions being made directly to God without the need for an intermediary.[28]

The resonance between the seven angels of Revelation and an angelic priesthood is strengthened by Davidson's suggestion that angelic priests exercise a teaching role. He argues that, in the Sabbath Shirot, angels are variously described as "angels of knowledge" (11QShirShabb 2:1–9 5), "godlike beings who draw near to knowledge" (4Q400 1 i 6), "holy ones who establish understanding" (4Q403 1 I 24), and "spirits of knowledge and understanding" (4Q405 17 3).[29] These titles suggest that angels act as messengers, bringing knowledge and understanding from the divine into the presence of human beings. However, suppose the angel of the church is seen as the heavenly equivalent of its earthly congregation. In that case, it might be argued that when the angel comes before God, it carries the spirit of the earthly community into the heart of the divine presence. Of course, this has both positive and negative connotations. Bringing the spirit of an imperfect community into the presence of God invites judgment as well as acknowledgment, which is exactly what the letters in Revelation portray. However, as well as offering a divine insight into the nature and function of each of the seven congregations, each letter concludes with an opportunity for redemption. This possibility of redemption is important to the outworking of Wink's concept of the angel of the church, and it allows for the weak areas of a congregation's ethos or practice to be transformed.

---

28. Davidson, *Angels at Qumran*, 309–10.
29. Davidson, *Angels at Qumran*, 241.

The Angel of the Church as Heavenly Representatives of an Earthly Congregation

The possibility that the angels of the churches might act as heavenly representatives of earthly congregations is explored by G. K. Beal. He suggests that Rev 19:10 and 22:9 support his argument that angels are heavenly beings that represent the corporate nature of the church. Beal notes that in each of these passages, the angels describe themselves as servants. Commenting further, he addresses the concerns raised by scholars, such as Hughes, who find it difficult to accept the idea that God would address his church through an angel. Beal suggests that the reason for this process is both the responsibility and accountability of the angel for the actions of the church and the mutual benefit the church receives from having a heavenly representative. He contends that by addressing the letter to the angel, the churches are reminded of their heavenly status and are strengthened in their faith amid a pagan culture. He supports this argument further by reminding the reader that the images of believers and angels worshiping together in the heavenly realms are woven throughout the book of Revelation.[30] Beal's comments imply that the church worshiping on earth amid pagan opposition derives strength and encouragement by seeing itself as part of a larger and ultimately victorious community consisting of human and spiritual entities.

The close relationship between the heavenly angel and the earthly church also forms the basis for Judith Kovacs and Christopher Rowland's view that the angels should be seen as heavenly guardians. Pointing to The War Scroll from the Qumran community, they suggest that there is a theological precedent for the involvement of angels alongside human beings in an earthly struggle.[31] Although not referenced in this way by Kovacs and Rowland's theory, the angel of the church represents the heavenly equivalent of the earthly struggle that a congregation faces, as it contends for faithfulness and authenticity within its sociological context.

In addition to the belief that viewing the angels as heavenly beings is congruent with the apocalyptic genre of Revelation, Boxall also believes that the church is a theological organization as well as a sociological community, with each congregation having a spiritual guardian.[32] This position

---

30. Beal, *Book of Revelation*, 217–18.
31. Kovacs and Rowland, *Revelation*, 53.
32. Boxall, *Revelation of St John*, 45.

is similar to Wink's, although Wink is willing to extend the presence of heavenly guardians beyond the church to secular organizations.[33]

The arguments presented by Beal and Boxall provide important points of reference for this thesis, and in the exploration of different facets of church life, they provide the foundation for a study that extends beyond a sociological understanding of the church. Although not explored in this thesis, Wink's work takes the concept of heavenly guardians representing the church in the heavenly realms beyond the boundaries of faith communities into every organization. It, therefore, opens the door to reflecting on how organizations are structured and function from a theological as well as sociological and anthropological perspective.

The Angel of the Church as a Fravashis

While accepting the concept of the angels as spiritual entities, George Beasley-Murray raises an objection to the angels of the churches acting as heavenly guardians. Noting that there is nothing intrinsically wrong with the argument, Beasley-Murray finds it difficult to comprehend John writing letters of instruction to spiritual entities.[34] Although he accepts that the references in Dan 10 and 20 create a case for the link between angels and nations, he sees the angels acting as Persian fravashis or guardian spirits that are, in effect, heavenly counterparts of earthly churches.[35] Thomas Kelper lists the possibility that there are parallels between angels and fravashis in his contribution to the *Dictionary of the Bible*.[36] Aune notes this, along with the fact that Swete embraces this possibility.[37] However, Aune argues that it is Beasley-Murray who develops this concept.[38]

According to Julia Cresswell, fravashis are found in Zoroastrianism and act as spiritual guides or guardian angels.[39] Cresswell suggests that God forms them, and while they will not involve themselves directly in the way humans make decisions, they do act as guides.[40] For

33. Wink, *Unmasking the Powers*, 79.
34. Beasley-Murray, *Book of Revelation*, 69.
35. Beasley-Murray, *Book of Revelation*, 69.
36. Kelper, "Angels of the Seven Churches."
37. Aune, *Revelation 1–5*, 110–11.
38. Aune, *Revelation 1–5*, 110.
39. Cresswell, *Watkins Dictionary of Angels*, loc. 2176.
40. Cresswell, *Watkins Dictionary of Angels*, loc. 2176.

Beasley-Murray, this concept of a heavenly guide should not be viewed as an angelic being residing in the heavens acting and reacting to an earthly congregation. Instead, he believes that the angel lives on earth while also existing transcendentally.[41] The basis for this viewpoint is that the church is made up of men and women whose status is in Christ. Thus, the lives of church members exist both physically on earth and simultaneously in heaven in Christ.[42] In this context, there is a synergy between the church's earthly and heavenly existence and actions.

The Angel of the Church as a Visionary Counterpart of the Community Prophets

Aside from the possibility that the angel of the church could be some form of human messenger or transcendent entity, an argument exists that sees the angel as a visionary construct within a visionary literary genre. This viewpoint is presented by Elisabeth Schüssler Fiorenza and Anne-Marit Enroth, who consider the possibility that the angels of the churches are visionary counterparts of the community of prophets. This concept is explored in Fiorenza's *The Book of Revelation: Justice and Judgement*[43] and Enroth's article "The Hearing Formula in the Book of Revelation."[44] Although cited by Aune, Enroth's comment on the nature of the angel of the church is restricted to one paragraph, of which the reference to the angel as a visionary counterpart is explained in a single sentence.[45] This leaves Fiorenza's description as the primary exploration of the angel as a visionary counterpart of earthly prophets.

Using a form-structural approach, Fiorenza contends that the seven letters are a type of visionary writing. Within this visionary form of literature, the angels are incorporeal spirits representing individual communities. Fiorenza argues that understanding the angels in this way addresses the issue of the resurrected Jesus instructing John to write to a human community via a heavenly entity. Furthermore, Fiorenza contends that understanding the angels as visionary interpreters of the will of Christ resonates with the presence of the angelic interpreter in Rev

---

41. Beasley-Murray, *Book of Revelation*, 69.
42. Beasley-Murray, *Book of Revelation*, 69–70.
43. Fiorenza, *Book of Revelation*, 145–46.
44. Enroth, "Hearing Formula in the Book of Revelation," 598–608.
45. Enroth, "Hearing Formula in the Book of Revelation," 603–4.

19:10 and 22:9, who on both occasions refer to themselves as fellow servants.[46] Thus the angels act as incorporeal counterparts to the physical prophets resident within the faith communities. The idea that the angels only exist within a visionary context and function as a literary construct for Christ's prophetic message is an elegant alternative to understanding the angel as either a human emissary or transcendent entity. Its strength is in placing the angel in neither an earthly nor transcendent residence. Arguably, viewing the angel as a literary prophet without physical or transcendent form also overcomes the linguistic difficulties raised by Aune.[47] However, the question raised by Fiorenza's thesis is whether her interpretation of apocalyptic literature reflects the way the early church interpreted the Revelation text. Wink's work assumes not. He argues that dismissing the existence of spiritual entities such as angels and demons is a symptom of a modern, materialistic mindset.[48]

The Angel of the Church as a Colony of Heaven

In addition to viewing the angel of the church as a transcendent entity, the angel might be seen as a heavenly colony. Kiddle uses this term as he describes each of the recipient churches in Revelation. He argues that the churches addressed by the letters should disassociate themselves from the pagan lifestyle of their city hosts and that the letters are not messages intended exclusively for the named churches.[49] Although Kiddle is essentially correct that the letters are intended for a wider readership, they are, nevertheless, specific to seven churches geographically located in Asia Minor.[50] Likewise, while the case studies contained in this thesis are focused on three churches in England's West Country, the principles emerging from their stories are applicable to other local congregations and, arguably, to a broader understanding of the church.

---

46. Fiorenza, *Book of Revelation*, 145.

47. Aune, *Revelation 1–5*, 109.

48. Wink, *Unmasking the Powers*, 1.
Jean Daniélou's research supports Wink's position. He argues that there is a very early tradition believing that angels existed as spiritual entities and were given a position of governance over the church. Daniélou, *According to the Fathers of the Church*, 57.

49. Kiddle, *Revelation of St. John*, 18.

50. Ramsey, *Book of Revelation*, 122.

Summary

The opening sentence of each of the seven letters in the second and third chapters of Revelation is the basis of Wink's belief in the angel of the church. However, as has become evident, exactly how the term "angel of the church" is understood is debatable.

Of the commentators who have examined the language and imagery used in the book of Revelation, Aune provides the most comprehensive description of how the angel of the church might be understood. Aune's review is divided into three categories: viewing the angel of the church as some form of human emissary, understanding that it is a form of transcendent entity, and viewing it as a visionary construct within a visionary form of literature.[51]

Wink's understanding of the angel of the church as a spiritual entity rather than a human emissary is interesting as it represents a shift in his theological approach. From Wink's comments on his theological training in a liberal tradition, it would be easy to perceive that he would interpret the word *angelos* rationally. Therefore, it would be safe to assume that Wink would interpret the angels of the churches as human recipients of the letters expressing Christ's view of their churches. However, this does not seem to be the case. Wink adopts the position that angels of churches are transcendent representations of earthly congregations. He reaches this position by considering links made in the intertestamental literature between angels and nations, guardian angels and angels of churches, and the use of individual and plural language within the letters to each of the seven churches in chapters 2 and 3 of the book of Revelation.[52]

The support of the intertestamental literature for Wink's case is invaluable, and while not referenced by Wink, the work of Newsom on the Sabbath Shirot and Davidson on the understanding of angels at the Qumran community provides a rich theological resource from which support for Wink's position can be drawn.

In addition to understanding the angel of the church as a transcendent entity, Wink's view that the transcendent angel forms the interiority of the church is also helpful, as it explains the gyroscopic nature of congregational behavior. As will become evident, the gyroscopic effect of the angel causes a church to repeat certain character traits over numerous

---

51. Aune, *Revelation 1–5*, 108–12.
52. Wink, *Unmasking the Powers*, 69–73.

generations. It can also cause a church to become focused on a specific part of church life to the point of obsession.

In the chapters that follow, most of the comments will be on the way sociological and architectural influences affect the way a church functions. However, while these aspects of a congregation's life represent their external nature, they also provide an insight into the nature of the church that resides within its interior. As will become evident, this inner nature often causes the congregation to repeat patterns of behavior or to be continually infatuated by a particular area of church life. Although this makes for an interesting way to interpret how a church functions, it has a deeper significance with respect to implementing change within the life of a congregation. This is because, if, as Wink argues, there is a transcendent aspect to earthly actions, it will be impossible to bring about a permanent change to the pattern of earthly actions without also adjusting the activity taking place in the heavenly realms.

In the chapters that follow, the practical aspects of church life that are explored have each been raised by Wink. He believes that in each case, they provide an insight into the nature of the angel of the church. Thus, while some of the areas to be discussed appear to be either historical or sociological conversations, in each case, they are a means by which part of the angel of a church can be observed.

2

Architecture and Ambience

INTRODUCING THE SECTION OF *Unmasking the Powers* that deals with understanding the nature of the angel of the church, Wink outlines the difficulties associated with observing the angel within the confines of a congregation. His argument is primarily that Western culture has become too individualistic in its mindset and fails to perceive the full extent of the interrelated factors that form an organization such as the church.[1] Furthermore, he states that the rational philosophy that permeates Western culture makes it difficult to perceive something invisible to the eye.[2] Therefore, to appreciate the full nature of an organization, one must find ways of viewing what sits beneath the visible aspects of church life.'[3]

To assist in answering this question, Wink outlines six broad areas of church life that contribute to the nature of a congregation's angel. While some of these areas, such as "architecture and ambience," have a specific focus, others appear to be simply a collection of loosely connected titles that await development. Furthermore, although Wink illustrates some of these aspects of church life from his own experience, he does not bring the core subjects into conversation with other authors who specialize in these areas of study. In his defense, Wink acknowledges that the facets he highlights are only suggestions, and additional aspects of ecclesiology

---

1. Wink, *Unmasking the Powers*, 73.
2. Wink, *Unmasking the Powers*, 73.
3. Wink, *Unmasking the Powers*, 73.

may reveal further dimensions to the congregation's angel.[4] The purpose of this chapter and the five that follow is not to add further facets to Wink's list but rather to explore the aspects of church life that he has mentioned but left underdeveloped. To achieve this, six areas of church life that Wink lists will be examined in the light of other authors working in each specific field. These conversations between Wink's work and these authors do not provide an exhaustive study of each subject. However, in each case, they have been selected to represent a specific field of study. Their work will offer insights that will support or critique Wink's contention that different facets of church life shape the angel of the church. This chapter will explore the effect of the architecture and the ambience of the building has on the way a congregation functions.

Architecture

Commenting on the relationship between church buildings and the angel of the church, Wink suggests that the structure of the building and the feeling that it engenders reveal something of the nature of the angel. What is more, the buildings that a congregation inhabits also say something about the values of a congregation's forefathers, even if a single member provided the finance for the construction.[5]

Of course, those who come from a Baptist tradition might well argue that a congregation can gather and worship in any form of building. Even so, Wink's comment suggests that when a church chooses to construct a building, a statement regarding a congregation's identity and vocation is given physical expression.

The Dialogue Between People and Buildings

Although not describing a church building, the relationship between how a building is constructed and the identity of an organization is aptly illustrated by the debate over the rebuilding of the House of Commons after the Luftwaffe bombed it on May 10, 1941. Addressing the Members of Parliament on the rebuilding of the Commons chamber, Winston Churchill argued that the shape of the building not only said something about what happened within the structure, but it also affected the way

---

4. Wink, *Unmasking the Powers*, 73.
5. Wink, *Unmasking the Powers*, 73–74.

the inhabitants acted within.[6] The significance of this is highlighted in Churchill's belief that if the Commons chamber was rebuilt in a semi-circular format, Members of Parliament would subtly change the way Parliament functioned. Churchill contended that by rebuilding the chamber in a rectangular format, Members of Parliament would be prevented from making subtle changes in their political stance.[7]

Churchill's belief in the influence of a building resonates with Wink's assertion that architecture and ambience affect the nature of a congregation's angel as it suggests that, rather than being passive vessels, buildings can influence what happens within them. Furthermore, with respect to Wink's understanding of vocation as the culmination of what a church might become in Christ, the relationship between the building and a congregation might also form a catalyst that will either enable or constrain the ability of a church to fulfill its vocation. In the context of the House of Commons debate, Churchill believed that the shape of the rebuilt House of Commons would affect how politics was conducted in the chamber. He argued that by retaining a rectangular format, the tradition of a clear divide, and thus debate, between the two principal political parties would be continued.[8]

Dynamic Energy

Describing the design of early nonconformist meeting houses, Martin Briggs argues that they were usually simple in their construction.[9] Richard Kieckhefer uses a similar description when he explores the design of the Walpole Chapel in Suffolk.[10] Likewise, A. J. Rhodes describes the first Baptist chapel in Newton Abbot as being of simple construction of mud walls, a few small windows, and basic seating.[11] The aspect of simple seating resonates with Briggs's understanding as he argues that the simplicity of early nonconformist buildings was also reflected in their furniture and, unlike the elongated form favored by Anglican and

---

6. "House of Commons Rebuilding."
7. "House of Commons Rebuilding."
8. "House of Commons Rebuilding."
9. Briggs, *Puritan Architecture and Its Future*, 26.
10. Kieckhefer, *Theology in Stone*, 44.
11. Rhodes, *Newton Abbot*, 97.

Roman Catholic traditions, nonconformist churches were designed as an auditorium with the preacher as the focus.[12]

On the internal design of nonconformist church buildings, Kieckhefer concurs with Briggs by suggesting that purpose-built evangelical churches were built to focus attention on the preacher. However, he also believes this creates a dynamic interaction between the preacher and the congregation.[13] Through the reading of the Scriptures, congregational hymn singing, and the sermon, the preacher and congregation interact. This interaction is designed to be verbal, intimate, and without excessive movement. According to Kieckhefer, these criteria are achieved by creating smaller buildings and filling them with seating.[14] The chapel at Little Knowle in Budleigh Salterton provides an example of this sort of intimate space. The small number of pews and their close proximity to the speaker creates an easy environment within which preacher and congregation can interact.

The Phenomenology of Architecture

Kieckhefer's discussion of the interplay between preacher and congregation introduces the concept of a phenomenology of architecture. Phenomenology is usually associated with understanding phenomena from either a philosophical or a psychological perspective.[15] In this respect, architectural philosophers offer insights into Wink's contention that architecture and ambience affect the nature of the angel of the church. The idea that the space created and defined by a building's structure affects its spirit and energy has been explored by bringing phenomenology into conversation with architecture. Christian Norberg-Schulz initially developed this in *Intentions in Architecture* (1965), *Existence, Space and Architecture* (1971), and later *Genius Loci* (1980).

Writing in the journal *Logos*, Almantas Samalavičius argues that, as an architectural historian and theorist, Norberg-Schulz has made a significant contribution to the rediscovery and application of the concept of *genius loci*. According to Samalavičius, this concept of localized spirits, that dates to the Roman era, is useful for describing the

---

12. Briggs, *Puritan Architecture and Its Future*, 27.
13. Kieckhefer, *Theology in Stone*, 21.
14. Kieckhefer, *Theology in Stone*, 44–45.
15. *Shorter Oxford English Dictionary*, 2180–81.

interaction between the physical construct of architecture and the less tangible experience of a place. Citing a meeting of the International Council on Monuments and Sites, Samalavičius argues that the spirit of a place is shaped by a combination of physical attributes, memories, and stories attached to a location.[16]

Exploring how the interaction between the tangible and intangible attributes of a location affects a person's experience, Norberg-Schulz builds on Martin Heidegger's concept of "dwelling."[17] For Norberg-Schulz, when a person "dwells" in a place, they are able to orient their inner selves and identify with their environment.[18] This relationship between internal orientation and external identification within a limited locality resonates with Wink's belief that a church building can affect the social interaction within a congregation and its attempt to fulfill a theological mission among a wider community. Wink illustrates this by telling the story of visiting a church in Peru that he described as feeling "dead."[19]

Developing the idea that a specific building or location influences orientation and identity, Norberg-Schulz uses the term "settle" to describe how a person or people develop a relationship with a place, and as a result, they give the location meaning.[20] Therefore when a congregation builds a church, the people not only create a fixed place from which they can orient themselves and launch their mission activity, they also create a meaningful focus point from which these activities can extend. Norberg-Schulz is clear in his assertion that the meaning invested in a building has a direct correlation with the design of its structure. Furthermore, as Harold Turner suggests, there is a school of ecclesial architecture that regards a church building as the house of God (*domus Dei*).[21] This link between church premises and encountering the transcendent is further supported by Norberg-Schulz's contention that each man-made construction has its own *genius loci* and that this spirit is related to what is "visualized, complemented, symbolized or gathered."[22] Holding this position on the spiritual essence of a place aligns Norberg-Schulz with Wink, who believes that each organization, secular and sacred, has its own spirit or

16. Samalavičius, "'Spirit of Place,'" 120.
17. Norberg-Schulz, *Genius Loci*, 5.
18. Norberg-Schulz, *Genius Loci*, 5.
19. Wink, *Unmasking the Powers*, 74. This story will be explored later in this chapter.
20. Norberg-Schulz, *Genius Loci*, 50.
21. Turner, *From Temple to Meeting House*, 157.
22. Norberg-Schulz, *Genius Loci*, 58.

angel.²³ Norberg-Schulz develops the concept of *genius loci* by arguing that there are some buildings within which the sensation of a mysterious force is prominent. He contends that this sensation is most prevalent in what he terms as "Romantic Architecture."²⁴

For Norberg-Schulz, architectural design can be categorized into four types: Romantic, Cosmic, Classical, and Complex. He contends that the principal contrast between the Romantic and Cosmic forms of architecture is found in its functionality. In this context, Cosmic architecture might also be called "modern" as it is distinguished by its rational application to function, uniformity, and lack of atmosphere.²⁵ This contrasts with the strong sense of atmosphere coupled with a creative application to function and diversity in design found in Romantic constructions.²⁶ Classical architecture falls between the Cosmic and Romantic versions and contains the logic and function of the Cosmic and the energy of the Romantic. However, within the Classical form, the energy is not as dynamic as it is in the Romantic. Instead, Norberg-Schulz describes it as being full of expectation and natural life.²⁷ As for the Complex form of architecture, its description is self-explanatory in that it describes constructions that contain a mix of the Romantic, Cosmic, and Classical forms.²⁸

The significance of these forms of design to Wink's contention that architecture and ambience affect the nature of the angel of the church is that Norberg-Schulz's descriptions each release different forms of dynamic energy that influence the way individuals and groups function. This release of energy represents the *genius loci* and arguably forms part of the nature of the angel of a church.

Domus Dei or Domus Ecclesiae

When placed into a theological context, a question arises over the nature of the *genius loci*. In this respect, Turner's work *From Temple to Meeting House: The Phenomenology and Theology of Places of Worship* is helpful. Exploring the nature of church buildings, Turner argues that

---

23. Wink, *Unmasking the Powers*, 79.
24. Norberg-Schulz, *Genius Loci*, 69.
25. Norberg-Schulz, *Genius Loci*, 71.
26. Norberg-Schulz, *Genius Loci*, 69.
27. Norberg-Schulz, *Genius Loci*, 73.
28. Norberg-Schulz, *Genius Loci*, 76.

there are two phenomenological forms by which we understand church buildings: *domus Dei*, the house of God, or the place where God is encountered, and *domus ecclesiae*, the house of the church or the practical meeting place of the people of God.[29]

Although the distinction Turner draws between the *domus Dei* and the *domus ecclesiae* resonates with a Baptist understanding of the church, it does not necessarily represent a consistent view of the sacredness of a church building. While not representative of all, twentieth-century Baptist publications of liturgy provide an insight into how some Baptists view their worship space and artifacts. For example, *Patterns and Prayers for Christian Worship*[30] and its predecessor, *Orders and Prayers for Church Worship*[31] provided Baptist congregations with resources from which a service, or ritual, of consecration can be developed. Both of these publications contain prayers of blessing and commission for the opening of a new building[32] and the dedication of artifacts, such as the communion table, lectern, pulpit, and baptistery.[33] In view of this, it appears that during the middle of the twentieth century, some Baptists expressed a sacred view of their worship space. Furthermore, although the prayers for the consecration of premises and artifacts were removed from the latest liturgical resource, *Gathering for Worship*, the publication still contains a prayer inviting worshipers into a space that is described as holy ground.[34] Therefore, while Baptists tend to adopt the *domus ecclesiae* model, some of their literature acknowledges that when believers are gathered with the expectation of encountering their God, the meeting room becomes a *domus Dei*.

Ambience

Kieckhefer's work *Theology in Stone* considers how the architectural layout of a church building influences the practice of worship. Within this exploration, he identifies three broad traditions of church construction:

---

29. Turner, *From Temple to Meeting House*, 157.
30. *Patterns and Prayers for Christian Worship*.
31. Payne and Winward, *Orders and Prayers for Church Worship*.
32. Payne and Winward, *Orders and Prayers for Church Worship*, 211–14.
33. *Patterns and Prayers for Christian Worship*, 215–18. Payne and Winward, *Orders and Prayers for Church Worship*, 231–34.
34. Ellis and Blyth, *Gathering for Worship*, 298.

sacramental, evangelical, and communal.[35] According to Kieckhefer, the sacramental version is the oldest form and includes the earliest surviving church buildings. Examples of this form of architecture can be found in both the Eastern and Western Christian traditions. Kieckhefer also suggests that this form of building is the most complicated and difficult to interpret, as it is richly adorned with symbolic decoration and structural forms.[36] For Kieckhefer, the communal church is the most modern innovation in church design and is, likewise, the most disappointing. He explains that while this form is created to emphasize the gathering of the congregation, in his opinion, this design creates a disappointing environment for worship.[37]

Kieckhefer's comment raises the issue of ambience and highlights the difficulty in exploring the concept. When Wink raises it in relation to the angel of the church, his only reference to ambience is contained in his illustration of the lifeless Peruvian church, which will be discussed later.[38] The difficulty with this assertion is that it is Wink's personal perception of the building and is, therefore, subjective. The subjective nature of ambience is highlighted further by Norberg-Schulz, who supports the argument that the surrounding environment can influence the mood of an individual or group but fails to explore how different forms of architecture might achieve this.[39] Although Norberg-Schulz does not explore how a building feels, he does note that the feelings created within a building will differ for each individual and the same person on different occasions.[40] While these observations might mean that it is impossible to define the ambience of a church building, theologians, social geographers, and phenomenologists appear to agree that there is a link between architectural designs and how human beings feel and function.

Social Geography

In this arena, three authors provide helpful insights into the relationship between a specific location and the people who reside or congregate

---

35. Kieckhefer, *Theology in Stone*, 11.
36. Kieckhefer, *Theology in Stone*, 11.
37. Kieckhefer, *Theology in Stone*, 12 and 15.
38. Wink, *Unmasking the Powers*, 74.
39. Norberg-Schulz, *Intentions in Architecture*, 22.
40. Norberg-Schulz, *Intentions in Architecture*, 22.

there: Tim Creswell, David Harvey, and Edward Soja. While each of their insights will be explored later in this chapter, the way these authors use the term "geography" requires an explanation. Creswell provides a helpful distinction by suggesting that there are two types of geography: historical and social. Historical geography considers the physical environment and how human civilization is ordered upon the land. It also describes the physical elements of a landscape that provide a community with resources, whereas social geography is used to test economic, political, and social theories by locating them in a specific context.[41] Creswell argues that the geographical environment can provide insight into the underlying forces that affect our everyday behavior.[42] This highlights how the term "geography" can be used as a social motivator rather than as a physical descriptor. In this respect, his comments resonate with Wink's belief that the nature of a location, or a building, can affect the way an organization functions. However, Creswell's perspective differs from Wink's in that Creswell views the forces that shape how people function within a specific location as social rather than spiritual. Therefore, while Creswell's insights will add to Wink's assertion, they will also offer a critique. Likewise, the insights that Harvey and Soja bring to Wink's view of the influence of architecture and ambience will both support and critique Wink's thesis.

Ideology and Place

Describing his concept of the angel of the church, Wink argues that a building's structure can powerfully influence people along with its objects and symbols. He illustrates this with two personal stories. In the first, he describes leading a Bible study on Jesus' encounter with a wealthy young man in Matt 19:16–26 while sitting in a mansion on a twenty-five-thousand-dollar oriental rug.[43] As the participants in the study explored the Bible passage, they expressed their disbelief that Jesus would say that the rich cannot enter the kingdom of heaven and seemed confused and irritated by the study.[44] Puzzled by the reactions of those present, Wink considered his surroundings more closely and concluded that the

41. Sack, *Human Territoriality*, 2.
42. Creswell, *In Place/Out of Place*, 11.
43. Wink, *Unmasking the Powers*, 74.
44. Wink, *Unmasking the Powers*, 74.

opulence of the rug and its setting was promoting a subliminal message that was difficult to resist.[45] While it is difficult to accept that the resistance to Jesus' reaction to the rich young man was a result of the opulent surroundings, Creswell's contention that social geography can shape everyday behavior would suggest otherwise.[46]

Creswell's work *In Place/Out of Place* examines the relationship between ideology and place. Citing the work of Goren Therborn, Creswell contends that his use of the term "ideology" can also be interpreted as belief systems or cultural values.[47] He also argues that belief systems cease to become theoretical when they are brought into dialogue with a particular location. For Creswell, when geography is applied to ideology, the result is a specific way of doing things.[48] This relationship between what is believed about a certain place and the resulting actions gives a place a specific meaning. In this respect, Wink's assertion that the rug was sending subliminal messages that resisted the direction that the Bible study was taking is not unbelievable. For, if Creswell is correct, the ideology being promoted by the culture of wealth that surrounded the participants contrasted with the critique of wealth emerging from the study of Jesus' encounter with the rich young man.

Although Creswell's position appears to support Wink's argument, it also demystifies the reaction of the Bible study participants. In contrast to this, Harold Turner makes a similar argument for a relationship between a building and the reaction of people within its confines. Turner suggests that when considering the relationship between a place and its people, a form of theological inquiry is required that extends how the church understands its beliefs, worship, and ministry.[49] Turner's solution is to apply phenomenology to the historical development of church architecture.

By applying phenomenology to church architecture, Turner argues that the nature of the building affects the way Christianity is both experienced and expressed. He contends that the way a room or building is organized focuses on the experience of those within.[50] In view of this, it is possible that because the room within which Wink's Bible

45. Wink, *Unmasking the Powers*, 74.
46. Creswell, *In Place/Out of Place*, 11.
47. Creswell, *In Place/Out of Place*, 14.
48. Creswell, *In Place/Out of Place*, 16.
49. Turner, *From Temple to Meeting House*, 5–6.
50. Turner, *From Temple to Meeting House*, 9–10.

study took place was focused on opulence, it was difficult for the group to contemplate giving up their wealth to follow Jesus. This possibility is strengthened further by Turner's argument that sacred structures, such as churches, represent an earthly expression of a transcendent entity.[51] Although it is clear from Wink's description that the Bible study was not taking place in a sacred building, the issue being discussed was sacred values. In view of this, a conflict appears to have taken place between sacred values and an earthly ideology. Therefore, if Wink's Bible study experience is to be understood from a theological perspective, then phenomenology allows for the influence of the opulent surroundings to be a transcendent rather than a social experience. Likewise, while Creswell's concept might point to Wink's experience of the expensive rug and its surroundings as a form of sociological energy, Wink may be correct in his assertion that the surroundings were creating an influence on proceedings whose source was transcendent.

This relationship between the physical and the transcendent, in the physicality of a location, blurs the lines between cultural experience and theological encounter. The tension between interpreting the influence of a situation from a sociological or spiritual perspective is a particular concern of Wink, as his work on the angel of the church is a polemic against a purely sociological stance. In this context, David Harvey's postmodern perspective on town planning may offer insights into Wink's belief in a link between a building and how people function.

A Postmodern Perspective on Architecture

Harvey's interest is in the transition between a rational, modernist, and more fluid postmodern perspective in architecture and town planning. In *The Condition of Postmodernity*, Harvey explores the transformation of urban life in the light of a changing social philosophy. He argues that, since 1972, there has been a significant change in cultural, political, and economic practices.[52] Harvey contends that this change is directly related to a fresh understanding of the relationship between a space and a time.[53] Although not directly addressing the type of issues Wink is expressing when he suggests architecture and ambience help to form the

---

51. Turner, *From Temple to Meeting House*, 10.
52. Harvey, *Condition of Postmodernity*, vii.
53. Harvey, *Condition of Postmodernity*, vii.

nature of a congregation's angel, Harvey's introduction to his chapter "Postmodernism in the City: Architecture and Urban Design" highlights how architectural design and the layout of an inner city can change.[54] This change results from a dialogue between those designing new structures and the prevailing culture. In view of this, Harvey's work invites the questions: How much do church buildings change in response to cultural changes within their locality? And to what degree does the adaptation of architecture affect the ability of a congregation to fulfill its mission and vocation? In this respect, Richard Giles's *Re-Pitching the Tent* is helpful as he addresses a series of issues relating to adapting a building to meet a contemporary missional challenge. As part of this project, he considers what church buildings say about the church. Here, he is very critical of the image presented by decaying fabric and outdated resources. Giles argues that while the physical environment created by a church building is not the only reason why a church may or may not fulfill its mission, it does exercise a powerful influence.[55] This relationship between the fabric of a building and how a church undertakes its mission can be explored through the relationship between architecture and confidence.

Architecture and Confidence

Describing early nonconformist architecture, Briggs argues that, with their whitewashed walls and basic furniture, these buildings were austere and did not appear to be church premises.[56] G. W. Rusling concurs with Briggs's assertion and adds that early Baptist churches were often situated away from the main street and not built as architectural statements of the glory of God. For Rusling, the glorification of God came from what happened within the building rather than its architectural statement.[57] He contends that the reasons for Baptists situating church buildings away from the main thoroughfares are rooted in the persecution of nonconformist churches during the seventeenth century.[58] Clyde Binfield makes a similar point, arguing that nonconformist architecture took time to

---

54. Harvey, *Condition of Postmodernity*, vii.
55. Giles, *Re-Pitching the Tent*, 63.
56. Briggs, *Puritan Architecture and Its Future*, 27.
57. Rusling, *Baptist Places of Worship*, 4.
58. Rusling, *Baptist Places of Worship*, 4.

develop and, even after the Act of Toleration of 1689, reflected a feeling of inferiority in comparison with the Church of England.[59]

Although there is an argument that the design of early nonconformist meeting houses emerged from the nature of their ecclesiology, Rusling's and Binfield's comments relating to the confidence of a congregation are also significant. While the interior of a church building creates a specific dynamic between the worship leader and the congregation, a building's exterior might tell a different story. In this respect, A. W. W. Dale's argument that many early Baptist churches were built in inconspicuous locations for fear that their worship would be disrupted suggests an element of fear and a lack of confidence among the congregation.[60] While this might be considered the case among some early Baptist congregations, the first Baptists in Newton Abbot do not appear to share this lack of confidence. Constructed in 1697, their first chapel, while a small structure, was situated on East Street, which Rhodes describes as a primary street in the town.[61]

Following a period when the Newton Abbot chapel was unoccupied, the confidence was rekindled when, in 1819, a small group of Baptists moved to the town from Bovey Tracey and restarted the congregation. This church grew and, according to Rhodes, the original chapel was quickly demolished and replaced with a larger building.[62] By 1830, the congregation had once again outgrown its premises, and an even larger building was constructed on the same site.[63] The need for yet another building was reached in 1863 when a new chapel was built adjacent to the current building. This new chapel was opened with a lavish ceremony lasting in excess of eight hours.

By constructing a new building, the Baptists in Newton Abbot were not simply expressing a confidence born out of an increase in number; they were also making a territorial statement. From an announcement made at the opening ceremony, it appears that the new building was considered to be a flagship among the local Baptist congregations in the South West. The implication here is that the new East Street Chapel declared a continued rise in the influence of the Baptists, not only in the

59. Binfield, "Nonconformist Architecture," 257.
60. Dale, *Life of R. W. Dale of Birmingham*, 170.
61. Rhodes, *Newton Abbot*, 97.
62. Rhodes, *Newton Abbot*, 97.
63. Stirling, *History of Newton Abbot and Newton Bushel*, 27. This building still exists and is now used by a spiritualist congregation.

Newton Abbot locality but also in the surrounding area. This link between a church building and the territory it influences resonates with the connection that Wink makes between a church and its mission to proclaim Christ.[64] With the need to construct increasingly larger buildings, the Baptists in Newton Abbot were fulfilling their mission to both spread the gospel and build the cause of nonconformity in the town. The difficulty with the statement made by the new building is two-fold. Firstly, while the new building was opened with a lavish ceremony heralding its significance, the accommodation was, from the outset, inappropriate for the obvious mission opportunities facing the church. This is evident from the church meeting minutes dated May 10, 1864:

> A Sabbath School was commenced the first Sunday after the opening service, and there being no schoolrooms is at the present held in the chapel. The school at first consisted of 10 teachers and 56 children; there are now 12 teachers + 90 Children.[65]

Although the new building may have made a territorial statement among the Baptists of South Devon, the lack of Sunday School accommodation might be considered short-sighted. This relationship between the church building and the congregation's mission became significant in the 2000s when the church decided to sell the East Street Chapel and rent premises for worship from Highweek Junior School. This decision was formalized in July 2003. As part of a church profile written in 2006, the church leaders expressed their belief that moving to the school had provided a catalyst for church growth.

Despite the positive statement issued in their church profile, a large minority of members refused to accept the decision and resigned their membership.[66] Although the perceived wisdom suggests that the move from the chapel building to the school was the correct one, documents contained within the Devon Heritage Centre suggest that the issue of ambience within the school building played a part in the discontent. In this respect, it is perhaps unsurprising that a school hall does not create the same ambience and, thus, the dynamic energy as a purpose-built worship area. A lack of dynamic energy may explain several comments relating to a deterioration in the quality of the preaching. It might also account for

---

64. Wink, *Unmasking the Powers*, 73.

65. Church meeting minutes, May 10, 1864, box 6916-1-1, Newton Abbot Baptist Church minute book Sept. 27, 1863–July 30, 1894, DHC.

66. Minister's report, 2004, box 6916, Newton Abbot Baptist Church, DHC.

some members' belief that they are no longer receiving anything from the services.[67] The perception that the space within Highweek School was affecting the dynamic energy among the congregation is further addressed in a letter dated October 2, 2004, where it was suggested that using a smaller room might enhance the experience of worship.[68]

The suggestion that using a smaller room might enhance the worship experience resonates with Kieckhefer's belief that a smaller space filled with seating enhances the dynamic interaction between the preacher and the worship leader.[69] If Kieckhefer is correct, using a smaller room for worship might also have solved the issues raised in respect of the minister's preaching.

In addition to raising the issue of the ambience of the building, the available documents also hint at a lack of confidence among the congregation. This is highlighted by comments regarding a lack of unity within the congregation and a belief that the decision to move from the East Street Chapel had been settled years before the congregation finally agreed to it. There is also a hint of this in a comment that they miss the church but feel that they should persevere with meeting in the school.[70] If there was a lack of confidence in the move to Highweek School, it may have been because the change of premises was motivated by economics as much as mission.

Confidence, Buildings and Mission

By the end of the twentieth century, the fortunes of the Newton Abbot Baptists had changed dramatically and despite their best efforts, the fabric of the building had deteriorated to a point where it was beyond economic repair. A report from the Architects Design Group dated October 13, 1998, suggests that continuing to maintain the church building would require a significant financial commitment.[71] As an alternative, the group offered two scenarios. The first was that part of the site could be sold and money raised used to fund the necessary refurbishment. Alternatively

---

67. Letter, Oct. 2, 2004, box 6916, Newton Abbot Baptist Church, DHC; Unsigned note, box 6916, Newton Abbot Baptist Church, DHC.

68. Letter, Oct. 2, 2004, box 6916, Newton Abbot Baptist Church, DHC.

69. Kieckhefer, *Theology in Stone*, 44–45.

70. Unsigned note, box 6916, Newton Abbot Baptist Church, DHC.

71. Architects Design Group, Oct. 13, 1998, Newton Abbot Baptist Church, South West Baptist Association Records.

they suggest that the whole plot could be sold for redevelopment and an alternative site sought for new accommodation.[72] As a consequence, the church considered its options and commissioned an evaluation report from Charles Blizzard and Beth Proudlock.[73] Blizzard and Proudlock's report noted that a site adjacent to the church was being redeveloped and suggested that the building be offered to the contractor for conversion into housing.[74] This proposition was accompanied by a "Church strategy report" suggesting that the church building was no longer helping the congregation to fulfill its mission.[75] Responding to these documents, the congregation agreed to experiment with meeting in a Highweek junior school. However, as discussed above, the congregation was far from united in their agreement to move to the school. In view of this, it is perhaps unsurprising that, while the congregation continued to meet for a further six years, the disruption caused by their move from the East Street Chapel appears to have seriously damaged the congregation's spiritual health. This disruption arguably contributed to their closing in 2009.

The Relationship Between a Congregation and Their Building

Kieckhefer's reflection on the nature of church buildings provides further insight into the connection between church members and their premises by describing the emotional energy that they invest in their buildings. He argues that entering a church building represents a spiritual process. Moreover, ecclesiastical architecture is designed specifically to assist and promote this process.[76]

Although the Baptists from the East Street Chapel never described their building as a sacred space, the bond that they maintained with it created a spiritual dynamism that lessened when they moved to Highweek School. This loss of dynamism is interesting in the context of the

---

72. Architects Design Group, Oct. 13, 1998, Newton Abbot Baptist Church, South West Baptist Association Records.

73. This report is undated; however, it is likely to have been commissioned either late in 1999 or in the early 2000s.

74. Charles Blizzard and Beth Proudlock, Report to the Minister, the Evaluation Group and the Deacons and Members of Newton Abbot Following a Visit by the Association Survey Team in the Action in Mission Project, box 6916, Newton Abbot Baptist Church, n.d., DHC.

75. Newton Abbot Baptist Church strategy, box 6916, Newton Abbot Baptist Church, n.d., DHC.

76. Kieckhefer, *Theology in Stone*, 21.

Newton Abbot Baptists as the energy that they appear to have derived from their building continues despite the amount of time and money they invested in repairing and renewing the building's fabric. In this context, the link that Wink makes between a church building, congregational identity, and the angel of the church suggests that the move to Highweek School created a breach between the congregation's identity and its angel. In view of this, it is unsurprising that the church lost its dynamism and eventually closed. Of course, this is not to say that the church, which was already in decline, would not have finally become unsustainable. However, the disruption caused by exiting a building, which at its opening had articulated a sense of confidence, appears to have played a significant role in their demise.

The Story of the Peruvian Church

In addition to using his experience of taking a Bible study in opulent surroundings, Wink also uses the story of his visit to a Peruvian church to illustrate the influence a building can have on a congregation. According to Wink, the church was situated in the central square of Cuzco in Peru and was significant because it was situated on the site of an Inca temple. For Wink, the fact that the temple had been razed by Spanish invaders, built with the aid of slave labor, and adorned with gold leaf that had been plundered from the original temple left an indelible mark on the church.[77] However, while Wink believes that the history of this building has led to the sensation that the church itself was dead, he contrasts the church with a similar congregation that appeared to have more spiritual life and concludes that "architecture does not equate to destiny."[78] In light of this comment and Harvey's exploration of how culture can inform architecture, Wink's assertion might be without foundation. For, if architecture can be adapted to address the needs of the current community, then whether the church is built on an ancient Inca site is of less consequence than the motivation of the congregation to fulfill their vocation.

While there might have been a belief in the continuing spiritual presence at the Peruvian site, the historical events that led to the sacking of the temple and the building of the church in its place cannot be overlooked. In this respect, Wink may be correct in assuming that the

77. Wink, *Unmasking the Powers*, 74.
78. Wink, *Unmasking the Powers*, 74.

guilt of the past was affecting the current nature of the church. However, if this is Wink's intention, his illustration may make more of a historical than a social-geographic or architectural point.

Buildings in Location and Time

Like Harvey, Edward Soja addresses geography within a postmodern context. However, his focus is on the relationship between a location and a time. He argues that, during the past century, the study of history held a prominent place in exploring social science.[79] Therefore, under the title *Postmodern Geographies: The Reassertion of Space in Critical Social Theory*, Soja presents a series of essays that seek to reclaim the importance of physical space in understanding a society. In this respect, because the Peruvian church in Wink's illustration is built on the site of an Inca temple, it might be thought that, even though the temple represents a different religious tradition, the construction of a new worship center represents a continuity of religious ethos. Turner develops this theory when he explores the history of constructing church buildings on the sites of pagan temples. He suggests that among the early church there was a desire to sleep in the newly constructed church in the hope God would reveal himself in a dream or vision. According to Turner, this desire was validated by the spiritual significance of the temple sites.[80]

Wink's illustration of the Peruvian church highlights Soja's contention that experiences are set in both a location and a time.[81] If the reason behind the Peruvian congregation's failure to fulfill their vocation is the guilt over the sacking of the temple. In that case, Soja's contention that history often provides the primary interpretation of geography is confirmed.[82] However, suppose the failure of the church to fulfill its vocation is associated with the significance of Cuzco as a center for the polytheistic worship of the Incas. In that case, Soja's argument for the influence of geography on society is supported. Either way, Wink's use of a lifeless church in Cuzco presents a weak case for the influence of a building over a congregation's angel. Despite this, it is possible to argue that, from a

---

79. Soja, *Postmodern Geographies*, 1.
80. Turner, *From Temple to Meeting House*, 172–73.
81. Soja, *Postmodern Geographies*, 14.
82. Soja, *Postmodern Geographies*, 14.

spiritual perspective, the territory occupied by the Peruvian church may be affecting its vocation.

The Relationship Between a Location, Its History, and Its Sacredness

Although she is not a social geographer, Susan White explores the relationship between a place, its history, and its sacredness. She suggests that there is a relationship between what happens at a location and the sort of energy it projects. White argues that a building or a location can lose its sense of holiness if it becomes associated with violence, greed, injustice, pride, or division. However, she also suggests that the sense of holiness might be regained if these associations are repudiated.[83] Commenting on this position, John Inge considers it to be too narrow a viewpoint. Pointing to Jerusalem, Inge argues that as a city, it has suffered a great deal of violence and yet is still considered to be a holy destination.[84] Although Inge's point is valid when taken from the perspective of pilgrims visiting Jerusalem, his argument does not address the spiritual dynamism present in a place. In Wink's illustration of the Peruvian church, the suggestion is that the violence inflicted on the original temple may have contaminated its spirituality and thus created the dead sensation he experienced. While not identifying the church in question, Eduardo Galeano's description of the pillage of Cuzco and the building of colonial buildings on the foundations of the previous Inca architecture resonates with Wink's narrative.[85] Furthermore, in the description of a second Peruvian church, where there was vibrancy and life in the congregation, Wink hints at the repudiation described by White.[86]

Summary

Of the six facets of church life that Wink highlights, "architecture and ambience" is one of the few that he devotes time to developing. However, having noted this, the development only extends to two illustrations: the Bible study in an opulent home and the visit to a Peruvian church. Although

---

83. White, "Theology of Sacred Space," 42.
84. Inge, *Christian Theology of Place*, 83.
85. Galeano, *Open Veins of Latin America*, 19–20.
86. Wink, *Unmasking the Powers*, 74.

both of these illustrations suggest a link between the architecture and ambience of a place and the spiritual energy of the location, each story has its weaknesses. In the case of the Bible study, because the focus of the story being explored was Jesus' exhortation to the rich young man to give up his wealth, the opulence of the context may have caused unease among the participants that related to their own social status. Likewise, as Wink indicates, the issue in the Peruvian church that appeared dead may have been the collective guilt that the congregation felt over the sacking of the temple that provided the site for the new church. Despite these weaknesses, the essence of Wink's argument that architecture and ambience affect the dynamic energy of a location appears to be valid.

Further support is given to Wink's argument by social geographers such as Creswell, Harvey, and Soja. In each case, these scholars argue that there is a relationship between a location and its residents. For Creswell, this relationship demonstrates that the outcome of the dialogue between a people and their location represents the physical manifestation of theoretical concepts. In this respect, Kieckhefer's work on the relationship between theology and architecture is important. In the context of a local church, Creswell's and Kieckhefer's arguments point to a building representing a practical expression of the ideology of a congregation's forefathers. Thus, the design of the building will contribute to a continuity of theology and liturgical practice being passed from one generation to another. This resonates with Wink's belief and is evident, in different ways, in the construction of the chapels at Budleigh Salterton and Newton Abbot. Whereas the compact interior of the church at Budleigh Salterton draws the congregation into an intimate relationship between the preacher and congregation, the increased size and statements of importance made at its opening in 1863 created a vocation that the Newton Abbot Baptists failed to sustain.

Vocation

If the statements made at the opening ceremony at the East Street Chapel in Newton Abbot did reflect the mind of Christ, it would have, using Wink's understanding of the term, represented the congregation's vocation. Thus, moving from the East Street Chapel to Highweek School for economic reasons would represent a failure to aspire to Christ's calling. This apparent failure might have been augmented if the new site had been purchased using the funds from the sale of the East Street Chapel. However, the presenting difficulties relating to the move to Highweek School appear to relate more to the ambience of the room they were using.

It would seem obvious that the reason for the lack of ambience within the school hall was due to the premises being designed as an educational establishment rather than a place of worship. However, as many of the complaints regarding the move to the new venue occurred shortly after the transition, the apparent lack of ambience may also be attributed to the fact that there had been little time for congregational memories to be formed. Of course, this argument might also be applicable to a congregation moving to a new building of their own. However, in this context, the congregation would have the shared experience of raising funds for and outlining the designs of the new premises.

Moving to Highweek School also involved moving to a place where the space was not dedicated to their sole use. This shared usage meant that the congregation was not at liberty to furnish the space in a way that would have augmented worship. In a letter held at the Devon Heritage Centre, church members reflect on their experience of worshiping both in the East Street Chapel and in Highweek School. As their argument unfolds, they explore the relationship between church furniture and worship and muse that the artifacts used to adorn a worship space may have more value than they had previously considered.[87] Despite this being mentioned in a letter sent to the deacons, the minute books do not record any discussion regarding furnishing the room used at Highweek School in such a way as to improve the atmosphere for worship. This oversight may highlight that the underlying reasons for moving to Highweek School were functional rather than vocational. If this were the case, it might also explain the anxious nature of the church and its angel.

The Nature of the Angel

In the chapters that follow, the results of the relationship between the people and their buildings will be revealed in different ways. In the case of the church at Budleigh Salterton, the intimate relationship between preacher and congregation, accentuated by the nature of their building, may explain the commitment the congregation shows to employing a minister.

---

87. Unsigned typed letter noted "Please distribute to each deacon," box 6916, Newton Abbot Baptist Church, n.d. (possibly 2004), DHC.

Likewise, the expectation expressed at the opening of the building in Newton Abbot may go some way to explaining the anxiety expressed by the church when it moved to Highweek School. In this respect, the link that Wink makes between a building, congregational identity, and vocation provides a significant challenge to a church that can no longer maintain its premises. While the Newton Abbot Baptists were clear in their assertion that the move to Highweek School would aid their missionary endeavor and thus contribute to fulfilling their vocation, the records of their discussions suggest that the church had not fully considered the emotional link between the congregation and the East Street Chapel. Exactly how much of this emotional link is bound up with the collective memory relating to the vocational statement made at the opening ceremony is unclear. However, the high level of anxiety recorded in the church records and accompanying correspondence is evident, as will become apparent later as the anxious nature of the Newton Abbot Baptists and their angel reveals itself in other areas of church life. This anxious nature contrasts with the nature of the angel of the Baptists in Budleigh Salterton, who, in a variety of scenarios, demonstrate their tenacity and creativity when dealing with practical issues facing the church.

Architecture and Changing the Nature of the Angel

According to Wink, the nature of the angel of the church is shaped by a congregation's vocation as much as it is by the social interaction of the congregation.[88] Harvey's contention that the change of architectural design adopted by urban planners has taken place in response to a cultural transformation might provide an insight into how the nature of the angel of the church can change. If the design of a building changes in response to cultural transformation, a reciprocal change might also occur within a church and with its angel, as the newly designed buildings influence the nature and culture of the community in new ways. In view of this, Giles's argument that architecture can and should be adapted to meet new cultural challenges is significant. Along with Harvey's insights on the dialogue between culture and architectural design, Giles's work on adapting church buildings to meet contemporary missional challenges invites a local congregation to explore its relationship with its buildings.

---

88. Wink, *Unmasking the Powers*, 73.

It also invites a church to consider how that relationship aids or hinders the fulfillment of not only its mission but also its vocation.

Soja's contribution to Wink's contention is linking experience and location. When juxtaposed with White's work on the spirituality of locations, Soja's argument supports Wink's thesis by articulating the link between personal stories and their locations. When discerning the angel of a church, Soja's and White's works provide a reminder of the importance of the relationship between memorable events and church building. This link between story, memorable events, and a building appears to have resonated with the Newton Abbot Baptists as they moved to Highweek School. By leaving the chapel in East Street, the Baptists at Newton Abbot left behind a building rich in memories to inhabit a hall that was designed for a purpose other than worship. This, along with the struggles that the congregation faced in coming to terms with the move, may have resulted in the church failing to thrive in their new location.

Finally, working with the tools of phenomenology, Turner's and Norberg-Schulz's exploration of the dynamic energy created by different types of architecture and locations provides an important source of support for Wink's argument. The concept of *genius loci* offers a basis from which the concept of a transcendent angel representing an earthly church can be discussed further. If, as Norberg-Schulz suggests, when a people settle in a place, it provides a venue from which they can orient themselves and identify with the construction of a church building, it not only creates a place within which people can gather to worship, it also forms a base from which a congregation's vocation can be expressed.[89] In this respect, Turner's review of *domus Dei* and *domus ecclesiae* is helpful because it questions the focus of a congregation's endeavor. If the church is seen as *domus Dei*, the emphasis of its vocation will be focused on drawing new members into the presence of God. In view of this, it might be argued that while the architecture of Budleigh Salterton Baptist Church is very basic, the intimate dynamic created by the proximity of the pews to the preacher might be seen as creating an environment where God is more easily encountered. Therefore, while there is no indication that the Baptists at Budleigh Salterton viewed their building as a *domus Dei*, the simplicity of the interior design may have created this effect.

Although Wink's concept is underdeveloped, his suggestion finds significant support among the group of social geographers and

---

89. Norberg-Schulz, *Genius Loci*, 50.

phenomenologists included in this conversation. Furthermore, even though the works referenced in this exploration represent both sociological and theological standpoints, they all point to a relationship between people, a location, and a dynamic energy. From Wink's perspective, and in the context of a local church congregation, this relationship and energy forms part of the angel of the church. However, as will become evident, the nature of the angel cannot be ascertained by a single facet of church life. Therefore, the next chapter will explore Wink's contention that demographics affect the nature of the church and its angel.

3

Demographics

ALTHOUGH THE SECOND FACET of church life that Wink considers in his advice on observing the angel appears to be a list of social descriptors, collectively, they form the basis of a demographic profile. Therefore, in this chapter, the aspects of a congregation's demographic profile listed in the following quotation from Wink's work will be explored and illustrated with stories from Baptist congregations. Wink states:

> A great deal of what a church is and does is determined by the economic class and income of its members, their racial and ethnic background, level of education, age, and gender balance. These show how the members talk, what they expect the church to do, where they live, where the church is located, and the ideological and political preferences of the members. Class extends even to unwritten dress code and behavior norms.[1]

While he does not elaborate on this subject in the way he does with architecture and ambience, his statement provides a significant starting point for a conversation about the relationship between the social demographic of a congregation and the ability to fulfill its vocation. The difficulty with this facet of Wink's concept of the angel of the church is that its application is predominantly sociological. Although many of the demographic aspects of church life listed by Wink can and will be illustrated with stories of Baptist congregations, it is difficult to define these

---

1. Wink, *Unmasking the Powers*, 74.

experiences as theological.² In this respect, it is possible that although the Powers Trilogy expresses Wink's journey toward a more mystical view of theology, some aspects of his work continue to reflect his rationalistic starting point. Therefore, the lack of an illustrative story might reveal that Wink's experience of the spiritual has failed to inform his theology in these areas of church life.

Despite this, the link between a church and its vocation remains an important issue for Wink. However, it is important to note that, in Wink's understanding, a congregation's vocation represents what they might become in Christ and not necessarily the things that they achieve. It is the correlation between the nature of a congregation and the possibility that is held in Christ that differentiates a church from other forms of organization. For this reason, while sociological studies can describe how a church is formed and embarks on its mission, it is the nature of its vocation that transforms it into a theological organization. Therefore, while this exploration of congregational demographics will look like a sociological study, it remains tethered to the belief that the church's vocation is to connect the earthly world with the transcendent God.

Economic Class

In the exploration of Wink's contention that demographics affect the nature of the church, the missioner Donald McGavran's comment "men [sic] like to become Christians without crossing racial, linguistic or class barriers"³ is interesting. Supporting his comment, McGavran suggests that every community has its own unique dynamic, and he uses stories from several different nations to illustrate this argument.⁴ Although these stories are not appropriate in a study of English Baptist churches, his understanding that communities are separated into different social strata offers an important insight to Wink's angel of the church. Furthermore, McGavran's reflection on the power structure within a community

---

2. Until this point in the study, Wink's concept of the angels of churches has been illustrated with stories drawn from the records of four Baptist congregations in the West Country. However, the records kept by these congregations do not offer sufficient material to illustrate every aspect that Wink raises under the umbrella of demographics. Therefore, in this section the illustrative stories that either support or critique Wink's contention will be taken from a broader selection of Baptist records and writing.

3. McGavran, *Understanding Church Growth*, 198.

4. McGavran, *Understanding Church Growth*, 183–97.

resonates with the relationship between the established church and the nonconformists in England during the nineteenth century.

Non-Conformity, Class, and Power

According to B. G. Worrall, during the nineteenth century, nonconformist congregations experienced a period of growth in numbers and confidence.[5] Although the repeal of the Test and Corporation Acts allowed increased freedom for nonconformists to serve the local community through public office, relationships with the Church of England remained strained.

The legislation contained within the Test and Corporations Acts dated back to the restoration of the monarchy in the seventeenth century and prevented nonconformists, such as Baptists, from serving the local community in public office. The Test Act passed in 1673, and the earlier Corporation Act of 1671 required office holders in civil and military authorities to take communion according to the rites of the Church of England.[6] Thus, refusal meant that nonconformists could hold neither public nor military office.

According to Worrall, while these acts were repealed in 1828, nonconformists continued to feel aggrieved that there was no change in the practice of the Church of England receiving a degree of prestige within society not given to the free churches. Furthermore, the established church continued to receive financial benefits not enjoyed by the dissenting congregations.[7] These grievances illustrate the power structure explored by McGavran. Whereas the Church of England, as the established church, represented the aristocracy with its inherited wealth and power, the nonconformists were regarded as belonging to a lower social class. Illustrating this, Worrall argues that members of nonconformist churches who were successful in business were, for social reasons, unlikely to leave their congregations and join the Church of England.[8] This insight into the social class division, reflected in the type of church attended, is not restricted to the divide between nonconformists and the Church of England. Recounting the story of the Baptists in

---

5. Worrall, *Making of the Modern Church*, 134.
6. Watts, *Dissenters*, 223, 51–52.
7. Worrall, *Making of the Modern Church*, 144.
8. Worrall, *Making of the Modern Church*, 140–41.

Barnoldswick, Keith Jones highlights how different social philosophies caused a Baptist congregation to divide and form two churches, each of which attracted members from different social classes.[9]

The Baptists of Barnoldswick

Writing in the *Baptist Quarterly* in July 1983, Jones recounts how the Baptist community in Barnoldswick, Lancashire, divided over a pastor's attempt to provide work for the unemployed. According to Jones, Thomas Bennett, a former print worker from Accrington, was called to be the minister at the Baptist church in Barnoldswick in 1844. At this time, the principal trade in the area was weaving, and opposite the church was a clough shed that housed three hundred looms. In 1860, due to the economic climate, the Bracewell brothers, who ran this operation, closed the business, relinquished their lease, and left the area. This caused a sharp rise in unemployment and led Bennett to explore ways of relieving the situation.[10] Jones's research shows that Bennett took over the tenancy vacated by the Bracewells and employed their staff. However, the difficulties in the weaving industry continued, and Bennett was forced into bankruptcy. The irony of this story is that it was Clayton Slater, a member of Bennett's church, who forced him into bankruptcy. According to Jones, Slater became a wealthy mill owner and, along with other families of similar social standing, left the church to form the New Chapel in North Street, Barnoldswick. Furthermore, Jones suggests that the separation was not to the detriment of the original congregation, as the two churches flourished: they were known locally as the employers' and employees' churches. Jones contends that the social differences between the congregations continued to be evident up until the 1950s.[11]

Reflecting on this story, Jones suggests that Slater and Bennett represent opposite positions on the exercise of leadership, with Bennett accepting the rule of the majority in the tradition of Baptist congregational government and Slater expecting assent according to his dictum as the owner/leader. Jones surmises that Bennett's values undermined Clayton's capitalist ethos and his ability to instill discipline among his workforce. This conflict in ethos led Slater to manufacture the circumstances

9. Jones, "Industrial Revolution."
10. Jones, "Industrial Revolution," 127.
11. Jones, "Industrial Revolution," 126–28.

necessary for Bennett's bankruptcy and was part of a larger struggle to remove him from the pastorate.[12]

The central part of this story illustrates Wink's assertion that the social values of the economic class from which a congregation is predominantly formed are difficult to overcome.[13] In Bethesda, the original Baptist chapel in Barnoldswick, the congregation continued to be predominantly working-class weavers, whereas the new North Street church echoed the middle-class management and factory owner profile of Slater, its founder.[14] However, the eventual outcome illustrates that this form of division can be overcome as, in 1971, the congregations at Bethesda and North Street were combined, and in 1977 they occupied a new set of premises.[15]

The significance of the two churches merging is accentuated when the membership returns submitted to the Baptist Union of Great Britain are examined. These annual records of church membership suggest that, while both congregations had experienced a decline,[16] neither had become so small as to be considered unsustainable. If, as their membership returns suggest, the congregations reunited for reasons other than sustainability, Wink's argument that the class divide can be overcome is also supported. The reuniting of these congregations also suggests that the nature of a congregation and its angel can be changed. However, in this case, the nature of the church and its angel are not simply changed by the ability of a single leader to overcome the history and tradition of each. The merging of two congregations that had separated acrimoniously requires skillful leadership in each church, along with an ability within each congregation to rise to the challenge of living by a higher set of ideals. This confluence of skilled leadership and the willingness to change that allowed the churches in Barnoldswick to reunite represents not only the transforming of two angels but the emergence of a third, new angel, as the merging congregations formed a new church. Just as it might be argued that the angel of the Baptist church in Newton

12. Jones, "Industrial Revolution," 136–37.
13. Wink, *Unmasking the Powers*, 74.
14. Jones, "Industrial Revolution," 137.
15. Jones, "Industrial Revolution," 135.
16. By 1971 the membership at North Street and Bethesda was 61 and 70, respectively. *Baptist Handbook for 1971*, 194. This marks a decline from 1900 when the number of membership totalled 178 for North Street and 136 for Bethesda. Avery, *Baptist Handbook for 1900*, 325.

Abbot died as the link between the congregation and its building was severed, so, in the case of Barnoldswick, a new angel is formed from the combination of two churches.

Aside from the fact that Slater participated in Bennett's bankruptcy, Jones's story is disturbing because of the violence and intimidation exercised by Slater in his attempt to remove Bennett from the pastorate. In this respect, the two events described by Jones illustrate the depths of Slater's animosity toward Bennett. The first is a report from the *Bradford Observer* dated December 14, 1868, recounting a court case where Slater is accused of using violence to remove Bennett from the pulpit.[17] In the second instance, having failed to convince the church meeting to remove Bennett from the pastorate, Slater approached the church trustees and persuaded them to withhold the part of Bennett's stipend that was raised by the renting of properties owned by the church. The withholding of the rental portion of the stipend continued for ten years when the High Court eventually settled it in favor of Bennett.[18]

The accounts of Slater's actions in his attempts to remove Bennett from the pastorate invite the question of whether, at this point in its history, the angel of the church at Barnoldswick had become demonic. In Wink's opinion, a congregation's angel becomes demonic when they turn away from the mission to which God has called them and focus on an alternative goal.[19] Therefore, the answer to this question appears to be that the angel had not become demonic. According to Jones's story, only part of the church rejected the values of collaboration and benevolence modeled by Bennett. Furthermore, Bennett remained pastor of Bethesda, the original Baptist church in Barnoldswick, until he died in 1886.[20] This suggests that while Slater's actions were unpleasant, they did not prevent the Bethesda church from continuing its mission.

Slater's actions that led Bennett into bankruptcy and then sought to drive him from the pastorate through violence and intimidation do appear demonic. However, once Slater had set aside his dispute with Bennett and concentrated on the new Baptist church in Barnoldswick, the fact that the church thrived suggests that any demonic influence was temporary. Furthermore, with both churches in Barnoldswick drawing members from different class statuses, it appears that the effectiveness

---

17. Jones, "Industrial Revolution," 130.
18. Jones, "Industrial Revolution," 131.
19. Wink, *Unmasking the Powers*, 78.
20. Jones, "Industrial Revolution," 132.

of the Baptists in the town to introduce people to the transcendent God was doubled. The difficulty with this conclusion is that the expansion is expressed by two churches dividing over social class. In view of this, whether the formation of the second church was a fulfillment of God's calling is debatable. Despite this, by eventually overcoming the divisions that had separated them, the congregations could be seen as fulfilling part of their vocation. This is because the reunification of the two congregations required each church to rise above the values of the social strata that had previously separated them.

Drifting into the Middle Class

In *The Making of the Modern Church*, Worrall notes that it was not uncommon for congregations to experience growth during the nineteenth century and that this expansion was particularly evident among the middle class. David Bebbington makes a similar observation in *Evangelicalism in Modern Britain*. However, from information contained in the 1851 census, he deduces that church attendance must have also comprised a significant number of people from the working class. Even so, he concedes that the nineteenth century attracted fewer members from the working class.[21] Despite this, Worrall notes that while many congregations had become middle class, they continued to be committed to taking the gospel to the poor. However, he argues that the lifestyle that accompanied membership in a nonconformist church inevitably led to a shift in class.[22] In view of this, Worrall argues that Free Churches not only extensively drew their members from the middle classes, they also helped create them.[23] While it is arguable whether this elevation in social class represents the adoption of the higher set of values, which Wink suggests lifts a congregation from the behavioral norm associated with their social class, it does represent a change in the values that inform their lifestyle. Worrall considers industry, thrift, and temperance as key for nineteenth-century nonconformists.[24] Worrall contends that the adoption of these principles resulted in church members becoming middle class.[25]

---

21. Bebbington, *Evangelicalism in Modern Britain*, 110–11.
22. Worrall, *Making of the Modern Church*, 140–41.
23. Worrall, *Making of the Modern Church*, 141.
24. Worrall, *Making of the Modern Church*, 141.
25. Worrall, *Making of the Modern Church*, 141.

The imposition of moral values was not the only reason for nonconformist congregations being transformed from working to middle class. Worrall also notes that during the expansion of the nineteenth century, the focus of nonconformist witness moved from villages and the inner city to the suburbs. This, in turn, led to the increase of predominantly middle class congregations that were formed.[26] Writing in 1880, Edward Smith observes and critiques migration to the suburbs:

> Godliness leads to sobriety and to additional power in the mind and prosperity is secured. To the prosperous, great temptation is presented. Trams and railways invite a movement towards, or into the suburbs, and thus the salt that once seasoned the thronging myriads extracts itself from them and goes where it is not so nearly needed.[27]

In addition to supporting Worrall's contention that the nineteenth century experienced an exodus from the villages and urban conurbations, Smith's comment is also used by K. S. Inglis to explore a similar phenomenon.

Inglis's approach to the migration to the suburbs is to explore its impact on rural and urban churches and chapels. He argues that nonconformists suffered more than the established church as their financial stability was more closely linked to wealthy individuals who supported their cause.[28] Commenting on the emigration from the urban centers, Inglis notes that nonconformists attempted to continue their links with the poor by financing charitable work in the areas that they had left.[29] The difficulty with this approach is that by financing a third party to attend to those who remained in the urban centers, nonconformists accentuated the social divide between themselves and those they had left behind.

The suggestion that congregations of a certain social stratum were formed because of their geographical position resonates further with the undercurrent of Wink's belief that there is a determinism within each social class that affects the nature of congregations. Whereas early Baptist churches were transformed from working to middle class through the aspiration of a high moral code, newly formed churches naturally adopted the demographic of their locality. This relationship between the social

---

26. Worrall, *Making of the Modern Church*, 141–42.
27. Smith, *Great Problem of the Times*, 3.
28. Inglis, *Churches and the Working Classes*, 63–64.
29. Inglis, *Churches and the Working Classes*, 64.

demographic of a community and the nature of the church is explored by the sociologist Max Weber in *Essays in Sociology*.

Weber is attributed with correlating religious practice with specific social classes.[30] For example, he is cited by Richard Niebuhr as linking Confucianism with the Chinese literary class and Islam with the Arabian military classes.[31] However, while Weber makes these connections, he believes that the correlation between types of religious practice and differing social strata are not absolute. He argues that while certain social demographics leave a mark on the nature of religious practice, their link with a certain social stratum is fluid.[32] Although, due to their ecclesiology, it is impossible to treat Baptists as a uniform group, broadly speaking, the history of English Baptists points to a demographic shift toward the middle class.

The demographic shift experienced by nineteenth-century congregations may have contributed toward the Baptist church meeting adopting a business model during the 1850s. Although Malcolm Egner does not reference this possibility, he does consider the transformation to be a reaction to the increasing complexity of church life.[33] In this respect, the move improved the functionality of congregations and enabled them to continue to fulfill their vocation amid changes in the prevailing culture. However, while the adoption of a business model of meeting enabled churches to become more complex institutions, it also caused the church meeting to become more confrontational.[34] Egner's research highlights the difficulties faced by nineteenth-century Baptist congregations as they became more institutionalized. While he does not reference the demographic shift experienced by Baptists in the nineteenth century, the subtle changes within the church meeting resonate with Wink's contention that the norms of a predominant social stratum can affect the way a church functions. This correlation between a congregation's demographic and its ability to attain its aspirations is seen in T. Dowley's research into the prevalence of church discipline among seventeenth-century Baptists.[35]

---

30. Niebuhr, *Social Sources of Denominationalism*, 77–78.
31. Niebuhr, *Social Sources of Denominationalism*, 77–78.
32. Weber, *Essays in Sociology*, 268.
33. Egner, "Re-Imagining the Covenant Community," 24–26.
34. Egner, "Re-Imagining the Covenant Community," 27.
35. Dowley, "Baptists and Discipline," 157.

Education

Exploring this phenomenon, Dowley contends that there is a link between the regularity of church discipline and the demographic of the early Baptists. Dowley's research suggests that the majority of members of seventeenth-century Baptist churches lacked a formal education.[36] Furthermore, their lack of education meant that they were predominantly in subservient occupations, such as laboring, domestic service, and retail. Dowley argues that these socio-economic factors caused early Baptists to struggle with the administration of church affairs. This, along with the demanding moral and ethical stance early Baptists required of their members, inevitably resulted in a high number of instances where church members were disciplined.[37] Egner's research into the process of Baptist church meetings suggests that the regular practice of church discipline continued into the eighteenth century. However, by the nineteenth century, the number of disciplinary incidences recorded became less, and meetings were dominated by applications for membership and the transfer of members to or from other congregations.[38] In light of Dowley's critique of Baptists' ability to manage church affairs in the seventeenth century and Egner's observations of church records in the nineteenth century, it appears that the shift in social demography equipped many Baptist congregations to develop a bureaucracy that enabled growing churches to be effectively managed. Of course, this does not necessarily mean that an increase in the number of educated church members affected the difficulties associated with making Christian disciples. However, Dowley's and Egner's research does support Wink's contention that the level of education within a congregation will affect its nature and how it functions. Furthermore, if the dynamics of an earthly congregation are changed by the level of education within the congregation, the nature of the angel of the church will also be changed.

Racial and Ethnic Background

In their publication *Churches and Churchgoers*, Robert Currie, Alan Gilbert, and Lee Horsley describe the spheres within which the church

---

36. Dowley, "Baptists and Discipline," 164.
37. Dowley, "Baptists and Discipline," 164.
38. Egner, "Re-Imagining the Covenant Community," 22.

influences its internal and external constituencies. According to Currie et al., while there are exceptions, a church usually recruits from these constituencies.[39] For these researchers, the term "internal constituency" relates to the group of people in immediate contact with the congregation. These include family members and individuals who attend church regularly but have not, as yet, fully committed themselves to the church. In a Baptist context, this latter group might be referred to as adherents rather than members. The external constituency represents members of the local community who have no previous relationship with the church but have an interest in religion. Currie et al. suggest that the distinctive nature of a church is drawn from its constituencies and argue that these constituencies represent and replicate a portion of the local society.[40] Drawing on the work of McGavran and Niebuhr, Currie et al. suggest that a congregation's external constituency is likely to be formed of a specific social demographic over which they have very little control.[41] However, for the church to continue to flourish, it must remain harmonious with and meet the specific requirements of this portion of its local community.[42] Of course, this assumes that all churches are local. In a Baptist tradition, where the church is defined by a gathered congregation, the church's meeting point can be far from the place where the church members are resident. Examples of this would be city center churches where, over time, an increase in industrialization and commerce has meant that church members who were once resident locally have moved away from the area. However, while there might be exceptions where Baptist congregations are local to their meeting point, the research carried out by Currie et al. is relevant.

Reflecting the relationship between a congregation and the racial and ethnic demographic of a community, Currie et al. note that some people groups identify themselves with a particular religious tradition. As an illustration of this phenomenon, they refer to the link between the influx of Irish and Polish migrants between 1900 and 1960s to England and the growth in numbers attending Roman Catholic churches during the same period.[43] Currie et al. also remark that a shared language can also create a specific constituency from which a church might draw

39. Currie et al., *Churches and Chuchgoers*, 6.
40. Currie et al., *Churches and Chuchgoers*, 46.
41. Currie et al., *Churches and Chuchgoers*, 6, 54–55.
42. Currie et al., *Churches and Chuchgoers*, 6–7.
43. Currie et al., *Churches and Chuchgoers*, 50.

members. Describing this, they note how Welsh-speaking congregations differentiate themselves from churches of a similar tradition in England and Scotland. From a Baptist perspective, while the Baptist Union of Great Britain contains member churches from Scotland and Wales, the majority of Scottish Baptist churches are affiliated with the Baptist Union of Scotland, and Welsh-speaking Baptist congregations tend to be affiliated with the Baptist Union of Wales.

Leadership and Responding to Demographic Change

Wink's belief that a congregation's ability to respond to a change in their demographic is linked to the practice of leadership is aptly illustrated by David Wise's experience at Greenford Baptist Church in Middlesex. Writing in *Ministry Today*, Wise, the pastor of Greenford Baptist Church, describes how the ethnic make-up of his congregation had changed during the twenty-seven years of his ministry. He explains that the church that had called him to be their pastor was "a traditional church with an almost completely 'white-English' congregation."[44] Over the course of his ministry, the ethnic demographic of the church changed, and currently, Wise suggests that there might be as many as forty nations represented at each worship service.[45] His response to the ethnic diversification of the congregation was to encourage representatives from different cultures to lead worship in the style of their own tradition. According to Wise, this development was not welcomed by the "all-white English group" that usually led congregational singing. As a result of his attempts to overcome the resistance to including new worship styles congruent with the new sections of the congregation, all of the original worship leaders resigned.[46]

Recovering from this situation, Wise's first action was to oversee the appointment of worship leaders who were willing to incorporate songs from different ethnic traditions. He also encouraged individuals from a non-English or non-white heritage to participate in leading worship. Initially, this did not produce the desired results. According to Wise, despite coming from a different ethnic background, the new leaders led Sunday worship in an English style. Illustrating this, he notes

---

44. Wise, "Multi-Ethnic Worship," 24.
45. Wise, "Multi-Ethnic Worship," 24.
46. Wise, "Multi-Ethnic Worship," 25.

that initially, the new leaders only chose songs written in North America or the United Kingdom. He explains that encouraging these new, non-English leaders to introduce songs written in their mother tongues and using their own cultural expressions took a long time.[47]

According to Wise's narrative, the church grew numerically throughout this process, and after several years, the church was able to appoint another member of staff. This new worker, Andy, was given the dual responsibilities of youth work and developing congregational worship. To encourage Andy to continue transforming Sunday worship from a traditional white, English format to one that represented the ethnic diversity of the current congregation, he was given an opportunity to experience a short course at All Nations College. Wise explained that encouraging the new worker to study the cultural differences in worship empowered him to continue transforming attitudes to congregational worship at Greenford Baptist Church.[48]

Although Wise does not mention the correlation between the growth in non-white members and the surrounding community, it is safe to assume that because the church continued to grow, it remained congruous with both its internal and external constituencies. According to Currie et al., this is one of the key requirements for recruiting new members.[49] By transforming Sunday worship services, Greenford Baptist Church ensured it continued to appeal to the portion of its external constituency that was disposed toward attending church.[50] Furthermore, the success appears to be due to Wise's desire and commitment to lift the congregation out of the constraints of their history as a white-English congregation and reach for a set of ideals that encompassed their new demographic. All of this resonates with Wink's belief that leadership plays a crucial role in the transformation of a congregation.

Significantly, Wise's experience also shows that the transformation undertaken by the church was not without its difficulties. Not only did he experience resistance from a white-English group who appeared to be becoming a minority within the regular congregation, he also met resistance from non-English groups to leading worship in ways that were other than English or North American. The fact that he can express the success of the transformation of Sunday worship is a testimony to his ability to lead the

47. Wise, "Multi-Ethnic Worship," 25.
48. Wise, "Multi-Ethnic Worship," 26.
49. Currie et al., *Churches and Chuchgoers*, 7.
50. Currie et al., *Churches and Chuchgoers*, 7.

congregation out of the constraints of its original traditional white English ethnicity. However, the difficulties that Wise overcomes also suggests that a church might struggle to overcome its historical demographic, even in the light of the make-up of its current congregation.

While the resistance to change exhibited by the white-English church members resonates with Wink's argument that the angel of the church has a gyroscopic effect that continually brings the church back to its original course, the resistance to change exhibited by a different ethnic group is interesting; an answer to this might be found in Wink's belief that people must be accepted before they can change.[51] It is possible that, by leading worship in an English or North American style, the members from different ethnic backgrounds felt that they would be accepted. However, while this might have been the case within the constraints of the congregation, by learning to lead worship in their native tongue and tradition, the members from a different ethnic community created a context where visitors from the ethnically diverse locality might feel both welcome and accepted. In the context of the angel of the church, this marks a significant transformation. By accepting the challenge to lead worship in their own tongue and tradition, the non-English members of Greenford Baptist Church added a new dimension to worship that enabled the church to remain congruent with its ethnically diverse community.

Although Wise does not account for the spiritual dimension in the process of changing the nature of worship services at Greenford Baptist Church, the fact that he refers to unpleasantness leading up to the transformation highlights the inertia created by the angel of the church.[52] This story also highlights Wink's belief that it is in the act of worship that the influence of the angel is most explicitly experienced and yet is often not recognized.[53]

Income

As might be expected among Baptist congregations, the nineteenth-century drift to the middle class was not a universal phenomenon. Writing to

---

51. Wink, *Unmasking the Powers*, 81.
52. Wise, "Multi-Ethnic Worship," 25.
53. Wink, *Unmasking the Powers*, 76.

the local Baptist Association on May 28, 1883, the church secretary from Budleigh Salterton Baptist Church stated:

> As a church our members are composed of the working classes to carry on the work of the Lord we stand in need of penury aid and we trust He will soften the hearts of those who have the means to render such aid by a grant of money from your association.[54]

Although the reference to the membership being predominantly working class is unique in the minute books kept by the Baptists in Budleigh Salterton, their appeal for financial assistance is a common occurrence. As will become evident, the ability to raise sufficient money with which to pay a stipend significantly impacted their ability to engage the services of a minister.[55]

Financing Ministry at Budleigh Salterton Baptist Church

The first mention of financial difficulties at the Baptist church in Budleigh Salterton is dated February 1, 1882, when Bro. Walters presented the quarterly accounts.[56] These showed a balance in hand of £6-17-10½;

---

54. Minutes, 3548D M1, Budleigh Salterton Baptist Church minute book Oct. 1843–Apr. 1883, DHC.

55. As part of a wider collective of nonconformist churches, Baptists have traditionally separated themselves from state involvement and, therefore, have not normally received funding from the state. While this situation has subtly changed in recent decades with the advent of tax refunds, in respect of covenanted giving, and, later, Gift Aid, the principle of self-funding remains a facet of Baptist ecclesiology. However, even this is not as straightforward as it might appear, for, in addition to funding their own ministry, most Baptist congregations are also committed to funding the work of local Associations and the national Union. In addition to contributing to these administrative bodies, many Baptist congregations also contribute to a Baptist expression of mission, through the Baptist Missionary Society. In return for funding the local Association and the national Union, Baptist congregations receive advice on issues such as safeguarding, administering property and financial affairs. They also receive assistance in finding a minister through the National Settlement Scheme and are able to participate in a pension scheme for their pastor.

In addition to the administrative assistance offered locally and nationally, with the implementation of the Ministerial Settlement and Sustenation Scheme 1912, local congregations have been able to apply to the Baptist Union for financial assistance. This assistance has also been known as a Home Mission Grant and, in the past, has been used to help smaller churches continue to pay their ministers. However, recent changes within the Baptist Union of Great Britain have seen Home Mission grants be directed toward time-limited mission projects rather than sustained support of local ministers.

56. The notation Bro. is used to designate a brother in the faith and is common in

however, as Walters explained, the church also had outstanding debts of £8-13-9.[57] As a result, the members agreed that there should be an additional monthly collection specifically to clear the shortfall.[58] Two years later, the church expressed their financial difficulties in their annual report to the local Association. On this occasion, they looked beyond the immediate members for financial aid.[59]

Although neither of these instances makes reference to paying their minister, the church at Budleigh Salterton had employed a minister since 1844.[60] Furthermore, the brief history of Budleigh printed in 1993 suggests that the cost of the building had been repaid in 1849, and there is no mention of an outstanding debt relating to the Sunday School hall that was constructed twenty years after the church building.[61] In view of this, it is safe to assume that the minister's stipend was the major part of the expenses that caused the church financial difficulties in 1882 and 1884. Perhaps the surprising factor in the 1884 appeal is that the Baptists at Budleigh Salterton were willing to appeal to the local Association for financial assistance before considering whether they should continue to employ the services of a minister. Clearly, the Baptists in Budleigh Salterton valued their minister, as is evident in their 1884 letter to the local Association. Here, they included a comment stating that they "enjoy the faithful ministry of our Pastor [the Rev. J. R. Brown] who labors away among us with great earnestness."[62] This obvious commitment to their minister led to the church continuing to employ the services of the Rev. Brown, even though this continued to place a financial burden on both the congregation and their pastor.

The tension between the desire to employ a minister and being able to pay the stipend is a recurring theme in the life of the Baptists at Budleigh Salterton. Furthermore, this disparity between a desire for a minister and the ability to pay a stipend resulted in the minister being

---

church minute books.

57. Prior to decimalization on February 15, 1971, currency in the United Kingdom consisted of pounds, shillings, and pence. There were twelve old pence to a shilling and twenty shillings to a pound.

58. Minutes, Feb. 1, 1882, 3548D M1, DHC.

59. Minutes, Apr. 30, 1884, 3548D M2, Budleigh Salterton Baptist Church minute book Aug. 1883–May 1902, DHC.

60. *Baptist Church, Little Knowle, Budleigh Salterton*, 1.

61. *Baptist Church, Little Knowle, Budleigh Salterton*, 1.

62. Minutes, May 28, 1883, 3548D M1, DHC.

underpaid when compared to the income received by other Baptist ministers. Alfred Piper highlights the poor amount of financial support offered to their minister by citing the example of the stipend of the Rev. T. Collings being set at £30 per annum in 1843 and the Rev. Daniel Cork being offered the same stipend in 1885.[63] According to the research carried out by F. M. W. Harrison among the Nottingham Baptists, by 1857, most Baptists ministers in the Nottingham area received less than £80 and some as little as £40 per annum.[64] In this context, while Rev. Collings's stipend was less than the norm, it was not unduly so, unlike that of Daniel Cork, whose stipend was significantly less than the norm for 1885. Ian Sellers's research into the Baptists of Yorkshire, Lancashire, and Cheshire highlights the disparity. According to Sellers, stipends in the Yorkshire, Lancashire, and Cheshire Association during the 1880s were £150 per annum.[65] When compared to the £30 received by Cork, it is clear that his stipend could be described as meager.

By 1916, the church was still only paying their minister, William A Baker, a stipend of close to £80 per annum, and even to reach this level, the Baptists at Budleigh Salterton required help. At the meeting held on April 27, 1916, the church reported to the Baptist Union that despite raising £45-5-0 in the previous year and receiving £8-0-0 from the Bristol Baptist Fund, they still needed to apply for a grant of £26-10-0 to meet the pastor's stipend. In making the application, the church assured the Baptist Union that "our people are doing their very best amid difficult surroundings" and justified their application for money by stating that their fellowship was the only congregational church in the area.[66] The consequences that the Budleigh Salterton Baptists faced as a result of struggling to pay an adequate stipend are apparent in the time and effort taken to find a successor to the Rev. Shaw (1898–1909). This is a protracted story that bears telling in full as it illustrates how a lack of finance frustrated the efforts of the Baptists in Budleigh Salterton.

---

63. Piper, *Short History of Ebenezer Chapel*, 4, 7.

64. Harrison, "Church Relations," 175–76.

65. Sellers, *Our Heritage*, 50.

66. Minutes, Apr. 27, 1916, Budleigh Salterton Baptist Church minute and registry book Mar. 27, 1913–Dec. 20, 1936, DHC.

Appointing a Successor to Rev. Shaw

The resignation of the Rev. Shaw was first discussed at the church meeting held on October 13, 1909, and the process of finding a successor began in December of the same year. Initially, the Rev. Case from Tiverton suggested that his brother from Sandhurst would be interested in the appointment. However, at the time of the introduction, there were other candidates, and at a church meeting held on December 15, 1909, it was agreed to extend an invitation to the Rev. Oare to preach with a view to the pastorate.[67] It is impossible to tell whether the Rev. Oare actually preached at Budleigh Salterton Baptist Church, as the minutes do not record his visit.

As for the Rev. Case of Sandhurst, while there is no record of an invitation to the pastorate being extended to him, there is a note stating that he had withdrawn his interest in the pastorate at Budleigh Salterton.[68] As a result of the congregation's inability to secure a pastor, the Rev. Durbin from the Devon and Cornwall Baptist Association wrote to the church suggesting that they link with the Baptist church in Exmouth and accept the spiritual oversight of their pastor, the Rev. Good.[69] Suggesting that the churches at Budleigh Salterton and Exmouth should link and share resources was not inconceivable due to their geographical proximity. Furthermore, relationships between the Baptists in Budleigh and Exmouth were good and remained so throughout the period under inquiry. As a result of the Rev. Durbin's suggestion, the church invited the Rev. Good to visit them and discuss the possibility of sharing in his spiritual oversight. However, at the next church meeting, the church secretary reported that he had been in further contact with the Rev. Case of Tiverton. Apparently, Case had persuaded the church secretary that his brother, from Sandhurst, was prepared to be their pastor. As a result, the Rev. Case of Sandhurst visited the church on a trial basis and was subsequently sent a unanimous call to the pastorate. Despite the strength of the invitation and assurance from his brother, the Rev. Case of Sandhurst once again turned down the invitation.[70]

---

67. Minutes, Dec. 10, 1909, 3548D M3, Budleigh Salterton Baptist Church minute book Oct. 1902–Feb. 1913, DHC.

68. Minutes, Jan. 26, 1910, 3548D M3, DHC.

69. Minutes, Jan. 26, 1910, 3548D M3, DHC.

70. Minutes, Mar. 10, 1910, 3548D M3, DHC.

Following the rejection from the Rev. Case of Sandhurst, the issue of the pastorate was not raised again until August 3, 1910. At this meeting, the Rev. Durbin conveyed the news that the church in Exmouth was unwilling to form a link with Budleigh Salterton and share the ministry of the Rev. Good. In view of this, it was suggested that the church approach the Rev. Fairburn from South Moulton. The Rev. Fairburn was known to the church and had conducted their recent anniversary service. According to the records, the Rev. Fairburn's ministry had been greatly appreciated. In view of the comments above, relating to the level of stipend that the Baptists at Budleigh Salterton paid their ministers, it is interesting to note that the church's inquiry regarding the pastorate also asked the level of stipend the Rev. Fairburn would require.[71] However, despite hinting that the church would meet the stipend requested by the Rev. Fairburn, the meeting held on August 31, 1910, was advised that he had also declined their invitation.[72]

Following the Rev. Fairburn's rejection, the church was informed that Mr. Oster of Exmouth had been corresponding with Mr. Henson of London. Mr. Henson had been working overseas but had suffered poor health and, as a result of his illness, had been advised to live and work in the Devon area. Mr. Henson also came with a warm commendation from the Rev. Shakespeare.[73] This was a lofty commendation as, at the time of the commendation, Rev. Shakespeare was secretary of the Baptist Union.[74] The church was advised that Mr. Henson would be happy to visit for any length of time, providing his train fares were paid and accommodation provided in Budleigh Salterton.[75] The minutes hint at the fact that Mr. Henson was considering regularly commuting from London; however, conscious of the financial commitment, the Baptists at Budleigh Salterton only invited Mr. Hanson to spend a weekend with them "in view of the pastorate."[76] Whether or not Mr. Hanson accepted the invitation to visit the church at Budleigh Salterton is not on record; however, the fact that on October 5, 1910, a letter from Mr. Onley of London was

71. Minutes, Mar. 10, 1910, 3548D M3, DHC.
72. Minutes, Aug. 31, 1910, 3548D M3, DHC.
73. Minutes, Aug. 31, 1910, 3548D M3, DHC.
74. John Howard Shakespeare was appointed secretary of the Baptist Union in 1898 and served in that position for twenty-six years. See Shepherd, *Making of a Modern Denomination*, 19–20.
75. Minutes, Aug. 31, 1910, 3548D M3, DHC.
76. Minutes, Aug. 31, 1910, 3548D M3, DHC.

read recommending the Rev. H. A. Burleigh as a suitable minister for the church suggests that Mr. Hanson was unwilling to take the pastorate.[77] The church responded to Mr. Onley's letter by inviting the Rev. Burleigh to "take services in view of the pastorate."[78]

The Rev. Burleigh's visit was a success, and the minutes record how well the members spoke of him; however, for the church to call him to be their minister, they had to consider an increase in financial commitment to meet a stipend of £120 per annum. The initial proposal was that the church members raise the additional £50 while simultaneously writing to the local Association explaining how earnest they were to recruit the Rev. Burleigh. This implies that the church was hoping to receive help in raising the additional money required to meet the expense of the Rev. Burleigh's stipend. As a concession to this request, Messrs. Collins and Gooding suggested that the application to the Association include the caveat that, once the Rev. Burleigh was in post and active in the community, the amount of grant required would probably be reduced.[79] The minutes do not record how the local Association responded to the church's proposal; however, at the church meeting held on November 28, letters were read from the Rev. Burleigh declining the invitation to the pastorate on the grounds of the stipend.[80]

When the church met on February 1, 1911, the first order of business was a discussion over the pastorate. At this meeting, the church considered inviting the Rev. Willingbly from Abergavenny to preach with a view. However, the initial proposal was amended, and a two-week delay agreed, as it was considered prudent to inform the local Association prior to approaching the Rev. Willingbly.[81] Although no mention is made of why the church felt the need to inform the local Association before approaching the Rev. Willingbly, it is possible that the inability to secure financial assistance in respect of the Rev. Burleigh's stipend led them to exercise caution.

The pastorate was not discussed again until April 26, when there was no mention of the Rev. Willingbly. At this meeting, the conversation regarding the pastorate centered on the Rev. W. A. Barker, who had

77. Minutes, Oct. 5, 1910, 3548D M3, DHC.

78. Minutes, Oct. 5, 1910, 3548D M3, DHC.

79. Minutes, Nov. 1910. 3548D M3, DHC. The exact date in November is not recorded.

80. Minutes Nov. 28, 1910, 3548D M3, DHC.

81. Minutes, Feb. 1, 1911, 3548D M3, DHC.

recently led a week-long mission in Budleigh Salterton. The records state that the Rev. Barker had left a lasting impression on the church members and they discussed the possibility of approaching him to be their pastor. However, with only seven members present, the church decided to postpone any decision until the following Sunday evening when more members could be present.[82] On Sunday, March 5, 1911, a special church meeting was held, and the church once again discussed the Rev. Barker. On this occasion, the members instructed the church secretary to send an invitation to the pastorate. The Baptists at Budleigh Salterton had to wait until the meeting held on April 26, 1911 to receive a positive reply from the Rev. Barker. At the same church meeting, the members agreed to pay him an annual stipend of £50 per annum, with a further provision that the church would contribute an additional £10 to the Baptist Union so that they might receive an augmentation grant.[83] In addition to the stipend and the grant from the Baptist Union, the church also agreed that any surplus income held in the account at the end of the financial year also be given to the pastor. The clause stating the minister would receive any surplus monies was further nuanced by an agreement that any finance required for repairs or renewals to the fabric of buildings would be raised by separate collections.[84] Presumably, this agreement was intended to sweeten a deal that still left the church paying a stipend that was less than was being paid by the Baptist churches in Yorkshire, Lancashire, and Cheshire thirty years earlier.

With the appointment of the Rev. Barker in 1911,[85] the church's search had ended, and although it is seldom explicit in the notes, there is a clear sense from the records that the difficulty in securing the services was related to the level of stipend offered. It is also clear that, despite their requests, the church did not receive any financial help from the local Association. Whether or not the difficulties faced by the Baptists in Budleigh Salterton were due to their financial constraints is an interesting question.

---

82. Minutes, Feb. 1, 1911, 3548D M3, DHC.
83. Minutes, Apr. 26, 1911, 3548D M3, DHC.
84. Minutes, Apr. 26, 1911, 3548D M3, DHC.
85. The date that the Rev. Barker accepted the call to the pastorate is not recorded. However, a meeting held in October 1911 (the exact date is not referenced) records the application for the transfer of membership to Budleigh Salterton in respect of the Rev. and Mrs. Barker.

The refusal of so many prospective ministers to accept the call to the pastorate at Budleigh Salterton does not appear to be due to the level of emotional support given to the initial call. As for the issue of accommodation, while the records suggest that the church did not have a manse,[86] the provision of housing is not recorded as part of the discussion over offering the pastorate to any of the prospective successors to Rev. Shaw. With a significant level of emotional support offered to each prospective minister and the question of accommodation not recorded, it appears that the level of stipend offered may have been the stumbling block for each of the prospective candidates. However, even here, the issue is not clear cut as, while there was a realization that raising the £120 annual stipend for the Rev. Burleigh's services would be a struggle, it was not considered insurmountable. Furthermore, it was only in response to the suggestion that the church meet train fares for Mr. Hanson to travel to and from London on a regular basis that the church refused to consider paying the expense.

In respect of Wink's contention that income affects what a church is able to achieve, it appears that financial constraints affected the ability of the Budleigh Salterton Baptist Church to recruit a minister. However, while their ability to pay for ministry was limited, the fact that they were willing to consider paying the £120 required by the Rev. Burleigh and pay £10 to the Baptist Union in the hope of receiving a grant toward the cost of the Rev. Barker suggests a willingness to overcome their financial difficulties. This creativity is exemplified in their decision to give all the surplus money to their pastor at the end of the year. This ingenuity, along with their willingness to seek financial help from both the local Association and the National Union, enabled the Baptists in Budleigh Salterton to employ the services of a minister despite their financial constraints. Although, in this instance, there is no record of a specific leader enabling the church to reach beyond the restrictions caused by their lack of income, their desire to employ the services of a minister clearly acted as a motivator sufficient to raise aspirations beyond what might be considered achievable. When considered in this light, the limitations placed on the Baptists of Budleigh Salterton might be considered a positive influence on the nature of the church. However, in view of information contained within the church records, it is clear that

---

86. When Rev. Stanley was appointed minister, in 1949, the church records detail the difficulties encountered in securing accommodation for him and his wife.

in addition to acting as an inspirational motivator, the lack of finances also corrupted the nature of the church.

Finance and the Nature of Budleigh Salterton Baptist Church

The creativity expressed in financing Rev. Barker's ministry is only one aspect of the preoccupation the Baptist church at Budleigh Salterton had with raising money. Examples of this are regular sales of work held by the fellowship and the reports of the profit made from the Harvest Supper and the Good Friday teas. Furthermore, in the annual report for 1944, the records show that having borrowed £2-0-0 to purchase materials for making calendars, the Sunday School had subsequently repaid the funds.[87] This suggests that even the work carried out among children was expected to pay its way.

In addition to expecting that all the church activities should be self-funding, there is a developing dependency on financial assistance from the Baptist Union. As has already been noted in the struggle to find a replacement for the Rev. Shaw, the church did not receive any financial assistance from the local Association. However, it is clear that they were expecting help from the Baptist Union. By 1949, the records from Budleigh Salterton Baptist Church show a clear expectation that the Baptist Union would assist the church in meeting the cost of a stipend:

> Mr Farnham explained that if the Rev Stanley accepted the pastorate of the church, we were not bound in any way to keep him more than a term of three or even five years and could give or receive three months' notice from him if need be. Furthermore if [the] Rev Stanley deal fell through, we could still apply for a hundred and twenty pounds a year plus a house from the Baptist Union.[88]

This is an interesting statement as it hints at the church's willingness to separate themselves from an incumbent minister. Furthermore, it suggests that Mr. Farnham believed that if the Rev. Stanley's ministry was cut short, the church might still benefit financially from the support of the Baptist Union. While this position might be considered a pragmatic

---

87. Minutes, Feb. 22, 1945, 3548D M6, Budleigh Salterton Baptist Church minute book Nov. 1944–Apr. 1949, DHC.

88. Minutes, 3548D M7, Budleigh Salterton Baptist Church minute book no. 7 May 31, 1949–Apr. 16, 1958, DHC.

response to the church's difficulties with financing and accommodating a minister, it does have a sinister overtone. The emphasis that Mr. Farnham appears to place on not having to employ the services of the Rev. Stanley for a specific period, coupled with the suggestion that the grant from the Baptist Union would be continued in the pastor's absence, invites the question, Has the perpetual lack of money changed the nature of the church and its angel? In this respect, Wink argues that "the angel of the church becomes demonic when the congregation turns its back on a specific task set before it by God and makes another goal its idol."[89] In view of this, Mr. Farnham's comments suggest that a change may have taken place and, rather than pursue the services of the Rev. Stanley, the church had become fixated on obtaining money from the Baptist Union. If this is the case, a further question emerges: Does a long-term struggle with a specific issue lead to a change in the nature of the angel? This question is not easy to answer. In the case of the Baptists at Budleigh Salterton, the long-standing tension between the desire to employ the services of a minister and the financial struggle that entailed appears to have affected the church's judgment. However, if this is the case, and obtaining finance has replaced the desire for ministry, it is difficult to see how the Baptists at Budleigh Salterton could be satisfied with receiving the additional finance without enjoying the benefits of a minister. Therefore, even if the goal had changed and the angel had become demonic, in the light of Wink's belief in the gyroscopic effects of the angel of the church, it is likely that the congregation's experience of not having a minister might quickly address their desire to simply receive funding from the Baptist Union.

Even if the Baptists at Budleigh Salterton did not intend to benefit financially from the Baptist Union without employing the services of a minister, the money they did receive was not always accompanied by a willingness to comply with the directions that accompanied the grant. An example of this is found in 1959. By this time, the circumstances related to financial assistance and the payment of ministerial stipends had been regularized, and the Baptist Union suggested the level at which stipends should be paid. As a result, on April 8, 1959, the church secretary informed the members that the Baptist Union had suggested raising the stipend paid to ministers by £20 per annum. Following a discussion, the

---

89. Wink, *Unmasking the Powers*, 78.

church agreed that they could not afford this increase and would, therefore, apply for a grant to cover the additional cost.[90]

The issue of increasing the minister's stipend was revisited at a special church meeting held on August 19, 1959. On this occasion, the church secretary reported that the Grants Executive Committee was unable to exempt the church at Budleigh Salterton from the increase when other congregations found themselves in a similar financial position.[91] Furthermore, the wording of the reply suggests that the General Executive Committee expected the increase to be found by the church and not by grants from the Sustentation Fund. However, according to the secretary's report, if the church required a review of the recommended stipend, the committee was willing to do so in the coming September. According to the records, the church decided not to request such a review and, instead, raised the stipend by £10 per annum.[92]

The Generosity of Budleigh Salterton Baptist Church

The fractious relationship that the church had with the Baptist Union in respect of receiving grants and the level of stipend it should pay to its ministers does not fully reflect the nature of the church. In other areas of its life, the church presented the generous side of its character. For example, where details of their annual letter to the Association are recorded, the minutes always note the enclosure of two gifts, the first for expenses and the second either for "letters"[93] or for the Widows and Orphans Fund.[94] Furthermore, there was also a tradition of recognizing those who served the church as members and outside advisors with financial gifts. For example, during the nineteenth century, the church paid for their quarterly accounts to be compiled by an external auditor, and on February 1, 1882, the members agreed not only to pay the auditor £2 but also to give an additional £1 to his wife.[95] No reason for this additional gift is recorded, and it can only be assumed that it was given as an act of generosity. A

90. Minutes, Apr. 8, 1959, 3548D M8, Budleigh Salterton Baptist Church minute book no. 8 Apr. 23, 1958–1975, DHC.
91. Minutes, Aug. 19, 1959, 3548D M8, DHC.
92. Minutes, Aug. 19, 1959, 3548D M8, DHC.
93. Minutes, May 19, 1850, 3548D M1, Budleigh Salterton Baptist Church minute book Oct. 1843–Apr. 1883, DHC.
94. Minutes, May 27, 1849, 3548D M1, DHC.
95. Minutes, Feb. 1, 1882, 3548D M1, DHC.

further example of a payment in lieu of additional services is recorded on January 24, 1935, where the church agreed to give the organist, Mrs. Jewel, an honorarium of £1-1-0 in respect of the additional work she had been involved with, organizing a series of musical concerts.[96]

This generous aspect of the nature of the Baptists in Budleigh Salterton highlights the complexity involved in discerning the nature of the angel of the church. While it is clear that the stipend the church was able to offer prospective ministers was often meagre in comparison with other Baptist congregations, they were generous in the emotional support. Furthermore, their inability to offer a stipend in keeping with other Baptist congregations appears to reflect a financial hardship among the congregation rather than a meanness of spirit. Moreover, in seeking a successor to the Rev. Shaw, the church demonstrated a tenacity that would eventually overcome the lack of monetary resources. In view of this, and despite Mr. Farnham's comments discussed above, the Baptists at Budleigh Salterton demonstrate both a practical and emotional commitment toward their minister. In addition to this, their generosity toward people serving the church community suggests an underlying spirit committed to the well-being of those working on behalf of the church.

Age

In addition to social status, ethnic background, and financial ability, Wink also cites age as a determining factor in the nature of the angel of the church.[97] Once again, while Wink suggests that the age profile of a congregation might affect the nature of the angel of the church, he does not develop his argument.

Placing the Age Demographic of a Church in a Wider Context

Exploring the wider context of age and the church and writing in *Future First*, Graham Hedger contends that there is no secret to the fact that the population of the United Kingdom is aging. With a falling birthrate and increase in longevity the proportion of the over-sixty-fives is increasing.[98]

---

96. Minutes, Jan. 24, 1935, 3548D M4, Budleigh Salterton Baptist Church minute book and registry Mar. 27, 1910–Dec. 20 1936, DHC.
97. Wink, *Unmasking the Powers*, 74.
98. Hedger, "Challenge of an Ageing Population," 6.

The significance of Hedger's argument is brought into focus by Peter Brierley's "The Elderly in the Church." Brierley notes that in 2000, 15 percent of congregations were aged sixty-five or over, and in 2010, this figure had risen to 17 percent, and by 2020 it had risen to 19 percent.[99] His research also suggests that among those who attend church, the age demographic has grown older. According to Brierley, in 2000, 25 percent of those attending church were aged over sixty-five, and by 2020 that number had risen to 36 percent. Brierley argues that this increase is due to a decrease in the number of young people attending church. He speculates that if this trend continues, by 2050, the number of over-sixty-fives in English churches could rise to 41 percent.[100]

The Nature of an Older Congregation

In view of these statistics, it might be argued that the demographic shift experienced by churches in the twenty-first century will change the nature of how a congregation functions. In this context, Brierley suggests that while older churchgoers will be more committed to attending and participating, they will be less healthy, less energetic, less creative, and resistant to change.[101] Although Brierley's observations have merit, the relationship between the individual traits of the aging and the corporate nature of a congregation are not without critics.

Exploring the nature of pastoral care among an aging congregation, James Woodward cautions against applying the type of research Brierley cites to a church's pastoral ministry. Woodward argues that it should not be presumed that just because a church population ages, it will lack initiative and be constrained by tradition.[102] As laudable as this assertion is, Woodward's belief that an organization like the church should not be understood as adopting the nature of its participants is difficult to justify in the light of Wink's understanding of the angel of the church.

According to Wink, the angel of the church reflects every aspect of a community and presents it before God.[103] Therefore, if a congregation is

---

99. Brierley, "Elderly in the Church."
100. Brierley, "Elderly in the Church."
101. Brierley, "Generations of Older People," 3; Brierley cites Julia Whitworth's address to the summer event of the Social Research Association on July 1, 2010, and applies her comments to church life.
102. Woodward, *Valuing Age*, 8–9.
103. Wink, *Unmasking the Powers*, 73.

made up of predominantly older people, the nature of its angel is likely to be shaped by the prejudices, aspirations, strengths, and weaknesses of the dominant generation. Furthermore, the age profile of a church will not only affect its attitudes, it will also affect the congregation's ability to embark on and sustain certain activities. Therefore, while Woodward argues against denigrating an older congregation, the nature of a congregation and how it functions will be affected by its age profile. In this respect, Hedger's research suggests that churches with an aging demographic will find it increasingly difficult to attract younger people.[104]

Engaging with a Younger Generation

Hedger's argument appears to be supported by the research of Currie et al., who argue that for a church to recruit from a specific portion of society it must be in close proximity to that constituency.[105] Furthermore, Brierley's article "Twenty Truths About Twenties" provides additional data supporting this conclusion. His paper also highlights the widening cultural gap between younger people and an aging church. Together, the works of Hedger, Brierley, and Currie et al. provide a robust argument for a link between the age of a congregation and what it can achieve.

In a wider context, Brierley's research into the twenties age group suggests that, after the over-sixties, people in their twenties are the next largest social group in the United Kingdom.[106] Reflecting on this data, he surmises that the size of this portion of the population has been boosted by immigration, with 41 percent of people in their twenties being immigrants. Despite the size of this population cohort, Brierley's research suggests that people in their twenties represent the smallest proportion of society that attends church. Furthermore, where they do attend a church, they are more likely to gather in small independent groups that do not meet in a church building.[107] Separating themselves from traditional meeting points and congregating in age-related groups

---

104. Hedger, "Challenge of an Ageing Population," 1.

105. Currie et al., *Churches and Chuchgoers*, 7. The use of the term "proximity" in the work of Currie et al. is ambiguous. However, the structure of their argument suggests that the term is being used in relation to a type of demographic rather than geographically.

106. Brierley, "Twenty Truths About Twenties," 1.

107. Brierley, "Twenty Truths About Twenties," 1.

makes this younger element of society who are interested in the Christian faith even more difficult to reach.

The difficulties in reaching the twenties age group are accentuated by their lack of a historical link with traditional churches, as only 7 percent of people in their twenties ever attended a Sunday School. However, where traditional churches reach people in their twenties, and relationships are formed with an older generation, younger people remain committed to attending church even when they move away from their locality to attend university.[108] Hedger's research into the long-standing relationship between an older and younger generation may provide a counterpoint to any entrenched values held by a congregation formed predominantly by older people. This, in turn, will affect the way the church understands itself and practices theology. In this respect, Wink argues that self-understanding and the practice of theology both reveal the nature of the angel of the church.[109] Therefore, the change of congregational dynamic that the influence of long-standing relationships between young and older people bring will be reflected in the congregation's angel.

The Benefits and Challenges That Younger People Bring to a Church

According to Brierley, young people can make a positive contribution to a church. He believes this is particularly true for people in their twenties. Developing this argument, Brierley cites the commitment younger people bring to relating biblical truths to the moral issues of life and their grasp of new technology.[110] However, in addition to these assets, they also offer considerable challenges to an older congregation. For example, Brierley highlights the fact that people in their twenties are more likely to have had multiple sexual partners than previous generations and are more likely to cohabit prior to marriage. Furthermore, people in their twenties are often committed users of social media, communicating through email and text, and frequently participate in online computer games. Brierley's research also reveals that the online aspect of their lives often becomes addictive and, therefore, time-consuming.[111]

108. Brierley, "Twenty Truths About Twenties," 1.
109. Wink, *Unmasking the Powers*, 76–77.
110. Brierley, "Twenty Truths About Twenties," 1–2.
111. Brierley, "Twenty Truths About Twenties," 1–2.

When juxtaposed with the statistics and research relating to older people and the church, the insight that people in their twenties bring with respect to technology and concern for social issues suggests that, as an age group, younger people have a great deal to offer to a congregation. However, the life issues that Brierley highlights also suggest that a congregation experiencing a large influx of people in their twenties would face a significant challenge to some of the theological positions traditionally held by the church. What is more, Brierley's and Hedger's research also indicates that the age demographic of a church will shape its attitudes to theological and moral principles. Therefore, a church that is successful at attracting a younger age group is likely to experience a shift in its theological stance, particularly in the sphere of interpersonal relations and human sexuality. While this shift in theological stance is likely to alter the nature of the angel of the church, the transformation is unlikely to be straightforward. This is because, while the angel of the church does not actively oppose change, its gyroscopic influence will create resistance.

The Danger Facing an Aging Congregation

Considering the research carried out by Currie et al., an aging congregation that fails to address its demography in a timely manner may enter an increasing spiral of aging. Furthermore, if the differences between generations are as Brierley suggests, the aging spiral will cause the church to become detached from contemporary moral and theological thinking. This, in turn, will make it more difficult for the congregation to recruit new members who are sufficiently different from themselves to redress the internal dynamics of the church. In view of this possibility, it is unsurprising that Wink highlights age as a factor in the church's ability to fulfill its vocation. Furthermore, if the transcendent angel of the church is indivisibly linked with the demography of the congregation there is a question as to whether the nature of the angel ages. Of course, it isn't easy to perceive a transcendent entity aging in the same way that human beings age. However, it is possible that an angel who reflects a theological or missiological position that has not adapted to current thinking and sociological changes might be deemed to have aged. In this respect, it might also be argued that a church that fails to adapt to meet the challenges posed by successive younger generations might have failed to fulfill its vocation. What is more, if this were the case, it is possible that the angel of that church would have become demonic due to the congregation's focus on something other than its calling in Christ.

Gender Balance

Commenting on how piety became feminized, Callum Brown makes an interesting observation regarding the artistic portrayal of angels.[112] He argues that, until the 1790s, angelic beings were portrayed in British art and literature as being masculine. However, by the middle of the nineteenth century, this had changed, with angels being portrayed in a feminine form.[113] Although the artistic interpretation of angels might appear to have little to do with the angel of the church and its relationship to the nature of a congregation, Brown uses this example to introduce a broader sociological and theological change. Following his observation of how the artistic interpretation of angels changed, Brown argues that from around 1800, sacredness and femininity combined and dramatically changed the nature of Christianity in the United Kingdom.[114] He develops his thesis by comparing how women and men are portrayed in the obituaries printed in religious magazines during the nineteenth century.[115] Brown contends that prior to the nineteenth century, religious piety was understood as a masculine character trait; however, at around 1800, this viewpoint changed dramatically, and piety became a feminine attribute.[116]

Linda Wilson also uses obituaries as a source for her research into nineteenth-century female spirituality. While agreeing with Brown's contention that obituaries were often written to reinforce certain attributes of Christian life and service, she also notes that many of the accounts of a woman's life and death were actually written by men.[117] Of course, as she acknowledges, this does not mean that if an obituary were written by a woman, it would be any less stylized in its portrayal of a woman's spirituality.[118] However, it does suggest that the men and women writing at the

---

112. Brown, *Death of Christian Britain*, 58.
113. Brown, *Death of Christian Britain*, 58.
114. Brown, *Death of Christian Britain*, 59.
115. Brown, *Death of Christian Britain*, 60.
116. Brown, *Death of Christian Britain*, 58.
117. Wilson, *Constrained by Zeal*, 24.
118. Wilson, *Constrained by Zeal*, 26.

turn of the nineteenth century were either noticing a shift in how religious piety was understood or were wanting to promote such a shift.

If there was a shift in how religious piety was understood in the nineteenth century, there also appears to have been a corresponding transformation in the dissipation of responsibility within church life. David Bebbington argues that this was the case in his work *The Dominance of Evangelicalism*.[119] According to Bebbington, the nineteenth century saw women playing important roles in visiting the sick, raising money, and educating children.[120] In 1890, women's pastoral role in caring for the sick was formalized by the London Baptist Association with the appointment of a small community of deaconesses.[121] This marked the beginning of what later became known as the Baptist Order of Deaconesses.[122]

Although neither the Baptist congregations at Newton Abbot nor Budleigh Salterton appoint deaconesses, the records of the Baptist church in Budleigh Salterton do reveal a growth in the number of women who actively participated in church life and were appointed to positions of responsibility between 1850 and 1910.

Women in Budleigh Salterton Baptist Church

Within Baptist ecclesiology, the process of accepting new members is important.[123] Following a request for baptism and/or church membership, applicants are usually interviewed to establish the validity of their faith. This interview is usually carried out by two visitors appointed by the church meeting. After they have visited the prospective member, a report is presented to the church, and a vote is taken. In addition to interviewing potential applicants, the church meeting might also discuss the transfer from or to other congregations. At Budleigh Salterton, votes in respect of applications for membership or transfer were initially proposed and seconded by male members. However, this trend changed on January 28, 1852, when a letter transferring Louise Payne's membership

---

119. Bebbington, *Dominance of Evangelicalism*, 202–12.
120. Bebbington, *Dominance of Evangelicalism*, 206–8.
121. Bowers, "For God and the People," 473.
122. Bowers, "For God and the People," 473.
123. The importance of membership in Baptist ecclesiology is discussed in the next chapter.

to a Baptist congregation in Oxford Street, London, was proposed by Bro. Elliot and seconded by Sister Dean.[124]

By 1881 women were proposing as well as seconding the acceptance of membership reports.[125] Furthermore, at a church meeting held on August 28, 1883, the role women took in membership applications and transfers was extended even further. At this meeting, not only did Sister Bowden second Mr. Cowd's proposal that visitors should be sent to Sister Brown as part of her application for membership, but Sisters Bowden and Walters were appointed as visitors.[126] As previously noted, while the visiting of potential new members is a significant responsibility within a Baptist congregation, it does not represent a leadership role. However, in this respect, the Baptists in Budleigh Salterton Baptist also demonstrate mutual respect and participation for its female members as, in 1910, they appointed a woman to the position of church treasurer.

Miss Cork

On June 10, 1908, with her father, the church treasurer, unable to attend the church meeting, Miss Cork was called upon to give the quarterly financial report.[127] Having received the report, the members extended a vote of thanks to both the Rev. and Miss Cork. The reading of the quarterly financial statement and the expression of thanks to both Miss Cork and her father was repeated on October 7, 1908. Then, on August 27, 1909, the minutes record not only the death of the Rev. Cork but the appointment of his daughter to the post of church treasurer.[128] Miss Cork subsequently served as church treasurer until April 27, 1916, when, citing an illness that had affected her eyesight, she resigned from the post. The fact that Miss Cork was responsible not only for keeping the church accounts but also for signing checks on behalf of the church is confirmed by the comments made by her successor, Mr. Page. Accepting the position of treasurer, Mr. Page stated that the position he

---

124. Minutes, Jan. 28, 1852, 3548D M1, Budleigh Salterton Baptist Church minute book Oct. 1843–Apr. 1883, DHC.

125. Minutes, Dec. 28, 1881, 3548D M1, DHC.

126. Minutes, Aug. 28, 1883, 3548D M2, Budleigh Salterton Baptist Church minute book Aug. 1883–May 1902, DHC.

127. Minutes, June 10, 1908, 3548D M3, Budleigh Salterton Baptist Church minute book Oct. 1902–Feb. 1913, DHC.

128. Minutes, Oct. 7, 1908, and Aug. 27, 1909, 3548D M3, DHC.

now held was an honorable one,[129] thus reinforcing the significance of Miss Cork holding the office.

Of course, it might be argued that the appointment both of women to visit prospective members and Miss Cork as church treasurer were due to the lack of available male members within the church. According to the research carried out by Ruth Gouldbourne and David Bebbington there may be credence in this argument. According to Gouldbourne, the female/male balance among early Baptist congregations was weighted in favor of women. Illustrating this, she points to the Bunyan Meeting in Bedford, which was founded in 1650 with twelve members, eight of whom were women.[130] Likewise, Bebbington argues that roughly two-thirds of the members in nineteenth-century Baptist congregations were women. If Gouldbourne's and Bebbington's observations are correct, the prominence of women in Baptist congregations throughout their history does not explain the lack of women ministers among Baptist congregations.

Reflecting on the relationship between the gender balance and the ability of women to play a significant role in ministry within Baptist congregations, Gouldbourne argues that there is an unhelpful pattern at play. Gouldbourne contends that as religious movements grow and, by necessity, begin to implement institutional structures, the roles open to women become more restricted.[131]

Gouldbourne's argument goes some way to explaining the reason why, despite a positive gender balance, responsibility within church life is disproportionately adopted by men. This difference is most evident in the appointment of ministers. In this respect, Gouldbourne suggests that because of the separatist nature of the early Baptists and the subsequent opportunities for women to preach, minister, and participate in the decision-making process, churches often attracted more women than men. However, as Baptists became more institutionalized, these opportunities appear to have reduced.[132] Commenting on women in leadership during the nineteenth century, David Bebbington also observes that while women played a significant role in auxiliary and missionary organizations, they were seldom allowed to preach in English

---

129. Minutes, Apr. 27, 1916, 3548D M4, Budleigh Salterton Baptist Church minute book and registry Mar. 27, 1910–Dec. 20 1936, DHC.
130. Gouldbourne, *Reinventing the Wheel*, 9.
131. Gouldbourne, *Reinventing the Wheel*, 17.
132. Gouldbourne, *Reinventing the Wheel*, 9.

churches.[133] This prohibition is evident in the life of Budleigh Salterton Baptist Church, as while they are happy to appoint Miss Cork as church treasurer, their church records reveal that they do not, at any point, consider calling a female minister.[134]

Women Ministers

Of course, this is not to say that opportunities for women to train for and practice ministry did not exist in the nineteenth and early twentieth centuries. However, these opportunities may have arisen due to a combination of the positive gender balance and a reduction in men willing to act as ministers. According to Kenneth Brown's research, the period between 1800 and 1930 saw a large number of men leaving the ministry. While there is a bias toward the Methodist ministry in his statistics, the research suggests that as many as half of Baptists who began their pastoral ministry between 1861 and 1881 had left their posts within fourteen years.[135] In addition to this loss, the latter part of the nineteenth century also saw a fall in the number of ministerial candidates applying to Free Church theological colleges. Responding to this decline, Bristol Baptist College opened its training courses to women in 1919.[136] Despite this, the first woman was not accepted for ministerial training by a Baptist College until 1922, when Violet Hedger felt the call to ministry and, having been refused admittance by Spurgeon's, was accepted by Regents Park College.[137]

Although Hedger was the first woman to be accepted by a Baptist college, she was not the first woman to be called to the pastorate. According to Gouldbourne, Edith Gates became the pastor at Tew and Cleverly in Oxfordshire in 1918 and subsequently passed an exam set by the Baptist Union for those entering ministry without spending time at a training college. Gouldbourne also notes that, in 1922, Maria Living-Taylor was accepted as a probationer minister in a joint pastorate with her husband.[138] Michael Collis's research reveals that the first woman being called to the

---

133. Bebbington, *Dominance of Evangelicalism*, 209.
134. The records available for inspection range from 1843 to 1975.
135. Brown, *Social History of the Nonconformist Ministry*, 125.
136. Brown, *Social History of the Nonconformist Ministry*, 229.
137. Gouldbourne, *Reinventing the Wheel*, 27.
138. Gouldbourne, *Reinventing the Wheel*, 27.

pastorate in Wales was also in 1922.[139] Even so, Collis notes that there was a significant debate among Baptists as to whether or not they should be appointed to ministerial positions.[140] At the heart of this debate was the issue of interpreting Bible texts such as 1 Tim 2:11–12 and the individual freedom each church had to apply their understanding to how the church functioned. Although the relationship between theology and the angel of the church will be discussed later, it is worth noting that, in Faith Bowers's opinion, the appointment of women ministers came more quickly to congregations with a liberal theological outlook.[141]

In view of all that has been said above, assessing the impact of gender balance on the nature of the church and its angel is not as straightforward as Wink might portray. From the research carried out by Bebbington and Gouldbourne, it is evident that, throughout most of their history, the gender balance in Baptist congregations has been biased toward women. Despite this, there have been long periods of time when the roles that could be fulfilled by women and the influence they could exert on the life of the church have been limited. In view of this, it is possible that social attitudes to the role of women in society may have influenced many Baptist congregations more than the male-female balance within their congregations. If this is the case, then there is an argument to be made that external forces might have as much of an influence on the nature of the church and its angel as a congregation's demographics. However, it is also clear that the theological outlook of a congregation might also affect the level to which women could serve and exercise influence among Baptist congregations.

Summary

Wink's suggestion that what a church does is determined by the demographic of its members opens a wide spectrum of studies for both sociologists and practitioners of congregational studies.[142] This has been illustrated by the brief discussion of economics, ethnicity, education, age, and gender balance carried out above. However, while these studies might be interesting, their significance, with respect to the angel of the

---

139. Collis, "Female Baptist Preachers," 465.
140. Collis, "Female Baptist Preachers," 466.
141. Bowers, "Liberating Women for Baptist Ministry," 463.
142. Wink, *Unmasking the Powers*, 74.

church, is found not in what a church does but in what it might become in Christ. Therefore, seeking to understand the nature of the angel by observing a congregation's demographic must consider what Christ is calling the church to become.

Vocation

The above review of demographic attributes listed by Wink reveals that while it is theoretically possible for a congregation to transcend the limitations imposed by its demographic profile, reaching for its vocation is not an easy process. This can be seen in Jones's account of how the Baptists in Barnoldswick split and lived, for several generations, as two congregations divided by social class. It is also visible in Wise's account of encouraging the Greenford Baptists to adopt a form of worship that was congruent with its multi-ethnic congregation.

Although these two stories suggest that a congregation's demographic creates an inertia that potentially restricts its ability to fulfill its calling in Christ, this effect is universal neither within a Baptist church nor the wider Baptist movement. This is illustrated by the experience of the Baptists in Budleigh Salterton. Although their economic situation appears to have frustrated their desire to employ the services of a minister, it did not thwart their efforts. Furthermore, the economic frustrations experienced by the Baptists at Budleigh Salterton do not appear to have influenced their attitude toward gender. This is illustrated in the smooth transition of the post of church treasurer from Rev. Cork to his daughter.

The Nature of the Angel

While the above accounts from Baptist congregations appear to support Wink's hypothesis that demographics can affect what a church does, they also illustrate the nature of the angel of the church creating a resistance to change. What is more, although Wink might be correct in his belief that the angel of the church is neither a positive nor negative influence on the life of the congregation, its neutrality appears to add to the inertia caused by aspects of a congregation's demographic. The case of the Baptists in Greenford illustrates this. In their case, the fact that the transformation of the worship style required more than simply replacing the worship leaders illustrates the inertia inherent within the nature of the angel of the church. However, as with all aspects of the nature of the angel of the church, not every experience is negative.

The Angel at Budleigh Salterton

The tension between economic austerity and the desire to employ a minister experienced by the Baptists in Budleigh Salterton reveals tenacity within the nature of their angel. The fact that they were willing to continue a conversation with the Rev. Case of Sandhurst even when he had already turned down a call to the pastorate suggests a desire to pursue a perception of God's will until all possibility of it being fulfilled was exhausted. This tenacity not only continued throughout their search for a new minister but also gave birth to creativity that enabled the congregation to see beyond the financial constraints of the weekly offering. This creativity allowed the Baptists in Budleigh Salterton to consider other funding streams, such as grants from the Baptist Union, as well as creative ways of stretching their own finances.

The congregation's creativity in funding a stipend is, perhaps, most effectively highlighted by the agreement that, at the end of the financial year, the pastor should receive the balance of any funds remaining in the church bank account.[143] Of course, there is also a darker side to the financial creativity of the Baptists in Budleigh Salterton. This is revealed in the discussion over receiving a Baptist Union grant to assist in paying for a stipend. While not actually advocating deception, there is a hint in the church records that the church was willing to continue receiving the grant even if they decided to terminate the minister's employment.[144] If a positive viewpoint were to be adopted, it could be argued that even if this was a correct interpretation of the church records, and the leaders at the time were inclined toward a financial indiscretion, this was only ever a passing phase and does not reflect the predominantly generous nature of the congregation.

Demographics and Church Records

When it comes to revealing the nature of the angel of the church, demographics clearly have a great deal to offer. What is more, church records appear to provide an ample supply of stories and information that reveal

---

143. Minute book Oct. 1902 to Feb. 1913, Apr. 26, 1911, Budleigh Salterton Baptist Church, DHC.

144. Church minute book no. 7, Budleigh Salterton Baptist Church, DHC.

the nature of a church and its angel. In this respect, Runcorn's call for his students to read their church minute books has much to commend it. However, having stated that church records provide a good supply of information from which the nature of the angel of the church can be discerned, it is clear that not all the demographic aspects listed by Wink are easy to deduce from the records. Although church finances are often well documented in the records examined for this thesis, the minute books have not always revealed the age profile of the congregation or its level of education. In these areas, it is possible that only by being present in the church could an observer consider whether age and education affect the nature of the church and its angel.

In addition to only offering a partial view of how demographics enable the observer to understand the nature of the angel of the church, the records kept by congregations also reveal how individual churches faced different challenges. Examples of this can be seen in the contrasting circumstances experienced by the Baptists in Barnoldswick, Greenford, and Budleigh Salterton.

Leadership

Finally, from Wise's experience at Greenford Baptist and Jones's account of Barnoldswick, it is evident that leadership can encourage a congregation to overcome the internal inertia created by the angel of the church. What is more, having overcome the angel's gyroscopic effect, a good leader can assist in the transformation of at least part of the angel's nature. Wink acknowledges the significant role that leadership can take in forming and transforming the nature of the angel of the church. Furthermore, he suggests that the attributes of authority, ministry, and power are significant in exploring and illustrating the role of leadership.[145]

Using these attributes as headings, the next chapter will explore the nature of leadership among Baptist congregations. As will become evident, the relationship between ministry and power among Baptists is complex, and whether or not the minister has the authority and power to affect the nature of the angel is open for debate.

---

145. Wink, *Unmasking the Powers*, 74–75.

4

Authority, Ministry, and Power

THE LETTERS TO THE churches in the book of Revelation each address the strengths and weaknesses of the congregation. However, each letter is written by John under the direction of Christ. In view of this, Wink explores why a human being should address a transcendent angel. Wink is clear that true change within the transcendent angel can only be accomplished by Christ. However, the reason why a human being is given the task of addressing the angel is because the transcendent exists within the interior of the church.[1] Although Wink's theory that the transcendent angel represents the interiority of the church will be discussed later in this thesis, it is sufficient at this moment to note that this concept allows for a human emissary to directly address the transcendent angel and bring about change. In view of this, the role of the emissary in addressing the angel is vital to the well-being of the church. While the minister will not always adopt this role, the person whose God-given task is to address the angel of a church will, undoubtedly, have to adopt some form of leadership role and be granted authority to identify the areas where transformation is required. Therefore, in addressing issues surrounding authority, ministry, and power, this chapter will explore the strengths and weaknesses of the pastor's role within a Baptist congregation, along with the authority they are able to exercise to bring about change and thus enable the church to fulfill its vocation.

---

1. Wink, *Unmasking the Powers*, 81.

Introducing the significance of authority, ministry, and power in respect of the angel of the church, Wink argues that although some of how a congregation functions are determined by denominational polity, differing theological outlooks, leadership styles, and approaches to authority will also affect the nature of the church.[2] In this respect, although, historically, Baptist churches have often appointed ministers, and have credited them with hard work in promoting the gospel, the relationship between church and minister is not without its tensions. As will become evident, embedded in Baptist ecclesiology are beliefs regarding authority that, when explored, reveal a power dynamic that has the capability to prevent the transformation of the angel of the church.

Authority

In its simplest form, a Baptist understanding of authority within an ecclesial context is that Jesus is the head of the church and that each congregation is at liberty to interpret his laws and apply them to their contemporary situation. This belief is enshrined in the first of the three principles that form the basis of the Baptist Union of Great Britain.[3] The reference to "his laws" in the declaration of principle is usually interpreted as the revelation of God in the Christian Scriptures. Although believing that Jesus is the absolute authority in the church and that the Scriptures reveal his will is not unique to Baptists, their insistence on the liberty of each congregation interpreting and applying scriptural principles locally adds an extra dimension to their ecclesiology. The liberty to do so places Baptists among those churches that are governed congregationally. While this is also not unique to Baptists, the bringing together of their commitment to discerning the will of Christ by interacting with the Scriptures and their locality, congregational government, and their doctrinal stance on believers' baptism does provide for a unique form of ecclesiology.

Having acknowledged that authority in a Baptist context is located in the lordship of Christ and his government is exercised within the local congregation, it is important to note that Baptist polity is not individualistic

---

2. Wink, *Unmasking the Powers*, 74–75.

3. Baptists Together, "Declaration of Principle." The first principle states: "That our Lord and Saviour Jesus Christ, God manifest in the flesh, is the sole and absolute authority in all matters pertaining to faith and practice, as revealed in the Holy Scriptures, and that each Church has liberty, under the guidance of the Holy Spirit, to interpret and administer His laws."

in nature. Traditionally, Baptist congregations have valued interacting with other congregations, have formed local Associations, and, eventually, have formed a national Union. However, commenting on the authority of a local Association, B. R. White notes that while a church might ask an Association for advice on an issue and would be expected to give a degree of credence to the Association's response, they would also be expected to weigh the reply themselves and make their own decision.[4]

Accountability

With a congregational polity, Baptist congregations are, generally speaking, not accountable to either the local Association or the national Union.[5] In light of this, a Baptist church meeting acts as a place of discernment and a place of accountability. Commenting on the nature of authority in a Baptist church, White suggests that membership of an early Baptist congregation depended on two criteria: professing a need for Christ and being willing to submit to the discipline of the local church.[6] This commitment to the church meeting having the authority to call a member to account is illustrated in this extract from the records of Kilmington Baptist Church, dated November 6, 1658:

> Brother Gill from the Brethren at Honiton informed the church that Bro. Farnaby was drunk in the street on Friday last. . . . The Church Appoints Bro. Gill and Bro. Gaylan from the Brethren in Honiton to give notice to Bro. Farnaby is to be at the next First day in the morning when the Church intends to talk with him about his miscarriage.[7]

The acceptance of being called to account in this way was a sign of the covenantal nature of early Baptist churches. Although the language of

---

4. White, *Authority*, 15.

5. The relationship between Baptist congregations and the national Union will be explored as part of a discussion on denominational polity in chapter 6. However, an example of when Baptists are obliged to adhere to instructions given by the Baptist Union is in administering the ecclesial exemption for listed church buildings. In this context, although there is latitude for negotiation, the church is compelled by legislation to comply with the ruling of the Listed Buildings Advisory Committee.

6. White, *Authority*, 14.

7. Minutes, Nov. 6, 1658, 3700D/M1, Kilmington Baptist Church minute book 1654–1795, DHC.

covenant raises some concerns among contemporary Baptists,[8] Stephen Finamore suggests that the commitment that members of a Baptist congregation make to being church in a specific location represents a covenant.[9] The use of covenantal language to describe the relationship between Baptist church members makes a significant statement as it emphasizes the mutual accountability of their relationship.

The mutuality of relationship among Baptists is also important when describing how Baptists understand the term "ministry." Stephen Holmes takes a strong stance on this aspect of Baptist ecclesiology, arguing that the ministry "is not a ministry of individuals in the church, nor even the ministry of every individual in the church, but a corporate ministry of the whole church that is indivisible."[10] This corporate understanding of ministry, along with a commitment to mutual accountability among church members, means that the minister is as accountable for lifestyle, actions, and ministry as any church member. An example of how this accountability might be expressed can be found in the records from Newton Abbot Baptist Church for 1985.

Calling the Minister to Account

On January 28, 1985, a special church meeting was held at the request of twenty-three church members. These members had all signed a resolution stating that they were concerned by signs of unrest in some sections of the congregation. Such was their concern that they urged the church leaders to call a church meeting. What is more, in light of the nature of their concerns, they requested that the area superintendent chair the meeting.[11]

Although this proposition does not directly critique the ministry of the pastor, the request that the area superintendent chair the meeting

---

8. Paul Fiddes notes that, while Baptists have traditionally resisted assenting to documents that restricted the expression of their faith, they have historically agreed on declarations, or statements of faith. Fiddes, "Covenant," 17. Furthermore, in 1996 the principals of the four English Baptist colleges produced *Something to Declare: A Study of the Declaration of Principle* in response to concerns raised over the use of the term "covenant" in *The Nature of the Assembly and the Council of the Baptist Union of Great Britain*. Fiddes et al., *Something to Declare*, 14.

9. Finamore, "Baptists in Covenant," 74.

10. Holmes, "Towards a Baptist Theology," 254.

11. Minutes, Jan. 28, 1985, box 6916-1-5, Newton Abbot Baptist Church minute book Jan. 1954–July 27, 1988, DHC.

suggests that the disquiet among the members involved the pastor. The credibility of this supposition is enhanced by the mention of a current lack of direction and that the quality of the preaching had deteriorated.[12]

The critique offered by the church members is interesting as, in addition to critiquing the pastor's performance as a minister, they also offer him support. Furthermore, while there is a critique of the direction that the church was taking, there is also an underlying concern that there were divisions within the congregation. These divisions appear to be highlighted in a lack of interaction between old and new members. A fifth comment highlights a further cause of concern as the deacons were described as a "Closed shop" or "Secret Society," and they were asked to explain why the church had not been informed that the deacons had met with the area superintendent.[13] This comment highlights the ability of the church meeting to critique the deacons as well as the pastor, together with an expectation that the church would be kept informed of all aspects of church life.

The calling to account of the Newton Abbot pastor raises a question regarding the minister's ability to implement change. From the above extract of the church meeting minutes, it appears that the members had differing opinions over the church's vocation. These disagreements appear to have become focused on the ministry the pastor exercised and their ability to implement change. Clearly, some members appreciated the pastor's preaching ministry and felt that, with the help of the congregation, they could implement the changes necessary for the continued well-being of the church. However, due to a significant number of members taking the contrary position, not only was the pastor's ministry called into question, the authority and power to implement change was also removed.

In response to the criticism leveled against his ministry, the pastor was given an opportunity to address the church members. He accepted and advised the meeting that he had "always intended to carry out the people's wishes."[14] Following his statement, the minutes do not reveal anything further except that the meeting closed with prayer.

The statement that the pastor's only intention had been to fulfill the wishes of the people reveals the perils of the chaplaincy form of ministry

---

12. Minutes, Jan. 28, 1985, box 6916-1-5, DHC. Although this material is in the public domain, the name of the pastor has deliberately not been used in this thesis.

13. Minutes, Jan. 28, 1985, box 6916-1-5, DHC.

14. Minutes, Jan. 28, 1985, box 6916-1-5, DHC.

critiqued by Wink.[15] However, although Wink envisages that this type of ministry provides a comfortable relationship between people and the pastor, the pastorate at Newton Abbot in the 1980s appears to be somewhat fractious. In this context, the pastor appears to be placed in an impossible position. While his ministry clearly garnered support from some members, there appears to have been a faction within the church that were unhappy with the results of his labors. The fractious nature of the church in Newton Abbot and the consequent relationship between minister and congregation contrast sharply with the relationship between Baptists in Budleigh Salterton and their pastor described in chapter 3. This contrast highlights how the nature of the angel of a church can differ between different congregations.

The impossibility of the Newton Abbot pastor's position is evident in the light of a further petition for a special church meeting presented to the church secretary on February 16, 1985. This time, the expressed concern was the "future pastorate of this church."[16] The requested meeting was held on March 6, 1985, and the minutes note that early in the proceedings, the area superintendent had read a letter of resignation from the minister.[17] As this is only a month after the meeting where the pastor appeared to receive support for his ministry, it is clear that whatever additional criticism had been reported was sufficient for him to tender his resignation. In the light of this, and the discussion that followed, a proposal was put to the meeting asking the pastor to withdraw his resignation. The fact that the proposal was carried by fifty-eight votes to thirty-four reveals that a significant minority of church members were unwilling to support their pastor. Of course, it is impossible to tell how many of the thirty-four votes represented members who felt that the compassionate approach was to allow the pastor to leave and how many had lost confidence in his ministry.

Despite the apparent support of a majority of the church and a request for him to reconsider his resignation, the church meeting held on April 24, 1985, confirmed that the pastor had decided to leave the pastorate.[18] Responding to this decision, the church discussed how they might

15. Wink, *Unmasking the Powers*, 74.

16. Request for special church meeting, Feb. 16, 1985, box 6916, Newton Abbot Baptist Church, DHC.

17. Minutes, Mar. 6, 1985, box 6916-1-5, Newton Abbot Baptist Church minute book Jan. 1954–July 27, 1988, DHC.

18. Minutes, Apr. 24, 1985, box 6916-1-5, DHC.

care for the pastor and his family during the period of transition. The records show that after some discussion, the church decided to allow the pastor and his family to continue living in the manse beyond his three-month notice period.[19] The fact that this discussion took place reveals that the loss of the family home is one of the pressures facing Baptist ministers that may lead to them deciding to placate the church members by conceding to their desires. In this respect, the deacons, who were also criticized at the church meeting held at Newton Abbot Baptist on January 28, 1985, do not face the same pressures. The fact that criticism was leveled at both the pastor and deacons and only the pastor resigned highlights the contrast between the vulnerability of the pastor's position and that of the deacons. This is particularly evident when the pastor relies on the church for their accommodation. The apparent contrast in vulnerability might also suggest that, as established church members, the deacons were not as likely as the pastor to face the discipline of the church meeting. In view of this, it is possible to surmise that if the deacons were united in their support of the pastor's ministry, their leadership position would have been more robust. It also suggests that any changes the pastor sought to implement would have been supported.

In the context of addressing the angel of the church, this episode in the life of Newton Abbot Baptist church is interesting as it highlights the need for wider support within the church leadership when addressing the angel of the church. It also highlights the vulnerability of the person who is called to address the weaknesses in the angel's nature and lifestyle. This vulnerability is enhanced by the practice of churches supplying their pastors with accommodation as well as paying a stipend.

Dependency and the Practice of Ministry

Exploring how power is exercised in the church, Paul Beasley-Murray suggests that the dependency caused by living in tied accommodation can be a cause of resentment, particularly among the minister's family.[20] Alternatively, the knowledge that the accommodation occupied by the minister and their family is directly linked to the office they hold may temper the minister's willingness to face any conflict arising from an attempt to address and transform the nature of the angel of the church. If this happens,

---

19. Minutes, Apr. 24, 1985, box 6916-1-5, DHC.
20. Beasley-Murray, *Power for God's Sake*, 29.

the ability of the minister to address the angel is neutralized, and they quickly simply become a chaplain to the congregation. In view of this, if the pastor is going to retain their position and authority to address the angel of the church and thus implement lasting changes, they will either require the support of the leadership team or have independent accommodation and financial means. In the first of these scenarios, the support of a diaconate who are securely embedded in both the church and the local community and are willing to advocate the changes suggested by the pastor will insulate the minister from the vulnerability that comes with being an outsider. Likewise, if the pastor is not dependent on the church for income or accommodation, they are free to address the issues facing the church without the fear of how or where they will live if the church dispenses with their services. Although each of these scenarios enhances the ability of the pastor to exercise their ministry, their authority to act is still open to critique by the church meeting. The difference is that with either the support of the deacons or the freedom of independent means, the pastor need not fear the outcome of the critique.

The story of the critique, apparent support, and resignation of a minister of Newton Abbot Baptist Church in 1985 demonstrates how, without actually demanding the minister's resignation, sufficient pressure can be applied to force them to leave. The record of proceedings is made particularly poignant by the minister's appeal to his desire to meet the requirements of the church members and not their desire to address the issues facing the church. In the context of Wink's critique of ministers who act as chaplains to the church members, this story reveals how the fickleness of a congregation may reject the ministry offered despite the pastor's attempts to assent to the congregation's desires.

The Church Meeting

The story of the Newton Abbot pastor in 1985 not only highlights the precarious position that a Baptist minister can find themselves in, it also reveals something of the nature of the church meeting. Although in *Something to Declare*, Paul Fiddes, Brian Haymes, Richard Kidd, and Michael Quicke are defending the use of covenantal language in respect of the relationship between churches, the Union, and Assembly, their arguments are nevertheless appropriate to describing the relationship at work within the church meeting.

Fiddes et al. argue that there are two axes in a covenant relationship: the horizontal, representing the relationship between individuals, and the vertical, between God and his people.[21] If the church meeting is a place where the liberty of the church to interpret Christ's laws and apply them to their context, then a congregation's relationship with God is as important as their relationship with each other.

Describing the nature of this axis, Baptist authors such as W. M. S. West, Fred Bacon, Wright, and Holmes describe the church meeting as a place where an interaction with God takes place, as his will is discerned.[22] The problem with this concept is highlighted by Wright and Holmes, who both acknowledge that the church meeting seldom functions in this way. Critiquing the church meeting from the perspective of an established church or the restoration movement, Wright suggests that the church meeting is a place where pride and the rebellious nature of the individual submits to the spiritual authority of the appointed leader. Citing Jdg 21:25, Wright also suggests that the humility and submission required for a church meeting to function well provide an antidote for the spiritual anarchy arising from everyone doing as they see fit.

Although Wright seeks to support his argument for revising the process of the church meeting, his point regarding the individualistic actions of members is insightful. Rodger Hayden argues that the contemporary church meeting has become a democratic process where decisions are made by majority vote rather than resulting from a process of discernment.[23] This critique of a meeting, where key decisions affecting the life of the church are made, is significant as it suggests that the integrated relationship between church members and God may have broken down. If this is the case, the activity of church members at a Baptist church meeting may provide a significant window into the nature of the congregation and its angel. A church whose decisions are being made purely on the basis of a democratic voting system will have lost sight of their vocation. If this is the case, the church will have ceased to be a church and instead will have become an organization regulated by a set of religious values. Of course, this does not mean that the congregation will cease to emulate a church by their use of religious language, but it will mean that their rituals will have lost their sacramental dimension. If this were the case, Wink's

21. Fiddes et al., *Something to Declare*, 12–15.
22. West, *Baptist Principles*, 17–19; Bacon, *Church Administration*, 80; Wright, *Challenge to Change*, 91–114; Holmes, "Knowing the Mind of Christ."
23. Hayden, "Baptists, Covenants and Confessions," 34.

definition of the angel becoming demonic would be appropriate.[24] However, even if the angel of the church has become demonic, this does not mean that the situation is irredeemable. If the church meeting is directed away from a purely democratic form of decision-making and returns to a process of discerning the divine will, the spiritual nature of both the church and its angel will be restored.

Ministry

With authority in a Baptist church vested in Christ and his will discerned through the church meeting, how the role of a minister is understood is open to discussion. Wright explores where Baptists disagree over how they perceive their minister in "Inclusive Representation: Towards a Doctrine of Christian Ministry"[25] and *New Baptist, New Agenda*.[26] Among the issues Wright addresses relating to ministry are questions over the wider role of a minister, how ordination is understood, and whether ministry is sacramental in nature.

A Local or Wider Ministry

Although, historically, Baptists have agreed that the local church has the authority to appoint its own officers, they have disagreed over the type of role these officers should fulfill and whether or not their roles might be exercised widely among other Baptist congregations. Under Thomas Helwys, the General Baptists appointed elders, who were expected to encourage and deepen the faith of church members, and deacons, who attended to the physical needs of the congregation.[27] This differs from the Particular Baptists who, in the 1644 London Confession, advocate the appointment of pastors, teachers, elders, and deacons.[28] While the section dealing with these appointments does not designate specific roles for each office, it does

---

24. According to Wink, an angel of the church becomes demonic when it rejects its God-given vocation and decides to pursue its own idol. Wink, *Unmasking the Powers*, 78.

25. Wright, "Inclusive Representation," 159–74.

26. Wright, *New Baptists, New Agenda*, 116–30.

27. See the English Declaration at Amsterdam, art. 20, in Lumpkin and Leonard, *Baptist Confessions of Faith*, 121–22.

28. The 1644 London Confession, art. 36 in Lumpkin and Leonard, *Baptist Confessions of Faith*, 166.

advocate that their appointments are to enable Christ to feed, govern, and build up his church.[29] The distinguishing feature of Particular Baptists' understanding of the wider role of the pastor is emphasized in article 10 of the Second London Confession, where the focus is serving the churches through attentiveness to prayer, preaching, and pastoral care.[30]

The subtlety of the charge to pastors to serve Christ in churches—plural—differs from the General Baptists, who believed that members appointed to an office were restricted to exercising their gifts within the church that had appointed them. The only exception to this rule was when a person was appointed to the role of apostle.[31] This link made by the General Baptists between ministry and a specific location is not restricted to the seventeenth century. Writing in 1944, Arthur Dakin described a Baptist minister as one who has a close relationship with the church that invited them to serve as pastor.[32] Dakin was principal of Bristol Baptist College when he expressed this view, and, in doing so, he excused himself from being understood as a Baptist minister.[33]

Writing in the same year, E. A. Payne contradicts Dakin's position, arguing that by including the office of apostle, General Baptists created a category of minister who could practice beyond the confines of the local church. For Payne, the fact that Thomas Helwys, the seventeenth-century General Baptist leader, included the office of apostle confirmed his contention that both General and Particular Baptists recognized a trans-local ministry.[34] Despite this, Payne tempered his argument by referencing the role that messengers played among the seventeenth-century General Baptists. Payne suggested that bishops were also known as messengers and their role was comparable to that of general superintendents and are now known as regional ministers.[35] Using this analogy, Payne seems to suggest that although messengers were entitled to undertake

---

29. These offices were amended to bishop, elder, and deacon in ch. 26, art. 9 and referred to as pastor in art. 10 of the Second London Confession. Lumpkin and Leonard, *Baptist Confessions of Faith*, 286–87.

30. The Second London Confession, ch. 26, art. 10 in Lumpkin and Leonard, *Baptist Confessions of Faith*, 87.

31. The English Declaration at Amsterdam, art. 22, in Lumpkin and Leonard, *Baptist Confessions of Faith*, 122.

32. Dakin, *Baptist View of the Church and Ministry*, 44.

33. Goodliff, "Inclusive Representation Revisited," 107.

34. Payne, *Fellowship of Believers*, 37.

35. Payne, *Fellowship of Believers*, 43.

the ministry of word and sacrament within a local congregation, their primary role was to appoint pastors to local congregations. If this is the heart of Payne's argument, it does little more than nuance Dakin's position. However, according to Paul Goodliff, this was not Payne's intention. Goodliff argues that at the time Dakin made his declaration regarding the nature of ministry, he was due to be inducted as the president of the Baptist Union. Therefore, Goodliff contends that, as the general secretary of the Union did not want any controversy surrounding his appointment, Payne was encouraged to significantly temper his argument.[36]

Broadening the Understanding of Ministry

If the disagreement among Baptists over whether or not ministry extends beyond the local congregation was not complicated enough, it was made more complex in 2006 by the publication of *Gathering for Worship*. The complication arises from *Gathering for Worship*'s provision of resources for ordaining church members called to fulfill a ministry other than the traditional pastor/teacher.[37] By offering these resources, *Gathering for Worship* fulfills the desire for a wider understanding of ministry expressed within the 1994 *Forms of Ministry Among Baptists* (*FMAB*) report. In addition to promoting the cause for national recognition of ministries other than the traditional pastor/teacher, the *FMAB* report also marks a distinction between British Baptists and those of the rest of Europe and the United States of America.[38] According to the report, Baptists in the United Kingdom were changing their perception that there was a fixed set of ministerial offices and, instead, were trying to identify the gifts that God had given to his church and were being exhibited by individual church members. Responding to this change, the *FMAB* report advocates a flexible approach to ordination and for churches to be ready to acknowledge different specialists, such as youth workers and evangelists, as they emerge.[39]

This recognition of ministries, other than that of the traditional pastor/teacher, provides local churches with a mandate to consider their ministerial needs in the light of their local vocation and call a person

---

36. Goodliff, "Inclusive Representation Revisited," 107.
37. Ellis and Blyth, *Gathering for Worship*, 121.
38. *Forms of Ministry Among Baptists*, 21.
39. *Forms of Ministry Among Baptists*, 21.

gifted in that area to assist them in their mission. Furthermore, by recognizing that the gifts God gives to his church extend beyond the traditional pastor/teacher role, local congregations are free to acknowledge church members gifted in areas of ministry that will strengthen the local and trans-local church. By recognizing gifted members of the congregation and acknowledging their ability to strengthen the church, Baptists in the United Kingdom are continuing their tradition of discerning the work of Christ among them. Although the wider recognition that God may call church members into roles other than that of the traditional minister is a positive step, there is a question as to whether local congregations will accept a specialist ministry in place of a traditional pastor/teacher role. Embracing the idea that the roles required to minister to the contemporary church may be different than they have been in the past will depend on the congregation's ability to overcome the inertia of its history and traditions. While the role that tradition plays in the life of the church will be explored later in this thesis, it is sufficient for the moment to acknowledge that it can have the effect of holding back change. Therefore, if Baptists in the United Kingdom are to overcome an attachment to the traditional pastor/teacher role of ministry, it will be because the gyroscopic nature of the angel has been overcome. If this is the case, then, like most things within Baptist ecclesiology, churches will react differently, with some embracing new ministries and others rejecting the concept. As for overcoming the internal resistance to change caused by the angel, the degree to which the congregation will overcome its prejudice toward a traditional pastor/teacher role depends on whether or not the new leader embraces new forms of ministry.

Understanding Ordination

With the recognition of new ministries and the introduction of material for ordaining church members exercising a wider selection of ministries, the question of what ordination means to Baptists needs to be addressed.

According to Wright, aside from a period during the nineteenth century, it has been the usual practice for Baptists to ordain their ministers.[40] However, the way Baptists understand ordination does not necessarily correspond with how other church traditions understand it. The 1957 report *The Meaning and Practice of Ordination Among Baptists*

---

40. Wright, "Inclusive Representation," 168.

(*MPOAB*) describes ordination as the church, having recognized the calling of God on a person's life and their gifting for ministry, publicly recognizes and commissions them.[41]

The significance of this description is that ordination among Baptists is a corporate event. It is the church that acknowledges the gifting and calling of God, and it is the church that commissions the minister in the name of Christ. The ambiguity in this statement is, however, in how the term "church" is understood. Among Baptists, there is a natural tendency to understand the church as a local congregation. Thus, ordination is the setting apart of a person for a specific ministry by a local congregation. The 1957 report on ordination acknowledges this understanding among Baptists. Furthermore, the recognition of a person's ministry in a specific location continues in some local Associations with respect to Locally Recognized Ministers.[42] However, while some Baptists recognize and ordain specific local ministries, ordination is generally accepted as a wider recognition of God's calling and gifting.

Is ordination sacramental?

Although Baptists generally accept the practice of ordination, there is nevertheless a disagreement over what ordination actually means. Addressing this issue, the *MPOAB* report simply states that it is impossible to tell what actually happens as a person is ordained.[43] However, it does consider ordination a blessing. It then seeks to explore how the church and the candidate at an ordination service might experience that blessing. This side-steps the issue of the ontological change and the enduring status of the ministerial candidate that may or may not take place during ordination. Accepting this difficulty, Holmes notes that when a Baptist minister stops performing the functions usually associated with their role, they are often removed from the list of "Covenanted Persons." He also notes that if a minister returns to pastoral practice and is welcomed back on the list of Covenanted Persons, they are not re-ordained.[44] Therefore, as Holmes points out, even if Baptists seek to understand ordination differently from other church traditions, they

---

41. *Meaning and Practice of Ordination*, 22.
42. *In This Place, at This Time.*
43. *Meaning and Practice of Ordination*, 25.
44. Holmes, "Towards a Baptist Theology," 258.

still practice, if not acknowledge, that something lifelong is confirmed on the minister when they are ordained.[45] Noting this, Wright suggests that because the idea of an ontological change and, therefore, lifelong transformation is linked with a sacramental view of the priesthood, Baptists have deliberately sought to understand ordination differently.[46] However, once again, it is impossible to state that Baptists are united in opposition to the sacramental nature of ministry.

John Colwell presents the case for a sacramental understanding of ordination from a different perspective. He argues for a dynamic understanding of sacrament, which, when applied to ordination, represents a place where God engages with human beings. This places ordination in a similar category as baptism and the Lord's Supper, where ordinary things provide a conduit through which God is encountered. Of course, understanding ordination this way opens a debate on the number of sacraments the church should recognize. This is an argument that Colwell is keen to avoid, concentrating instead on the idea that God is encountered as the minister is ordained.[47]

The starting point for Colwell's argument is the Augustinian thesis that a sacrament is a sign of divine activity or a dynamic example of a divine word.[48] In this context, the ordination service is a place where the activity of God is made visible. Having introduced the idea that the act of ordination provides a sign of God at work, Colwell draws on the work of Thomas Aquinas to argue that the sign of ordination is more than a symbol but is rather an act that confers grace.[49] Exploring this, Colwell is careful to emphasize the view that the gift of grace at ordination is bestowed by God through the Holy Spirit and is not dependent on human activity.[50]

Developing this argument for a sacramental understanding of ordination, Colwell considers John Calvin's view of a sacrament as making a commitment in the light of a prior promise of God as a useful way of understanding ordination.[51] This is a helpful illustration as, during a Baptist ordination service, it is usual for promises to be made by both the church

---

45. Holmes, "Towards a Baptist Theology," 258.
46. Wright, "Inclusive Representation," 168.
47. Colwell, "Sacramental Nature of Ordination," 233.
48. Colwell, "Sacramental Nature of Ordination," 233–34.
49. Colwell, "Sacramental Nature of Ordination," 234–35.
50. Colwell, "Sacramental Nature of Ordination," 236.
51. Colwell, "Sacramental Nature of Ordination," 236.

and the minister.⁵² Therefore, using Colwell's interpretation of Calvin's view, when promises are made at the ordination service, the initial desire of God is fulfilled, which, in turn, results in his blessing being bestowed.

In addition to exploring the link between ordination and the promise of God, Colwell also considers the link between the laying on of hands and the prayers offered at an ordination service. Here, in addition to Calvin, he also references the work of Karl Barth. Beginning with Calvin, Colwell argues that the act of ordination represents an event in which God interacts with his church. He then references Barth's view that baptism seals the prior promise and action of God and argues that ordination also represents a fulfillment of God's initial promise.⁵³ Developing his thesis in this way, Colwell's argument resonates with the point raised by Holmes. If the ordination service marks a place where God is at work and laying hands on the ordained seals the promise and action of God in the life of the minister, then Colwell, like Holmes, is advocating that an enduring change takes place at ordination.

The Sacramental View of Ministry

Despite both Colwell's and Holmes' clear rejection of a sacerdotal form of ministry, there is nevertheless an underlying belief among some Baptists that the act of ordination defines the position of minister in a way that is different from other forms of leadership. Wright attempts to address this issue in "Inclusive Representation." Here, he suggests that the contemporary disagreement over the sacramental nature of leadership can be simplified by first defining the opinions over the sacramental nature of ministry as the difference between "High" and "Low" Baptists. Using these distinctions, Wright suggests that High Baptists have a sacramental view of ministry and might represent a Presbyterian view of leadership. Conversely, Low Baptists have a non-sacramental view of ministry and might be represented by an Anabaptist view of leadership. However, having made this distinction, Wright acknowledges that while these definitions might provide a helpful way of understanding the disagreement among Baptists on this issue, the conclusions are not clearly defined.⁵⁴

52. Payne and Winward, *Orders and Prayers for Church Worship*, 194–95; *Patterns and Prayers for Christian Worship*, 176–81; Ellis and Blyth, *Gathering for Worship*, 122–27.

53. Colwell, "Sacramental Nature of Ordination," 237.

54. Wright, "Inclusive Representation," 166.

The difficulty in discussing the disagreement among Baptists over the sacramental nature of the minister's office is not simply related to what happens at the ordination service but also relates to how the ordained minister functions. According to Wright, the contention among Baptists is exemplified over the meaning of being ordained into "the ministry of Word and Sacrament." The difficulty here is that such a statement suggests that preaching, baptizing, and presiding at the Lord's Supper is the prerogative of the ordained minister.[55] This position is emphasized by two of the three significant publications offering suggested texts for ordination services.[56] However, having stated this, it is only *Patterns and Prayers for Christian Worship* that specifically uses the term "ministry of Word and Sacrament."[57] While the earlier *Orders and Prayers for Church Worship* does not use the phrase, it does suggest that the role of the ordained will be to lead worship, administer the sacraments, and preach and teach the Christian faith as revealed in the Scriptures.[58] In both instances, the act of ordination appears to differentiate between the role of the minister and the rest of the congregation in respect of preaching, baptizing, and presiding at the Lord's Table. Holmes legitimizes this differentiation by arguing that the ministry of Word and Sacrament is the ministry of the church and, as such, is a corporate ministry.[59] However, within the corporate exercise of ministry, the church recognizes that some of its members are gifted to fulfill certain roles. Thus, when the ordained minister preaches, baptizes, and presides at the Lord's Supper, they are not acting as individuals but as the church's representatives.[60]

Ministry as a Corporate Activity

Discussing the nature of ministry in *On Being the Church*, Haymes et al. present an argument that concurs with Holmes's belief that ministry is a corporate activity.[61] They base this understanding on the belief that

---

55. Wright, "Inclusive Representation," 166.

56. The three significant Baptist publications offering texts for ordination services are Payne and Winward, *Orders and Prayers for Church Worship*; *Patterns and Prayers for Christian Worship*; and Ellis and Blyth, *Gathering for Worship*.

57. *Patterns and Prayers for Christian Worship*, 170.

58. Payne and Winward, *Orders and Prayers for Church Worship*, 193.

59. Holmes, "Towards a Baptist Theology," 254.

60. Holmes, "Towards a Baptist Theology," 260.

61. Haymes et al., *On Being Church*, 157.

ministry is primarily the activity of God. In the opinion of Haymes et al., the role of the church is to tell the story of what God is doing in his world. Therefore, within this context, a person appointed to a ministerial role within the church is called upon to remind the church of what God is doing and help them to participate in his divine activity.[62] Within this definition, the person appointed to minister to the congregation also has a responsibility to reveal the areas of church life that need to be transformed so as to reflect the nature and will of Christ. Undertaking this action will involve addressing the nature of the angel of the church. However, as ministry in a Baptist church is considered a corporate activity, the power that a minister has to address and transform the angel of the church is only granted by the consent of the congregation.

Power

At the heart of Baptist ecclesiology is the belief that the church is formed out of the people called into a relationship with God, and this is evident in the early confessions of faith from both the General and Particular Baptists. Examples of this can be seen in article 12 of John Smyth's Short Confession of Faith in XX Articles and article 33 of the Particular 1644 London Confession.[63] Furthermore, as well as acknowledging that the call of God forms the church, Baptists have also historically adopted a position where church membership is intrinsically linked to the confession of sin and the atoning sacrifice of Christ. Once again, the early confessions of faith from both the General and Particular Baptists articulate this.[64] It is this link between membership and the confession of Christian faith and the vertical axis of the covenantal relationship that forms the basis for Baptists understanding the church as a priesthood of all believers.

By viewing the church as a priesthood of all believers, Baptists negate the need for a specific priesthood and create an opportunity for ordinary church members to preach, baptize, and preside at the Lord's Table. In view of this, it is unsurprising that the early confessions of faith attest to the first Baptists appointing officeholders from among

---

62. Haymes et al., *On Being Church*, 153, 58–59.

63. Lumpkin and Leonard, *Baptist Confessions of Faith*, 99, 147.

64. Article 20 of the General Baptist Short Confession of 1610 and article 21 of the Particular Baptist 1644 London Confession are examples of the early Baptists' stress on the importance of the atoning work of Christ. Lumpkin and Leonard, *Baptist Confessions of Faith*, 100–101, 150.

their own congregations.⁶⁵ Reflecting back on the corporate nature of ministry expressed by Holmes, it is significant that these early confessions considered ministry to be a corporate act and yet expected to appoint officeholders to fulfill pastoral and teaching roles. Their reason for making these appointments was that it helped ensure the well-being of the church.⁶⁶ The 1948 paper *The Doctrine of the Church* echoes this position, arguing that worship, preaching, baptism, and the Lord's Supper are all congregational acts. What is more, while the act of preaching or presiding over the Lord's Table is usually carried out by a person of status within the congregation, they are, nevertheless, held in equal standing with the other church members in Christ.⁶⁷

This stance on ministry provides an important key to understanding the tension Baptists face between the ministry that every church member can exercise and the appointment of individuals to specific offices. It also provides a further key to understanding the angel of a Baptist congregation, as knowing how a church interprets its role in ministry will affect the influence a minister will be allowed to exercise. By declaring the equality of each church member while also acknowledging that different individuals will exercise different gifts within the church, the 1948 paper underpins the belief that although some members are called into leadership positions, they remain mutually accountable to the rest of the church. However, while the 1948 paper acknowledges that different gifts are exercised within a congregation and the mutual accountability of church members, it does not address the strength of commitment Baptists have to the concept of the church being a priesthood of all believers. Addressing this, Wright suggests that this commitment is often used to close down an argument for leadership.⁶⁸ Thus, when an impasse arises over the direction a church should or should not take, reference to the priesthood of all believers removes the authority and the ability to act from the hands of the leadership and returns it to the body of believers. In view of this, when an impasse occurs between

---

65. Articles 23–25 in the General Baptist Short Confession of 1610 and article 36 of the Particular Baptist Confession of 1644, in Lumpkin, *Baptist Confessions of Faith*, 101, 154.

66. Articles 23 and 24 in the General Baptist Short Confession of 1610 and articles 36 and 37 of the Particular Baptist Confession of 1644, in Lumpkin *Baptist Confessions of Faith*, 101, 166.

67. *Baptist Doctrine of the Church*, 4–5.

68. Wright, "Inclusive Representation," 163.

the leadership and the church meeting, there is a temptation for the ministers and deacons to dominate the meeting and push their decisions through by force of personality. An example of this can be seen in the life of Newton Abbot Baptist church in 2006.

The Dominating Leadership

The relationship that the Baptists of Newton Abbot had with their building on East Street has already been explored in an earlier chapter. However, that discussion did not consider the tensions between the church leadership and the rest of the church members over the move.

Following the paper by Blizzard and Proudlock and the subsequent church strategy report,[69] the church experimented with meeting at a local school for worship. Although the strategy report outlines a period of preparation prior to the move, and on October 8, 2003, the deacons discussed the process of transition at length,[70] there is no indication in the church meeting minutes that the move was ever discussed at a church meeting during 2003. In the light of an ecclesiology founded on congregational participation and mutual accountability, it is significant that the practicalities of moving to new premises were not considered at the church meeting. This is not to say that conversations with the church members and the wider congregation were not held outside of the church meeting, but it is concerning that the church leaders did not consider updating the church meeting of their discussions as part of the normal process of spiritual discernment and church governance.

According to the Church Strategy report and the deacons' discussion on October 8, 2003, it is evident that the move to Highweek School was to be reviewed after three months. This review took place on January 19, 2004, with the minutes recording "an honest and wide-ranging discussion." Under the guidance of the regional minister, the discussion was brought to a close with a proposal that the church continue to worship at Highweek School. However, there was a caveat that this decision

---

69. Charles Blizzard and Beth Proudlock, Report to the Minister, the Evaluation Group and the Deacons and Members of Newton Abbot Following a Visit by the Association Survey Team in the Action in Mission Project, box 6916, Newton Abbot Baptist Church, n.d., DHC; Newton Abbot Baptist Church strategy, box 6916, Newton Abbot Baptist Church, n.d., DHC.

70. Minutes of Deacons Meeting Held on Monday 6 October 2003 at 19a Chudleigh Road, Kingsteignton, box 6916, 2, DHC.

should be reviewed again in July. The proposal was carried, but it is worth noting that of the thirty-five members present and voting, twelve voted against. This represents a significant minority and might go some way to explaining some of the tensions described above. Despite the clear division and the significant number voting against the proposal, the pastor advised that July would represent the last time their relocation would be discussed.[71]

Interestingly, the records show that this meeting was chaired by the regional minister and not the pastor. This action alone highlights the contentious nature of the meeting as it suggests that either the church or the pastor and deacons felt the necessity for a neutral chairperson. However, from the perspective of process, the fact that the records show a vibrant conversation took place is positive. The disappointing aspect of this meeting is that while there was a healthy exchange of ideas, very little discernment took place. This is evident in the result of the final vote. While the motion to continue worshiping at Highweek School was carried by a majority, approximately a third of the church members voted against. Although the next chapter will discuss the use of voting as a means of coming to a conclusion within a church meeting, it is difficult to see how, without further caveats, this decision could have reflected the mind of Christ. Of course, it is possible that a caveat, such as an agreement by those who voted against the proposal to support the decision because they believed that the mind of Christ had been reached, would show that this was not simply a democratic process in action. However, if this were the case, it might be reasonable to expect that the church minutes would note this position. Therefore, without such a statement or the notation of any other caveat that suggests that those who voted against felt that the mind of Christ had been discerned, it must be presumed that a democratic decision-making process was used as a method of discernment. If this was the case, the question of the nature of the angel returns to the fore. If, by using a democratic decision-making process rather than seeking to discern the mind of Christ, the church had reached a decision that led them away from their vocation, the angel of the church might have shifted toward being demonic. What is more, such a spiritual transition could be attributed to the power exerted on the members by the church leaders.

---

71. Church meeting minutes, Jan. 19, 2004, box 6916, Newton Abbot Baptist Church, DHC.

The Language of Leadership

Although the authority in a Baptist church lies with the church meeting, the center of power is less clear. In the illustration above, the pastor and deacons exercised sufficient power to push a motion to acceptance despite the objections of a large minority of members. While, in the case of the church in Newton Abbot, the minister and deacons were able to convince the church to adopt an unpopular, but arguably necessary, decision, leaders in other Baptist churches may not be granted a similar amount of power.

Whether or not a minister will be granted sufficient power to address the angel of the church will depend on how leadership is understood. Exploring this facet of Baptist ecclesiology, Wright suggests that the view of some Baptists can be summed up as there being no clear leader, with each church member serving the others.[72] While he notes that there is some validity in this concept, as it is based on the model of servanthood exemplified by God in Christ, Wright also suggests that such a position misrepresents Christ's relationship with his disciples. He also believes that the language of leadership, which is present throughout the Scriptures, is subverted by Christ's example. Thus, while Christ acts as a servant, he does so while still exercising leadership. Therefore, for Wright, the role of the minister is one of leadership that is exercised in a spirit of humility and self-sacrifice.[73]

Reflecting on Wright's comments, Robert Ellis notes that during the first decade of the twenty-first-century, the term "leader" has been increasingly used to describe a Baptist minister.[74] For Ellis, there is an inherent danger in this shift in language as it represents the adoption of a label that might not be wholly appropriate in describing the role of a minister. Illustrating his concerns, Ellis reflects on Israel's desire for a king in 1 Sam 8 and suggests that, just as Israel's desire for a king was born out of the experience of other nations, the language of leadership has been adopted from contemporary management theory.[75] In his view, the danger in using this form of language is the power inherent in the secular understanding of leadership. For Ellis, this power has the potential to corrupt

---

72. Wright, "Inclusive Representation," 164.
73. Wright, "Inclusive Representation," 164.
74. Ellis, "'Leadership of Some. . .,'" 71.
75. Ellis, "'Leadership of Some. . .,'" 72–73.

the individual and exploit the church.[76] Despite this, he is not completely dismissive of using leadership language to describe the role of the minister, as he believes that there are aspects of the secular understanding of the term from which the church can benefit. Thus, he contends that while the management theory from which the term "leader" emerges might be useful, it should not be without theological reflection.[77]

The Power to Paralyze

Commenting on the power that the minister exercises, Wink argues that although pastoral leadership can be significant, it can also be overstressed. In Wink's opinion, some congregations simply appoint ministers who share their values. He also notes that a minister with an authoritarian style of dominating personality might appear to change the dynamics of the church. However, sadly, this sort of ministry is unlikely to bring about a genuine spiritual change within the angel of the church.[78]

Although it was noted above that not all Baptist congregations would tolerate an authoritarian model of ministry, this is not the only form of power a minister might exercise. Exploring the concept of a minister's ability to paralyze a congregation in the pursuit of its vocation, Wink tells the story of being invited to advise a church on how best to adapt its mission strategy to the changing demographic of its local community. The consultation was due to last for five days, and as the process unfolded, Wink and his assistant found themselves floundering. Following the consultation, Wink's assistant spent some time investigating the source of inertia among the church's leadership. Her investigation revealed that the pastor suffered from an illness that was accentuated when he was placed in stressful situations. As a result, his fellow leaders sought to protect him from anything that would cause him undue stress. This attempt to protect the pastor led to a reluctance to engage with any new initiative within the church that would undermine the current status quo. In Wink's opinion, the actions of the other leaders to protect their pastor from additional stress paralyzed the church and prevented them from fulfilling their new mission.[79]

76. Ellis, "'Leadership of Some...,'" 73–74.
77. Ellis, "'Leadership of Some...,'" 80–81.
78. Wink, *Unmasking the Powers*, 75.
79. Wink, *Unmasking the Powers*, 75.

The Secession from South Street Baptist Church in Exeter

While the circumstances are not the same as in Wink's story, the power a minister has to inadvertently restrict a congregation's freedom to pursue their vocation is evident in the Baptist church in South Street in Exeter toward the end of the nineteenth century.

The story is recorded by a group of Baptists who had separated themselves from the church in South Street in Exeter and had begun to meet in the Royal Public Rooms in Exeter. According to their records, their secession from the church in South Street Exeter arose from their frustration at the inaction of the minister, the Rev. E. L. Pike.

In the recorder's view, the problem began around 1887 when the Rev. Pike advised the church that he intended to leave the church and serve the Lord in a new capacity. Describing what followed, the recorder notes that, initially, there were no objections to the minister's announcement that he was intending to leave. However, when four years later, he was still in post some dissension began to occur. Apparently, according to the recorder's notes this dissension began among those who were relatively new church members.[80]

These comments mark the beginning of a narrative that seeks to justify the separation of a group of members from the church in South Street, Exeter. They justified their frustration by pointing to the time taken by the Rev. Pike to discern where the Lord was calling him. It is also clear from this record that their frustration was accentuated when, after four years of deliberation, the Rev. Pike decided to stay at the church in South Street, Exeter. Reflecting on this, the recorder notes that the frustration was most acute among the younger members and that the older members failed to question Rev. Pike's actions out of their love for him and their desire to avoid the disruption that would be caused by removing him from his post.[81] This suggests that while the younger members were frustrated by the Rev. Pike's inaction, they also felt powerless to remove him from his post. The powerlessness of those who left the church in South Street, Exeter, is contrasted by the passive, though nevertheless powerful, actions of the Rev. Pike. However, unlike Wink's story, the records of neither the secessionists nor the church at South Street reveal the effect that the Rev. Pike's actions had on the church fulfilling its vocation.

---

80. Records of those meeting in the Royal Public Rooms in Exeter, 75-9-1-6, South Street Baptist Church Exeter, 1891–1983, DHC.

81. Records of those meeting in the Royal Public Rooms in Exeter, 75-9-1-6, DHC.

In this context, with the church's vocation stifled by the actions of the Rev. Pike, the influence of the angel is paralyzed. It cannot be deemed to have changed its nature as the congregation has not sought to fulfill an alternative vocation. Furthermore, the gyroscopic effect that the angel of the church might ordinarily be expected to create cannot continue to guide the church in its usual direction. In view of this, it might be argued that, with the spiritual state of suspension present in the main church, the angel moved with the secessionists to the meeting in the Royal Public Rooms in Exeter. While it is impossible to ascertain whether or not the angel moved or if a new angel was formed when some of the members moved away from the church in South Street, the fact that, following the removal of the Rev. Pike, the secessionists returned suggests that the state of spiritual suspension within which the church in South Street had been held had ended, in which case it might be assumed that the angel of the church had been restored to the heart of the congregation.

The Acceptable Outsider

Although the tensions inherent in Baptist ecclesiology make it very difficult for the minister to address the angel of the church, there is an aspect of their churchmanship that might make the process a little easier. While Baptist ministers are appointed by the local congregation and may be appointed from among the members, it has been common practice to appoint an outsider to the post. An example of this was explored in the previous chapter in the story of Budleigh Salterton Baptist Church's struggle to appoint a minister in the late nineteenth century. John Rackley also discusses this tradition in his article "The Acceptable Outsider."

Rackley begins his exploration of the "acceptable outsider" by reflecting on what he describes as an "unguarded" comment delivered to a church meeting. Having been provoked, he responded by saying that if the church had wanted someone to maintain the status quo, they should have appointed someone from within the congregation and not an outsider like himself.[82]

Rackley continues by revealing his expectation that the minister will be an outsider, and their task will be to critique a congregation's present circumstances and past history. In light of Wink's concern that a minister

---

82. Rackley, "Acceptable Outsider," 3.

appointed by a local congregation might become a paid chaplain, Rackley's statement is extremely positive.

For Wink, the implementation of lasting change can only take place when the agent of transformation comes from outside of the institution. By this, he means that true transformation can only take place when it comes as a result of the intervention of a transcendent God. In view of this, Wink finds it strange that the implementation of what is, in effect, a change in the spirit of a congregation should be brought about through a human being. Despite the strangeness of a human being acting as a messenger to the angel of the church, Wink believes that the detached position of the messenger is important for a church to be transformed. His argument is based on the premise that while a congregation might claim to know the will of God, their actions can only be critically assessed and, where necessary, condemned by someone who is outside of the situation.[83]

This resonates with the argument that Rackley develops. He contends that the minister must be kept on the margins of the story that defines the church in order to bring an alternative perspective to the congregation.[84] He bases his argument on Jesus' decision to pass through Samaria on the way to Jerusalem in Luke 17. Rackley contends that, by taking the route through gentile territory, Jesus enabled his disciples to see things that they would not otherwise have appreciated.[85] Furthermore, by journeying through Samaria, Jesus encouraged the disciples to see where they had come from and appreciate the new places that they might visit in the future. Rackley believes that, by holding a detached position and resisting the temptation to gain popularity within the congregation, the minister will be able to counter the priorities, prejudices, and preferences that naturally occur within the church. Although the story involves the appointment of a moderator, or spiritual overseer, rather than a minister, Rackley's position is illustrated by the Rev. Ives of Exmouth, as he oversees the appointment of Mr. Tuck to the Baptist church in Budleigh Salterton.

---

83. Wink, *Unmasking the Powers*, 80–81.
84. Rackley, "Acceptable Outsider," 5–6.
85. Rackley, "Acceptable Outsider," 6.

The Appointment of Mr. Tuck

On April 8, 1937, the Rev. Ives from Exmouth Baptist Church chaired the church meeting that paid tribute to the Rev. Durbin, who had recently died. Prior to his death, the Rev. Durban had been a regional minister in the Local Association and, since 1929, had assisted the church by chairing church meetings and occasionally taking services.

In response to the Rev. Durbin's death, the church expressed a desire for a new spiritual overseer, and the Rev. Ives suggested that the most appropriate course of action would be for the church to appoint a superintendent.[86] Prior to the Rev. Durbin acting as moderator, the church at Budleigh Salterton had accepted the spiritual oversight of the Rev. Isles of Exmouth Baptist Church. However, at the request of the Exmouth deacons, this arrangement ended on December 31, 1928.[87] From records of the meeting held on April 8, 1937, it is clear that the relationship between Budleigh Salterton and Exmouth Baptist Church was still a positive one and that there was an underlying desire for the Rev. Ives to adopt the role of spiritual overseer. However, the Rev. Ives dismissed this by suggesting that a superintendent be appointed at Budleigh Salterton until the church in Exmouth had appointed a new pastor.[88] This statement indicates that the Rev. Ives may have been exploring a call to leave the church at Exmouth and was therefore concerned for the well-being of both churches. In view of this, the Rev. Ives suggested that Mr. G. Tuck would make a good superintendent and commended the pastoral work he had undertaken in the church in Exmouth. Despite this strong recommendation, Miss Hatton suggested that Mr. Fray from the Budleigh Salterton church was well-liked and would make a good superintendent.[89] The fact that Miss Hatton was free to recommend an alternative illustrates the autonomy that a Baptist congregation has to appoint their leaders. It also illustrates Wink's fears that, if appointed from among themselves, a congregation will appoint someone whom they like rather than a person with the gifts and abilities that they need.[90]

---

86. Minutes, Apr. 8, 1937, 3548D M5, Budleigh Salterton Baptist Church minute and register book Feb. 1937–Dec. 1944, DHC.

87. Minutes, 3548D M4, Budleigh Salterton Baptist Church minute book and registry Mar. 27, 1913–Dec. 20 1936, DHC.

88. Minutes, Apr. 8, 1937, 3548D M5, Budleigh Salterton Baptist Church minute and register book Feb. 1937–Dec. 1944, DHC.

89. Minutes, Apr. 8, 1937, 3548D M5, DHC.

90. Wink, *Unmasking the Powers*, 75.

Despite Miss Hatton's interjection, the Rev. Ives persisted by arguing that, where possible, it was advisable to appoint a member from the Exmouth church.[91] While the Rev. Ives does not explain why the church at Budleigh Salterton should appoint someone from Exmouth, it may be that the possibility of a more substantial link between the two churches was still being considered. If this was the case, and the link became official, then the appointment would not fulfill the criteria of the acceptable outsider that Wink and Rackley consider necessary to address the inner nature of the church. However, following Mr. Tuck's appointment, he is referred to as either "Pastor" or "Lay Pastor" in the church records and is listed as a lay leader in the Baptist Union *Handbook* until 1940, suggesting that he fulfilled the role of the acceptable outsider.[92]

Summary

Vocation

Although Baptist congregations have a long history of appointing ministers, how the role is understood is not without its disagreements and tension. At the heart of these are two concepts: that the church operates as a priesthood of all believers and a congregational model of governance. By committing themselves to these principles, Baptists believe that God might call all church members to preach, baptize, or preside at the Lord's Supper. While this provides opportunities for members of the congregation to share in the corporate ministry of the church, it also has the effect of devaluing the roles traditionally performed by ministers. For some Baptists, the minister's role is devalued further by their reluctance to engage with the possibility that ministry might have a sacramental dimension. By removing the sacramental aspect of ministry, there is a question as to whether addressing the nature of the church becomes a sociological ritual rather than one that is spiritual.

The commitment to congregational government further weakens the ability of a minister to address the angel of the church. While the covenantal relationship practiced by Baptists suggests that members are mutually accountable, the balance of power given to the congregation suggests it is easier for the church to publicly critique the minister rather

---

91. Minutes, Apr. 8, 1937, 3548D M5, DHC.
92. *Baptist Handbook for 1940*, 69.

than vice versa. This imbalance of power is accentuated when the minister is an outsider and their income and living accommodation are dependent upon the congregation to whom they are called to minister. What is more, the pressures associated with being an outsider can also lead to a minister acting as chaplain to the congregation rather than addressing its angel. This possibility is made even more likely in a Baptist context due to the church's liberty to appoint their own minister and, therefore, appoint someone who shares their values, theology, and spirituality and is less likely to confront the weaknesses in their angel.

In light of these issues, it is evident that of the first three facets of church life introduced by Wink as a means to grasp the nature of the angel of the church, the question of authority, power, and ministry offers the most significant challenge to Baptists. The difficulty that Baptists face is that their ecclesiology impedes the ability of their ministers to address the angels of their churches. Furthermore, it is the commitment to a priesthood of all believers, congregational government, and the liberty of each congregation to discern and implement the will of Christ that makes Baptist congregations Baptist. Thus, addressing and transforming their ecclesiology is extremely difficult. In view of this, for the transformation of the angel to take place, Baptist ministers must be aware of the weaknesses imposed upon them by their ecclesiology and find ways to address the angel while avoiding the temptation to either dominate the church or become their chaplain.

In addition to the minister's ability to effect change within a Baptist congregation, the records of the period when a group seceded from South Street Baptist Church, Exeter, also illustrate the ability of the minister to stifle a church in the pursuit of its vocation. However, while the Rev. Pike's inaction appeared to restrict the ability and desire of some church members to pursue the congregation's vocation, it also led to the frustration of others. This frustration resulted in their secession from the church at South Street in Exeter. With the remaining congregation in a state of spiritual suspension, it appears that the secessionists continued the church's vocation.

The Nature of the Angel

In addition to revealing the relationship between ministry and the church's vocation, the above extracts from church records also highlight aspects of their angel's nature. In respect of the Baptists at Newton Abbot, a discussion over the continuation of Sunday evening services reveals a deeply ingrained anxiety. This anxiety reveals itself in the congregation's struggle to make a decision and stick to it. The desire to continually return to a decision with a view to overturning it is not just a trait of the Newton Abbot Baptists in the twenty-first century. As will become evident, the discussion over who should be allowed to participate in the Lord's Supper, described later in this thesis, also reveals a church that finds it impossible to accept a decision as final.

The records kept by the Newton Abbot Baptists also reveal occasions when the leadership were willing to exercise dominance over the church meeting. This is particularly evident in the discussions over the move from the East Street Chapel to Highweek School. Of course, just because the leadership seeks to dominate the church does not mean that the congregation is unwilling to call them to account. This is particularly evident in respect of their minister.

The anxious nature of the Baptist church in Newton Abbot is contrasted with the calm, reasoned discussions that take place among the Baptists in Budleigh Salterton. This is illustrated in the appointment of Mr. Tuck from Exmouth as moderator. Although there is some discussion over Mr. Tuck's appointment and Miss Hatton offered Mr. Fray's name as an alternative, the congregation accepted the advice of the Rev. Ives, who was chairing their meeting.

Although the Baptists at Budleigh Salterton seemed to be able to settle their issues relating to ministry amicably, this is not always the case in Baptist churches. What is more, as the following chapter will highlight, even in the records of Budleigh Salterton, there were times of conflict.

The records kept by the Baptists in Newton Abbot contrast sharply with minutes of the church meetings held at Budleigh Salterton. In Newton Abbot Baptist, the leaders appear to exercise authority, ministry, and power in a way that is often accompanied by conflict. In view of this, Wink's belief that the way conflict is handled reveals something of the nature of the angel is apposite. Therefore, the next chapter will explore issues surrounding conflict and its resolution within Baptist congregations.

5

Handling Conflict

AFTER RAISING THE ISSUES of authority, ministry, and power, Wink suggests that how a congregation deals with conflict will reveal a great deal about a congregation's angel. He argues that handling conflict reveals a great deal about the angel. With this in mind, Wink suggests that, as with some marriages, some congregations thrive on conflict, and their lives together are underpinned by constant bickering. Similarly, while some congregations treat their ministers well and enjoy long and fruitful ministries, others seem to treat them badly.[1]

Although it has already been argued that the relationship between the minister and congregation can have a significant impact on the nature of the angel, this is not the whole story. In the discussion that follows, the contrasting nature of the angels of the Baptist churches at Newton Abbot and Budleigh Salterton will be explored further. While this discussion will include an illustration of conflict between the minister and a member of the congregation it will also explore wider issues of disagreement common among Baptist congregations. However, prior to this, a broader basis for understanding the nature of conflict must be outlined.

The Types of Conflict

Addressing the issue of preaching into conflict situations, William Willimon identifies three types of conflict: intrapersonal, interpersonal,

1. Wink, *Unmasking the Powers*, 76.

and substantive.² According to Willimon, intrapersonal conflict is the internal stress faced by an individual as they face new challenges or seek to address conflict situations.³ As this is an individual's emotional response to a situation, any records are likely to be found in personal diaries rather than the corporate records kept by a congregation. Therefore, this study will not be exploring examples of intrapersonal conflict. As for interpersonal conflict, disagreements between church members are frequently recorded within church records. An example of this concerns Mr. Bulivant from the pastorate at Budleigh Salterton Baptist Church. This episode will be discussed later in this chapter.

Substantive conflict is a disagreement over matters of substance, such as the facts relating to a situation. However, substantive conflict might also include disagreements over what the church believes or the values it holds.⁴ In their exploration of substantive conflict, Speed Leas and Paul Kittlaus divide the subject into four categories: conflict over facts, method or means, ends or goals, and values.⁵ In this respect, two stories from the Baptist church at Newton Abbot are used to illustrate forms of substantive conflict. The first, a debate over whether to continue with Sunday evening services, engages with all four of the categories discussed by Leas. However, while the second, a debate over who should be allowed to participate in the Lord's Supper, only provides an example of a disagreement over values, the protracted nature of the debate also offers insights into the resilient nature of the church's angel.

The Nature of Conflict

Authors commenting on conflict in the church disagree over whether the experience is a positive or negative aspect of congregational life. Writing from a positive perspective, Willimon suggests that conflict brings energy to a congregation and causes believers to deepen their faith as they overcome the difficulties they face.⁶ Sara Savage and Eolene Boyd-MacMillan echo Willimon's belief that conflict is an essential phase in

---

2. Willimon, *Preaching About Conflict*, 10–11.
3. Willimon, *Preaching About Conflict*, 10–11.
4. Willimon, *Preaching About Conflict*, 11.
5. Leas and Kittlaus, *Church Fights*, 29–32.
6. Willimon, *Preaching About Conflict*, 15, 17.

the transformation of a congregation.[7] Carolyn Schrock-Shenk makes a similar point in *Making Peace with Conflict*, arguing that conflict is a natural part of life.[8] However, Larry McSwain and William Treadwell provide an alternative viewpoint, arguing that conflict is the result of a failure of expectations and is not part of God's plan for his creation.[9] Furthermore, in his foreword to *Journeying Through Conflict*, David Coffey reinforces this belief by arguing that conflict within the church is far from the will of God for his people.[10]

Viewing conflict from a Mennonite perspective, Menno Epp contends that purity and peace are to be highly valued, as they represent God's will for humanity.[11] Epp also suggests that pastors are expected to model these attributes to their congregations.[12] This idea of modeling peace and purity is taken further by Savage and Boyd-MacMillan, who suggest that one of the key contributing factors to the difficulties congregations experience when conflict arises is that it contradicts a desire to act as nice people.[13] Suppose Savage and Boyd-MacMillan are correct, and a commitment to "niceness" translates into a belief that conflict should not occur within a Christian community. In that case, the church may begin to suffer from a form of anxiety during a period of disagreement.

Part of Peter Steinke's contribution to congregational studies is his use of emotional systems theory to explain how anxiety affects congregations. While Steinke believes that anxiety can act as a motivator for change, he is also aware that when it reaches a certain level, it can prevent the change it instigated.[14] Developing this argument, Steinke contends that there are two types of anxiety: acute and chronic. A congregation feels acute anxiety as they enter a process of change or engage in a discussion where individuals or groups will disagree. In this context, anxiety makes a positive contribution to a church undergoing a process of change. Conversely, chronic anxiety has a detrimental effect on the life of a congregation. According to Steinke, chronic anxiety creates habitual behavior that can lead to repeated church splits, rapid changes in

---

7. Savage and Boyd-MacMillan, *Human Face of the Church*, 54.
8. Schrock-Shenk and Ressler, *Making Peace with Conflict*, 29.
9. McSwain and Treadwell, *Conflict Ministry in the Church*, 15, 19.
10. Lassetter and Walley, *Journeying Through Conflict*, 1.
11. Epp, *Pastor's Exit*, 24.
12. Epp, *Pastor's Exit*, 24.
13. Savage and Boyd-MacMillan, *Human Face of the Church*, 57.
14. Steinke, *How Your Church Family Works*, 14.

leadership, or continued resistance to change.[15] If Steinke is correct, then, from the illustrations below, it might be possible to argue that the Baptist church in Newton Abbot suffered periods of chronic anxiety between 1819 and 2009 and, therefore, its angel easily became anxious.

A Discussion over Sunday Evening Worship Services

Despite the consensus among scholars that conflict will be present in the life of a congregation, the records examined for this study provide very few accounts of interpersonal or substantive conflict. Therefore, the illustrative stories used in this chapter tend to be the exception rather than the rule of church life. This is particularly true in the church at Budleigh Salterton. Moreover, the records of conflict contained in the minute books examined tend to be more serious than the low-level disagreements that are easily resolved. Therefore, it might be assumed that the tradition of niceness, described by Savage and Boyd-MacMillan, has led to the recorder simply noting the decision and not the differing opinions that were overcome to reach a conclusion. Furthermore, where the emotion of the decision-making process is described, it is often in a redacted form. This minute from the records of Newton Abbot Baptist Church serves as an example of how a redacted discussion might appear:

Sunday Evening Service Discussion

Before proceeding to the discussion, the proposed voting system was explained: no vote will be taken at this meeting, a paper ballot will be taken at the next meeting, and postal votes will be available. There will be no further discussion at this meeting, and once a decision has been made, the subject will not be raised again for at least a year. The discussion followed, and various points were raised, including - 1) Some would prefer a traditional service to the suggested program, 2) would numbers voting for a service be a deciding factor, 3) Heating and lighting expenses should not come into the discussion if we want a service. 4) Most churches have low attendance at Sunday pm service; perhaps churches should join together 5) Sometimes we have to change are we going forward or backwards 6) Concern that we only meet together to worship as a fellowship for 1 hour on a Sunday morning 7) No biblical command to worship twice on a Sunday so we should not feel guilty 8) We live out our

---

15. Steinke, *How Your Church Family Works*, 20.

> Christianity where ever we are - not just in Church 9) Some lack of teaching when we only meet together on a Sunday.[16]

Although this is a redacted account of the proceedings, the anxiety and tension present in the discussion are still evident.

The first point of tension present in this meeting was whether a decision would actually be reached. This was obviously settled, and the records make it clear that this meeting was purely for discussion. The explanation of the decision-making process also points out that once the decision was made, the subject would not be revisited for at least a year. This suggests that whether or not to continue with an evening service was a recurring question within the church. It also indicates that there may be individuals or groups within the membership who, if dissatisfied, would seek to overturn the conclusion reached by the meeting and seek further discussion. As will become evident from an illustration over who should be allowed to share in the Lord's Supper, the Baptists at Newton Abbot have a long history of revisiting a decision in the hope of having it overturned.

Anxiety and Re-Orientation

The repeated revisiting of an issue might also be symptomatic of a chronically anxious church. Exploring the relationship between anxiety and how churches function, Steinke suggests that chronically anxious groups find it difficult to reorient themselves in challenging situations. He contrasts this with the acutely anxious who, once they have acknowledged the cause of their anxiety, are able to reorient their thoughts and actions to address the challenges they face.[17] Thus, in the case of the Baptists at Newton Abbot, the desire to continually revisit a question might represent a level of anxiety that prevents them from making a decision and living with the consequences.

Reflecting further on how churches act, Steinke suggests that the chronically anxious often provide a restricted response to a situation. Thus, they are more likely to constrain their answers to either yes or no and to describe actions as either right or wrong.[18] Steinke's belief

---

16. Church meeting minutes, June 24, 2002, box 6196, Newton Abbot Baptist Church, DHC.

17. Steinke, *How Your Church Family Works*, 20.

18. Steinke, *How Your Church Family Works*, 21.

that the chronically anxious church may not be able to address a point of contention might explain why the Baptists in Newton Abbot decide to reach a final decision on whether or not to continue meeting for evening worship by using a paper ballot.

Voting

Since the mid-nineteenth century, voting at a church meeting has been common practice.[19] However, as the purpose of a Baptist church meeting is one of discernment, the ideal situation is a unanimous agreement on the final decision. Reflecting on this, Bacon points out that, as human beings are imperfect, unanimity may not be achieved. In these cases, he suggests that decisions may be reached by a majority vote.[20] Bacon suggests that this could be achieved by either calling out "Aye" or "No" or by a show of hands.[21] He also acknowledges that in certain circumstances, such as the election of deacons, the vote may be secret and ballot papers used.[22] With respect to the voting procedure at a church meeting, Richard Fairbairn and Ronald Thomson point out that each church will have their own rules regarding the type of ballot used and whether postal votes are acceptable.[23] In the case of Newton Abbot, the rules they were operating under at the time their decision was made only mention the use of a ballot when calling a minister.[24] Of course, this does not mean that the church was prevented from using a ballot to reach a decision on a question such as whether or not to keep their Sunday evening services, but it might be considered unusual.

If using a ballot in this circumstance was unusual, the acceptance of postal votes is more controversial. Even though Fairbairn and Thomson acknowledge the liberty of Baptist congregations to allow postal voting, participating in this way might seem contrary to the aim of the church meeting. While not explicitly referencing postal voting, the 1948 paper on *The Doctrine of the Church* provides an important insight into the nature of the Baptist church meeting by arguing that, while a

19. Egner, "Re-Imagining the Covenant Community," 24.
20. Bacon, *Church Administration*, 81.
21. Bacon, *Church Administration*, 89.
22. Bacon, *Church Administration*, 89.
23. Fairbairn and Thomson, *Church Secretary's Handbook*, 31.
24. East Street Baptist Church Newton Abbot, rules, 1991, box 6196, Newton Abbot Baptist Church, DHC.

Baptist church meeting might appear democratic beneath the surface, something more significant is happening. This is because, in a Baptist context, the church meeting is a place where God's will is discovered as church members submit themselves to the leading of the Holy Spirit and the judgment of God.[25] It is, therefore, anticipated that while individuals vote to confirm a decision, the process of making that decision is one of communal discernment.

In light of this, the danger with allowing postal votes is that, while individuals might cast their vote believing that they have followed God's leading, their understanding of his direction will not have been tested by the discussion that takes place at the church meeting. Of course, in the situation where the discussion is held at one meeting and the vote held later, it might be argued that those present at the meeting and deciding to exercise a postal vote had been part of the discernment process. As the records of the subsequent meeting are not available, it is impossible to tell if this is what actually happened. However, if the congregation at Newton Abbot was chronically anxious, allowing postal votes might have reduced the anxiety by placating those members who wanted to contribute to the decision but were unable to participate in the meeting. If this were the case, while postal voting detaches the individual from the discernment process, it does insulate them from the anxiety expressed in the discussion and thus provides a context within which a more dispassionate decision can be made. Therefore, if, at this point in their history, the Newton Abbot Baptists were a chronically anxious congregation, confirming the decision of the meeting by paper ballot may have mitigated the influence of their anxiety by providing members the freedom to make their opinions known while retaining their anonymity.

Consensus

Of course, voting is not the only method by which a Baptist congregation might make or confirm their decisions at a church meeting. Because the focus of the church meeting is discernment, decisions might be made through consensus rather than simply by majority. Although Nigel Wright and Paul Fiddes both reference the use of consensus within

---

25. *Baptist Doctrine of the Church*, 3–4.

a church meeting,[26] the subject is more fully explored by Mennonite and Anabaptist writers.

Writing for the *Global Anabaptist Mennonite Encyclopedia Online*, Ralph Lebold suggests that decision-making via consensus was introduced to Mennonite churches in the 1950s.[27] Defining their understanding of consensus, the Mennonite World Conference "Guidelines for Making Decisions by Consensus" describe the term as a method of reaching a decision without the need for a vote. The advantage of seeking a consensus is that every member is encouraged to participate and this, in turn, creates harmony through collaboration.[28]

The idea of creating harmony through collaboration appears to echo the aspirations for the church meeting of Baptist writers such as Wright and Fiddes. However, as Fiddes indicates, the desire for small groups to exercise power and thus influence the outcome of the decision-making process is common among Baptist congregations.[29] In the discussion over the continuation of evening services, it appears that, due to the level of anxiety within the church meetings, the Newton Abbot Baptists were unable to form the "collaborative and harmonious context" described by Lebold. Therefore, because of its anonymity, the instigation of a secret ballot may have been the only way of reaching a decision that all the members would accept, even if they disagreed with the outcome.

Conflicting Opinions

Having settled the question of procedure, the minutes reveal four distinct groups of conflicting opinions:

i. Members who are advocating change vs. those who are resisting change.

ii. Members favoring a traditional liturgy vs. members wanting to experiment with new styles.

iii. Members who consider that meeting together is an important part of Christian discipleship vs. members who consider the church to be only one facet of the Christian experience.

---

26. Wright, *Free Church, Free State*, 134; and Fiddes, *Tracks and Traces*, 51.
27. Lebold, "Decision Making."
28. Mennonite World Conference, "Guidelines for Making Decisions."
29. Fiddes, *Tracks and Traces*, 51.

iv. Members concerned with the financial cost of an evening service vs. members who felt that financial considerations should not stand in the way of the church gathering for worship.

With these four groups forming in response to the nine points raised in the discussion over whether to continue with Sunday evening worship services, the nature of the discussion must have been extremely complex. Unfortunately, the limited nature of the records makes it impossible to tell how the members were divided in each area of conflict. However, what is evident is that there is an overarching tension between the members advocating change and those resisting it.

The first discussion over the format of the evening services hints at this tension. However, when juxtaposed with the opinion that change is necessary if the church is to progress, the level of anxiety becomes evident. By noting the opinion and question encapsulated in "Sometimes we have to change, are we going forward or backward?"[30] the minute-taker indicates that the level of frustration being expressed by some members was significant. With such a high level of frustration being expressed from one group it is, perhaps, unsurprising that some members were anxious over how the final decision would be made. This is highlighted by the discussion over the significance of the number of votes cast in support of either continuing or ending Sunday evening services.

Commenting on the proportion of votes required to formalize a decision at a church meeting, Rachel Tole, Fairbairn, and Thomson suggest that the church constitution or trust deed will indicate the majority required.[31] These comments are not helpful in this case as the rules that the Newton Abbot Baptists were operating under in 2002 do not stipulate the majority required to confirm a decision, except in the case of appointing a minister.[32] In view of this, while making the decision by secret ballot might allow members anonymity in expressing their opinion, by not stipulating the majority required for a resolution to be adopted, an element of uncertainty is introduced to the meeting. This element of uncertainty appears to have increased the level of anxiety among some members.

---

30. Church meeting minutes, June 24, 2002, box 6196, Newton Abbot Baptist Church, DHC.

31. Tole, *Nothing Spiritual About Chaos*, 20; Fairbairn and Thomson, *Church Secretary's Handbook*, 31.

32. The available records suggest that discussions regarding implementing a new set of rules were underway in 2002.

Dwindling Attendance

Although not recorded as such, the questions raised about heating and lighting the building for a small congregation might be considered a pragmatic reason for closing the Sunday evening services. In this respect, it is notable that the Newton Abbot Baptists acknowledge the fact that other churches were experiencing a dwindling attendance at evening services. Raising this point in the meeting may have been an attempt to reduce the level of anxiety among those struggling with deciding to cease the Sunday evening meeting. However, having sought to reduce the anxiety they felt by noting that their situation was not unique, the suggestion that the church may consider meeting with other congregations might have actually increased the members' anxiety. While the issue of collaboration with other fellowships will be discussed at length in the following chapter, at this point in the study, it is sufficient to say that, although each Baptist church is autonomous in identity and government, Baptists have a long tradition of association with other Baptist churches and, more latterly, with churches of other traditions. Of course, this does not mean that all Baptist congregations embrace the opportunity to engage with other churches.

Discipleship

The sixth discussion point recorded in the minutes raises the question of Christian discipleship and gives rise to the final three issues noted on the subject of evening services. These final comments reveal a division over the perception of what is necessary to maintain Christian discipleship.

Commenting on the relationship between discipleship and Baptist identity, Brian Haymes, Ruth Gouldbourne, and Anthony Cross note that Christian discipleship is more than what a person believes or good deeds.[33] According to Haymes et al., one facet of Christian discipleship is a state of being; thus, the eighth point in the discussion over evening services is correct. However, Haymes et al. also note that the link between the state of being and Christian discipleship has not been voiced as frequently as the way church members should behave or what they should believe. Furthermore, in their reflection on Christian discipleship, Haymes et al. argue that the mutuality expressed within the local

---

33. Haymes et al., *On Being Church*, 107.

church lies at the heart of Christian discipleship.[34] Therefore, while the sentiment expressed in discussion point eight bears some truth, it does not tell the whole story. In the light of the importance of the relationship between discipleship and the community of the local church highlighted by Haymes et al., the concerns recorded in discussion points six (concern for only meeting for one hour for worship each week) and nine (concern over a lack of teaching on a Sunday) are equally valid. As for point seven (there is biblical command to worship twice on a Sunday), this raises a further dialectic between points eight (Christian faith is a lifestyle) and nine (lack of teaching on a Sunday).[35]

By arguing that there is no biblical imperative for the congregation to meet twice on a Sunday, the speaker highlights the importance of the Scriptures in the life and worship of a Baptist congregation.[36] Although the use of the Scriptures will be explored in the next chapter, for now, it is sufficient to note that the second part of point seven, the members should not feel guilty for giving up the evening service, appears to suggest that the congregation should feel comfortable with meeting less often. If this is the speaker's objective, it appears to support the eighth point, Christianity is a lifestyle, in the records.

Although the records of the meeting where the outcome of this decision was taken are not publicly available, the record of this discussion does reveal a number of the tensions present among the Baptists of Newton Abbot during the last decade of the church's life.[37] In respect of Wink's concept of the angel of the church, the discussion over whether to continue with Sunday evening services reveals the gyroscopic nature of the angel that seeks to keep the church functioning in a specific way. This is evident in the differing opinions over liturgy, the need for Christians to meet regularly together, and the perceived need for change. Although in each case, there are advocates for change, the internal inertia generated by the angel can be observed in the reactions of those

---

34. Haymes et al., *On Being Church*, 105.

35. The record of the discussion on evening services is quoted on page X-REF of this thesis.

36. As has been previously mentioned in this thesis, point 3.1 of the Declaration of Principle of the Baptist Union of Great Britain notes the importance of the Scripture's role in revealing Christ and the church's role in interpreting and applying scriptural principles to their life together (Baptists Together, "Declaration of Principle").

37. The church that was founded in 1863 at the East Street Chapel finally closed in 2009. A new congregation named "This Hope Baptist Church" was subsequently started but did not own its own building.

members who favor a traditional form of liturgy and continuing to meet on a Sunday evening. Of course, this is not to say that the nature of the angel cannot be changed. In this respect, citing the lack of biblical command to meet twice on a Sunday is the sort of theological argument that is able to address the transcendent angel. Conversely, the practical arguments relating to the cost of heating and lighting and the experiences of other churches are more likely to address the earthly nature of the church. Moreover, the discussion over who would be voting in respect of the decision hints at a change in the spiritual nature of the angel of Newton Abbot Baptist Church. As discussed above, in the chapter exploring how authority, ministry, and power affect the nature of the angel of the church, when the decision at a church meeting is based purely on a democratic process, it is arguable whether or not the mind of Christ has been discerned. In view of this, as has already been mentioned, if, as a result of their decision, the church moves away from the vocation set by God, the angel may become demonic. While, in this discussion, there is no suggestion that the decision rested solely on the outcome of the vote, the fact that the procedure for voting was discussed is interesting, as it signals a change in how future decisions will be made.

In addition to revealing the gyroscopic influence of the angel of the church and hinting at a change in its spiritual nature, the discussion that the Newton Abbot Baptists have over Sunday evening services also reveals the emotions present in a church meeting. In the next example, it was the forceful expression of emotion that led the church at Budleigh Salterton to disagree over whether or not to accept their pastor's resignation.

The Resignation of Mr. Bulivant

Commenting on the nature of the angel of the church, Wink suggests that the demographics of a congregation require a code of conduct to be followed for a member to belong.[38] If this is so, along with Savage and Boyd-MacMillan's contention that a church expects a person to act nicely toward others. In that case, an expression of frustration or anger might cause conflict within a congregation. While this conflict may not be serious, it will create a discussion as individuals adopt different positions over what should happen in the situation that has arisen.

38. Wink, *Unmasking the Powers*, 74.

Willimon describes this as interpersonal conflict.[39] The resignation of Mr. Bulivant from the pastorate at Budleigh Salterton in 1948 is an example of this form of conflict.

Mr. Bulivant's resignation was discussed at a church meeting held on February 11, 1948. According to the records, after he had resigned in a fit of frustration, Mr. Bulivant later regretted his actions. In his defense, he argued that he had been provoked by Mr. Elston, the captain of the Boys Brigade company associated with the church. Mr. Bulivant explained to the members present how he had struggled to engage Mr. Elston in a discussion on a specific issue.[40] Eventually, he became frustrated with Elston's lack of response. Then, when a meeting between himself and the officers from the Boys Brigade had finally been arranged, Mr. Bulivant believed that the Boys Brigade officers acted particularly belligerently. This belligerence had led him to storm out of the meeting, leaving his church keys and membership card.[41]

In the discussion that followed, Mr. Watts argued that in view of the circumstances, the pastor's resignation should not be allowed to stand. However, Mr. Colds suggested that, as the pastor had come to the meeting with his keys and membership card, he had been prepared for his dramatic act of resignation. Mr. Bulivant rejected this assumption, claiming that he always kept his membership card at the church. He also argued that his actions had been a bluff and that he did not expect his resignation to be accepted. This revelation opened a further discussion on Mr. Bulivant's credibility as a leader. Mr. Roberts, a representative from the local Association who was chairing the meeting, spoke against Mr. Bulivant. He argued that, as a leader, the pastor was seen as an exemplar of Christian faith and thus should be prepared to resist such emotional responses to difficult situations.[42]

Stressing that there was little to be gained by continuing an argument over what Mr. Bulivant should or should not have done in that situation, Mr. Roberts guided the church toward a vote. This was a secret ballot and resulted in an even split between the membership, thirteen votes accepting and thirteen votes rejecting Mr. Bulivant's resignation. At this point, Mr. Roberts pointed out that although he was acting as

---

39. Willimon, *Preaching About Conflict*, 11.

40. The records do not stipulate the exact nature of the issue.

41. Minutes, Feb. 11, 1948, 3548D M6, Budleigh Salterton Baptist Church minute book Nov. 1944–Apr. 1949, DHC.

42. Minutes, Feb. 11, 1948, 3548D M6, DHC.

chairman, he was a representative of the Association and not a member of the church, and, therefore, he did not have a casting vote. However, he reminded the church that the rules of the Devon and Cornwall Baptist Association stated that in ballots like this, the pastor should receive the support of at least two-thirds of the votes; thus, the church must accept that it was the Lord's will that Mr. Bulivant should leave his post at Budleigh Salterton Baptist Church.[43]

Although Mr. Bulivant's actions may suggest that he did not have the sort of temperament necessary for pastoral leadership, the even split over whether to accept his resignation reveals a lack of consensus among the church members. This, in turn, questions whether the congregation had truly discerned the Lord's will. In view of this, Mr. Roberts's conclusion might appear somewhat clinical. However, the evenly split vote does suggest that Mr. Bulivant had lost the confidence of at least half of the church members. Therefore, it might be assumed that his ministry at Budleigh Salterton Baptist Church had come to an end.

Although the disagreement over the resignation of Mr. Bulivant is recorded, there are no preceding notations of the tension between Mr. Bulivant and the Boys Brigade. Likewise, there are no records of additional points of conflict suggesting that Mr. Bulivant's support was on the wane. This highlights a limitation of church meeting records when it comes to assessing the level of anxiety within a congregation. Despite this, the records do show that the church appears to have handled the situation with some care. By inviting Mr. Roberts from the local Association, the church employed the services of an outsider, whose authority would be accepted, to chair the meeting. Furthermore, while the minutes do not contain a large amount of detail, they do portray the members entering into a discussion over Mr. Bulivant's actions. They also illustrate the necessity of a chairperson to recognize when the fruitful period of discussion had ended. Finally, having made their decision, even if it was as a result of the direction of Mr. Roberts, the church upheld its decision.

In this example of an interpersonal conflict, the Baptists at Budleigh Salterton reveal an expectation that their minister will exercise restraint in a frustrating situation. When this expectation has not been met, the church is able to demonstrate their own restraint in the way they conduct a discussion at the church meeting. Furthermore, having

---

43. Minutes, Feb. 11, 1948, 3548D M6, DHC.

been evenly divided, the church is willing to base their decision on the advice of an acceptable outsider.

A Disagreement over Communion

According to Malcolm Grundy, disagreements over values and beliefs are one of the key areas that can lead to conflict within a congregation.[44] In the case of the Baptists at Newton Abbot, a protracted discussion over who should be allowed to participate in the Lord's Supper reveals a significant disagreement over the values expressed in their foundational document. According to the digest of church records compiled by Arthur Gabb, the question of whether non-members should be allowed to share communion was discussed on at least eight occasions.[45] Although aspects of theology present in this story will be discussed in the next chapter, a brief introduction to how strict communion is understood is necessary here.

Strict Communion

The policy of strict communion, adopted by the Newton Abbot Baptists, is deeply rooted among both General and Particular Baptists and emerges out of a doctrine of the church. As Michael Walker points out, the first Baptists had separated themselves from the Church of England on the basis that the church should represent the fellowship of believers.[46] This distinction led to a belief that baptism should be a mark of Christian faith and, therefore, not be open to children. This insistence that baptism was an act undertaken only by believers distinguished Baptists from other separatist forms of church.[47]

Having defined the church as the gathering of believers and insisted on baptism prior to membership, theologians such as Peter Naylor suggest that there was a consensus among early Baptists that only believers baptized by immersion should be allowed to participate at the

---

44. Grundy, *Understanding Congregations*, 121.

45. Arthur Gabb, Extracts from the minutes of the Old Church, 12, 14, 30, 31, 33, 24, 25, 39–40, 40–41, 6916D/68, Newton Abbot Baptist Church, n.d., DHC.

46. Walker, *Baptists at the Table*, 32.

47. Walker, *Baptists at the Table*, 32.

Lord's Supper.[48] This consensus does not mean that the restriction was uniform. Walker suggests that, broadly speaking, Baptists fell into two camps: those who believed that the Lord's Supper was an ordinance of the church and, therefore, only open to those who had been baptized as believers and those who emphasized the requirement of faith in Christ to share at the table and not the act of baptism.[49] At Newton Abbot, the articles of faith suggest that the members took a firm line on a closed communion table.[50] This is highlighted by the seventh article, which advocates that visitors from another Baptist congregation would only be allowed to participate in the Lord's Supper if all the members agreed to grant consent.[51] Despite this clear stance on communion, the Newton Abbot Baptists struggled to sustain their position in the light of pressure from a growing congregation.

The Fluctuating Stance on Communion

The pressure to open the communion table was first discussed at a church meeting in March 1826. The discussion is instigated by a number of townsfolk, who were already worshiping regularly with the fellowship, and had asked for permission to share communion.[52] According to this extract from the church records, while the question of regeneration[53] did not appear to be an issue; their views on baptism were:[54]

> March 1826
>
> Several persons resident in this Town, and attending the worship of God with us, having requested communion with us, whom we believe to be regenerate Christians, and whose conduct is as becometh the Gospel of Christ, who yet differ from us in their views of baptism, the question of admitting such with us to the privilege of the Lord's Supper was discussed and carried unanimously, it being understood at the same time that

48. Naylor, *Picking Up a Pin*, 88.
49. Walker, *Baptists at the Table*, 32.
50. Gabb, Extracts, 3–9, 6916D/68, DHC.
51. Gabb, Extracts, 6, 6916D/68, DHC.
52. Arthur Gabb, "Short History of the Baptist Cause," 10, 6916D/67, Newton Abbot Baptist Church, 1947, DHC.
53. Gabb, Extracts, 12, 6916D/68, DHC.
54. Although Gabb does not specify, it may be assumed that these townsfolk believed in paedobaptism.

they cannot have a voice in any of our church matters like our regular members.[55]

This record raises a question in respect of the link between church membership and attendance at communion. Having opened their communion table to the townsfolk, who were regularly attending their worship services, it is questionable whether or not the Newton Abbot Baptists, under their own rules, had the authority to prevent them from participating in church meetings. The rule regarding eligibility for membership reads:

> No person shall be admitted a member of this church who does not contentiously believe the above doctrines, and in a confession of his or her faith and experience before the Church, and if approved of by the whole membership then present, on his or her being baptized, shall be taken into full communion according to Regular Order.[56]

With the question regarding the regenerate nature of the townsfolk not under debate, the first part of this statement is satisfied. However, the difficulty is, having granted them access to the communion table, the Newton Abbot Baptists have, arguably, validated not only the faith of the townsfolk but also their baptism. Thus, while missiologically opening the communion table was a positive step, potentially, it changed how the doctrine of the church was understood. To avoid this potential shift in doctrine, the Newton Abbot Baptists decided that, although they would allow the townsfolk to participate in the Lord's Supper without the need to confirm their faith through baptism, they would retain the requirement for anyone wishing to participate in church affairs. In light of the tension created between their actions and beliefs over communion, it is perhaps unsurprising that the question was revisited on November 3, 1833.[57]

At this meeting, the decision to allow non-church members to share the Lord's Supper was overturned. Furthermore, according to Gabb's digest, the meeting also reaffirmed and strengthened the seventh article of their foundational document.[58] This article referred to restricted access to

---

55. Gabb, Extracts, 12, 6916D/68, DHC.
56. Gabb, Extracts, 2–3, 6916D/68, DHC.
57. Gabb, Extracts, 14, 6916D/68, DHC.
58. According to Gabb's research, the seventh article of the foundation document states, "That no member from any other Baptist Church shall be admitted an occasional communicant, without the consensus of all the members present." Gabb, Extracts, 6, 6916D/68, DHC.

the Lord's Table, even to members from other Baptist churches. In view of this, the church introduced a requirement for members from other Baptist congregations to be interviewed by the minister and his recommendation taken to the church meeting before they shared in the Lord's Supper. Only after the church meeting had granted permission could the visiting Baptist share the Lord's Supper with the Newton Abbot Baptists. Although no reason is given for the strength of sentiment expressed in this meeting, the suggestion that the member from another church should be "approved of by him [the minister] as a proper subject"[59] suggests that some impropriety had led to a review of procedure.

The position agreed at the meeting on November 3, 1833, was upheld for a further sixteen years. However, in 1849, the members revisited the question of who should be allowed to share the Lord's Supper on two occasions. On June 28, they agreed:

> The following paedobaptist friends who desire to sit down with us at the Lord's Table should be admitted to the privilege on the coming Lord's Day and in future similar occasions:
>
> Mr Ford
>
> Mrs Ford
>
> Mrs Bush
>
> Mrs. Dent
>
> Mr Panoll
>
> Mr Bartlett
>
> Resolved that the wishes of our friends be cordially complied with in the humble hope that mutual Christian affection and spiritual edification may thereby be procured. Agreed unanimously.[60]

The church met again on November 23, 1849 and, regarding admission to the Lord's Table, agreed:

> In order to meet the case of any persons in the congregation, who not being members of any other church and not seeing it their duty to be baptized, may yet desire to enjoy the ordinance of the Lord's Supper, it is agreed that such persons shall be allowed to sit down with us as paedobaptists on the testimony of the minister, and one or more members of the church, who shall

---

59. Gabb, Extracts, 14, 6916D/68, DHC.

60. Gabb, Extracts, 30, 6916D/68, DHC.

express their conviction that such persons are converted characters and are maintaining a walk and conversation becoming the Gospel, and their names shall be mentioned at the church meeting before the Ordinance Day on which they may be admitted to communion at the Lord's Table.[61]

The first point of interest in these decisions is not mentioned in the above extracts. Among the eight members listed as present and agreeing with the resolution taken at the June meeting were Stitson and Soper. While it is impossible to tell if they were part of the unanimous decision to close the table in 1833, they are recorded as agreeing to the adoption of a strict view of communion at the church's formation. Therefore, their inclusion among the members who unanimously agreed to open the table to the townsfolk in 1826 and June 1849 is surprising. In light of this, it might be surmised that Messrs. Stitson and Soper never actually agreed with the policy of a closed communion table. However, this does not seem to be the case. In 1863, when the church finally divided into two congregations over the question of who should be allowed to attend the Lord's Supper, Messrs. Stitson and Soper are not listed among the seventeen members who were removed from membership for supporting open communion.[62]

The second point of interest relating to these two meetings in 1849 is that paedobaptists are being granted access to the Lord's Supper upon the testimony of the minister and a church member. Once again, this decision changes the dynamic of the church. By allowing access to the Lord's Table upon the testimony of a church member and the minister and the agreement of the whole church, the faith of the paedobaptists was being validated without the need for believers' baptism. This is a significant contrast with the decision made in 1833 when even members of another Baptist congregation, who are likely to have been baptized as believers, were expected to have their faith validated prior to being allowed to take communion. Furthermore, by validating the faith of persons who had been baptized as infants and not requiring that they submit to believers' baptism prior to sharing at the Lord's Table, the Baptists at Newton Abbot have rejected their position on strict communion. Unfortunately, Gabb's extracts do not show if a vote confirmed the proposal made at the November 1883 meeting. It is, however, safe to assume it was carried, as the decision was overturned in 1854.

61. Gabb, Extracts, 31–32, 6916D/68, DHC.
62. Gabb, Extracts, 40–41, 6916D/68, DHC.

On June 2, 1854, Gabb's digest states that:

> At a church meeting held on this day, it was resolved the rule made in March 1826, being contrary to the formation of the Church (on the 5th day of February 1819) be henceforth void, and in consequence of which no unbaptized person can be admitted to the Table of the Lord with us![63]

This resolution is signed by thirteen members, among whom are Stitson and Soper. While this apparent indecision on the part of Messrs. Stitson and Soper invites an inquiry into the intrapersonal conflict they are facing, this is not possible from the records available. However, it is possible to explore the influence the ministers at Newton Abbot Baptist Church may have had on the issue of opening and closing the Lord's Table.

The Influence of the Minister

In Gabb's opinion, the choice of ministers had a significant effect on the Newton Abbot Baptists' move away from a closed position on the Lord's Supper. He suggests that none of the ministers who served the church between 1824 and 1859 held a strict position on communion.[64] However, of the four ministers that served the church during this period, Gabb only highlights the practice of two: Mr. Cross and Mr. Walker. He argues that Mr. Cross allowed unbaptized believers to participate in the Lord's Supper and had built relationships with ministers from the local Congregational churches. Gabb also notes that these Congregational ministers were allowed the freedom to preach in the Baptist chapel.[65] The implication in Gabb's account is that by allowing Congregationalists to preach in the Baptist chapel the sanctity of believers' baptism was undermined. However, this must be considered speculation as there is no record of this in his digest.

Having suggested that Mr. Cross's ministry was not in keeping with the expectations of a church holding a strict view of communion, Gabb

---

63. Gabb, Extracts, 33, 6916D/68, DHC.

64. Gabb, "Short History of the Baptist Cause," 12, 6916D/67, Newton Abbot Baptist Church, 1947, DHC.

65. Arthur Gabb, "Short History of the Baptist Cause in Newton Abbot," 12, in Extracts from the minutes of the Old Church, 6916D/68, Newton Abbot Baptist Church, n.d., DHC.

describes Mr. Walker as heterodox.[66] While not necessarily the case, Mr. Walker's position regarding the Lord's Supper was not in keeping with a strict position on communion. The records for December 1858 highlight this:

> The Pastor [Mr. Walker] having stated that it was desirable that the church should come to some decision on the subject of Open Communion, after some conversation, it was named by Bro Michelmare and seconded by Bro Gilpen, and resolved that unbaptized persons should be admitted to the Lord's Table, if approved by the church.[67]

Although this is the third time that the members decide to open the communion table, it is the first occasion that the records intimate that the minister initiated the discussion. Arguably, by revisiting the question of who should be allowed to share in the Lord's Supper, Mr. Walker adopted the position of the accepted outsider described in the previous chapter. However, by reopening the discussion, Mr. Walker appears to have instigated his removal as pastor.

The Removal of Mr. Walker

Mr. Walker's ministry is the subject of three successive meetings. Initially, on June 20, 1859, he asked the church for permission to continue as minister beyond the end of the year. On this occasion, the church is evenly split over whether he should continue as pastor. At the next meeting, held on July 5, the vote registered eighteen for and two against him continuing.[68] At the third meeting, held on August 2, the church attempted to censure Mr. Walker:

> Church meeting was held this evening to agree about the terms of the invitation to Mr Walker. There was much discussion which ended in a resolution being passed requesting the deacons to ascertain from Mr Walker whether he conscientiously believed in certain doctrines as stated in the church book, and which one of the rules required that the minister should believe and hold.[69]

66. Gabb, "Short History of the Baptist Cause," 74, in Extracts, 6916D/68, DHC.
67. Gabb, Extracts, 34–35, 6916D/68, DHC.
68. Gabb, Extracts, 35, 6916D/68, DHC.
69. Gabb, Extracts, 35–36, 6916D/68, DHC.

The implication here is that Mr. Walker's decision to revisit the question of who should be allowed to participate in the Lord's Supper indicated he may not agree with the position articulated by the church rules.[70] In view of this, the church members were correct in censuring Mr. Walker. However, as the church members had already agreed on two occasions to open the communion table without censure, it is possible that the church was using Mr. Walker as a scapegoat for their own indecision.

The Scapegoat

Wink addresses the use of a scapegoat in his work *Engaging the Powers*. Here, in a work that explores the nature of spiritual power within a matrix of non-violent response, Wink argues that the use of a scapegoat is common among human communities.[71] He develops this contention by referring to the work of René Girard and suggests that communities survive their own internal tensions by killing or expelling a victim.[72] Wink points out that the person treated as a scapegoat is often a marginalized member of the community. He also notes that the person being scapegoated is usually someone whom the rest of the community finds easy to blame for their current situation. In the case of Mr. Walker, as minister, he was an outsider and, therefore, the natural scapegoat for the members' frustration over their own inability to deal satisfactorily with the issue.

Concluding the Debate over the Lord's Supper

If Mr. Walker was used as a scapegoat, his removal did not successfully assuage the issue of who should be allowed to share the Lord's Supper. This indecision was finally resolved in 1863 when seventeen members were expelled from the church for supporting open communion.[73]

---

70. Rule 2 states, "That if any member shall hereafter change their sentiment, disbelieve, or deny either of the above points of doctrine, on being so proved before the church, shall no longer be considered a member of this Christian Society . . ." Gabb, Extracts 3–4, 6916D/68, DHC.

71. Wink, *Engaging the Powers*, 144.

72. Wink, *Engaging the Powers*, 144–46.

73. Gabb, Extracts, 40–41, 6916D/68, DHC.

The removal of these members is noteworthy for two reasons. The first is that John Branscombe is listed among the members expelled.[74] Branscombe was a founding member of the church at Newton Abbot and appears to have been an influential figure among the members. According to Gabb, Branscombe succeeded Stitson as church clerk on May 15, 1861.[75] Although Branscombe is never implicated in the decisions to open the communion table to non-members, his presence among the list of members withdrawn over the issue suggests that he may have provided a consistent influence toward opening the Lord's Table. Therefore, by ejecting Branscombe along with all the other members who took an open stance on communion, the Baptists at Newton Abbot finally dealt with their indecision.

The decision to remove the members holding an open view of the Lord's Table is also significant in that, while they only represented one-fifth of the church membership, they were sent to the new, larger building that had recently been constructed.[76] Although not recorded as such at the time, this action was insightful. While the original church maintained its stance on closed communion, it closed in 1919.[77] However, by contrast, the new congregation created by the separation in 1863 existed until 2009.[78]

Summary

The Nature of the Angel

The accounts from church records discussed above appear to confirm Wink's belief that the way a church handles conflict reveals something of the nature of its angel. In the case of the Baptists at Newton Abbot, the discussion over Sunday evening services reveals a deep-seated anxiety within the angel's nature. This anxiety causes the congregation to continually revisit a decision with a view of overturning it. Moreover, the

---

74. Gabb, Extracts, 40, 6916D/68, DHC.

75. Gabb, Extracts, 38, 6916D/68, DHC.

76. Gabb, "Short History of the Baptist Cause," 14–15, in Extracts, 6916D/68, DHC.

77. Gabb, "Short History of the Baptist Cause," 26, 6916D/67, Newton Abbot Baptist Church, 1947, DHC.

78. The date of closure was confirmed in an interview with Caroline Eglin. The interview took place on Wednesday, December 17, 2014. Rev. Eglin was the last minister of the Baptist church that was formed in Newton Abbot in 1863.

fact that they expressed a similar trait more than a hundred years earlier supports Wink's belief that the nature of the angel has a gyroscopic effect on some aspects of church life. This repetition of organizational character traits transcending a particular generation will be discussed later in the chapter on self-understanding. However, for the moment it suffices to say that the Baptists in both Newton Abbot and Budleigh Salterton exhibit this characteristic, albeit over different issues.

In addition to revealing a pattern of anxiousness that causes the congregation to return to a prior decision, the records kept by the Newton Abbot Baptists also demonstrate how the congregation uses scapegoating as a means to quell its unsettled nature. This is illustrated by the dismissal of Mr. Walker in 1859 and the questioning of the credibility of the pastor's ministry during the 1980s. Of course, the Newton Abbot Baptists are not the only church to treat the minister as a scapegoat.

Although not framed in this way, Mr. Roberts's advice to remove Mr. Bulivant from office might also be considered to be scapegoating. By reminding Baptists at Budleigh Salterton that it was usual to expect a minister to receive a two-thirds majority at a church meeting, Mr. Roberts provided the means by which the church could dismiss Mr. Bulivant without suffering the feelings of guilt associated with sacking their pastor.

The discussion over Mr. Bulivant's lifestyle also illustrates how a congregation might express an expectation that the minister would uphold a certain lifestyle. While lifestyle expectations were discussed in general terms in the chapter on demographics, the account of Mr. Bulivant's frustration demonstrates how the often unspoken expectations of a congregation can be easily transgressed.

A Change of Vocation

In addition to revealing how a congregation might resort to scapegoating as a means of dealing with its own sense of guilt, the records kept by the Baptists in Newton Abbot appear to reveal a disturbing shift in the congregation's vocation. During the discussion over the Sunday evening services, it appears that the church becomes frustrated with its inability to make a decision and then keep to it. This, in turn, leads to the conversation over who should be allowed to vote and the length of time that a decision should be kept prior to review. While the decision over whether to continue with Sunday evening services is not significant enough to suggest that the congregation is moving away from its vocation, the nature of the discussion marks a point of transition from discernment to democracy. Where the emphasis of the church meeting moves away from the process of discernment toward a purely democratic decision-making process, it could be argued that the church's vocation has changed. According to Wink, such a change in vocation would indicate that the nature of the angel had become demonic. While, at the point when Sunday evening services are discussed, it is unlikely that the nature of the angel had become demonic, it may have become so in the move to Highweek School.

Recording Emotion

Although the records used for this study provide some important insights into the angels of the churches studied, such as the inertia that an angel generates or how an angel of the church can move toward becoming demonic, there are areas where the information provided by church records is insufficient. Perhaps the most obvious weakness is the relationship between the emotions expressed by the church and how they might be understood with respect to the angel. This is particularly evident when disagreements are recorded, as the emotions present in a church meeting are very difficult to report. An illustration of this is the discussion held by the Baptists at Newton Abbot when considering the continuation of Sunday evening services. While there are obviously underlying tensions present in and influencing the outcome of, the meeting, the minute-taker only records the questions being asked. As a result, the level of tension and anxiety present in the meeting is not recorded. Likewise, while the debate over Mr. Bulivant's departure from the pastorate at Budleigh Salterton notes some of his frustrations, the records reveal very little of how the members felt about his actions. Furthermore, the minutes do not record how the members reacted to a split decision regarding the acceptance of Mr. Bulivant's resignation. They similarly make no mention of how the members reacted to Mr. Roberts's recommendation that Mr. Bulivant should leave the pastorate.

Despite this weakness, the records kept of disagreements between church members at church meetings are helpful. Furthermore, the description of how these disagreements are settled can offer important insights into the nature of the angel and, in the case of the angel of the

Newton Abbot Baptists, suggest when the nature begins to change. In addition to revealing the nature of the angel, the records of disagreements provide some examples of how theological arguments can be used as part of a wider discussion as an aid to overcoming the inertia caused by the gyroscopic influence of the angel of the church. While these examples are not necessarily significant, they do hint at how the church includes theology as part of its day-to-day life. In view of this, the next chapter will explore the relationship between a congregation's theology and the nature and vocation of its angel.

6

Denominational Rubrics, Theology, and Worship

WINK'S FIFTH FACET FOR defining the angel of the church encompasses denominational rubrics, theology, and worship. As with his introduction to demographics, Wink does not illustrate how these facets of church life affect the nature of the angel. He simply states:

> Within denominational rubrics, there is ample latitude for high or low liturgies, the whole gamut of musical tastes, and various types of preaching. The educational program quickly reveals what premium is put on spiritual growth, as do the special groups that meet during the week (are they limited to social occasions and Boy Scouts, or do they reach the deeper needs, like Alcoholics Anonymous, marriage enrichment, or singles and divorced groups?). The theology tends to be denominationally orientated, but not always recognisably so and the role of the Bible stretches all the way from pretext to pre-eminence. It is in worship that the majority of the congregation experiences the angel; paradoxically, it is in worship that the angel most flagrantly goes unnoticed.[1]

At the heart of this list lies the correlation between theological belief and practice and the nature of the angel of the church. Wink's comments invite anyone seeking the nature of the angel of a congregation to consider the external influence of churches of a similar tradition, para-church

1. Wink, *Unmasking the Powers*, 76.

organizations, and the internal pressures caused by differences in theology. His comment that the angel is both most fully experienced and yet simultaneously hidden in the way a congregation worships is significant, particularly as the focus of this study is strongly historical and thus has not collected data from real-time worship services. However, this does not mean that certain practices within worship cannot be explored from a historical perspective. Therefore, this chapter will revisit the accounts from Newton Abbot Baptist Church, where the continuation of Sunday evening services was discussed, and the congregation's extended vacillation over who should participate in the Lord's Supper. As the significance of each of these issues has been discussed with respect to the form of conflict they represent, this chapter will briefly consider the theology that lies behind the conversations.

Wink's statement also invites a comment on how a congregation teaches the Christian faith and the sort of organizations that a church allows to use its premises. In this respect, accounts from Budleigh Salterton Baptist Church describing their relationship to children and young people will be explored. Also, discussions that relate to the use of church premises held at both Budleigh Salterton and Newton Abbot will be considered. Finally, with particular attention to the calling of a minister to the pastorate, the relationship between preaching and worship among Baptist congregations will be examined. However, before these issues can be explored, the nature of Baptist denominational rubrics must first be discussed.

Denominational Rubrics

While this study has sought to focus on the experience of English Baptists, and in particular the experiences of three churches in the South West, the comments made by the American Baptist Bill Leonard highlight the distinctive nature of a Baptist denominational rubric. Leonard confesses:

> I remain a Baptist, less because of the constancy than because of the messiness of this strange and wonderful heritage. I cannot make it fit any more than I can make the gospel all fit into a nice package without contradiction, controversy and occasional confusion.[2]

---

2. Leonard, "Being Baptist," 87–88.

Although Leonard is writing from an American perspective, his comment encapsulates the complexity of Baptist ecclesiology both in America and in the United Kingdom.

As will become evident, the term "denominational rubric" is difficult to apply to British Baptists, even to those who are members of the Baptist Union of Great Britain. While the term suggests a set of rules that creates a framework that encapsulates and defines a specific form of church, in a Baptist context, even in the case of churches that belong to the Baptist Union of Great Britain, these rules do not exist. Instead, churches wishing to belong to the union of churches that encompasses all of England, much of Wales, and some Scottish churches are founded on a declaration of principle that only contains three brief statements. These cover the revelation of God's will, baptism by immersion, and participation in mission.

In the context of an exploration of a denominational rubric, the first point is the most significant, as it states:

> That our Lord and Savior Jesus Christ, God manifest in the flesh, is the sole and absolute authority in all matters pertaining to faith and practice, as revealed in the Holy Scriptures, and that each Church has liberty, under the guidance of the Holy Spirit, to interpret and administer His laws.[3]

This principle provides a rubric within which the latitude of theology and expressions of worship referred to by Wink can exist.

Christ the Head

Discussing the nature of the Baptist Union Declaration of Principle, Paul Fiddes, Brian Haymes, Richard Kidd, and Michael Quicke emphasized the importance placed on Christ being the final authority in all matters pertaining to Christian faith. They argue that this distinguishes Baptists from other forms of evangelicalism.[4] An alternative to this is to contend that the Bible provides the final authority on all aspects of faith and conduct. This is the position that the Evangelical Alliance adopts in the third point of their declaration of faith.[5]

---

3. Baptists Together, "Declaration of Principle."
4. Fiddes et al., *Something to Declare*, 29.
5. Evangelical Alliance, "Basis of Faith."

Although Fiddes et al. defend the wording of the Declaration of Principle, and all churches in the Baptist Union of Great Britain have to agree to these principles, it does not mean that some congregations might not articulate a different belief. For example, some Baptist congregations argue that the Bible is the supreme authority on all matters relating to faith. This argument places them closer in belief to organizations whose theology is more conservative than some fellow Baptists who have also signed the Baptist Union Declaration of Principle. It also highlights the messiness of Baptist ecclesiology, referred to by Leonard, as agreeing to the Baptist Union Declaration of Principle allows for a broad spectrum of theological interpretation.[6]

The Liberty to Hold a Different Opinion

According to the records examined in this thesis, the liberty to hold a different theological position is equally as evident among the members of a single congregation as it is between Baptist churches. The discussion over the nature of Sunday evening services that took place in a church meeting held at Newton Abbot on June 24, 2002 illustrates this. In the records of this conversation, a multiplicity of different opinions was expressed. These range from whether the cost of heating and lighting the building should influence their decision to a disagreement on the proposed new format for Sunday evening services.[7]

This liberty to express an opinion is also not limited to a contemporary time frame. In his 1947 notes on the history of Newton Abbot Baptist Church, the historian Arthur Gabb argues that between 1824 and 1859, none of the ministers had been "strict Baptists."[8] He also believes that this not only contravened the principles upon which the church was founded, but it also led to a lack of numerical growth during the period when the incumbent ministers were encouraging an open view of communion.[9] These comments are interesting in the light of the fact they were written in 1947 when the church in East Street Newton Abbot was not only thriving but had been practicing open communion

---

6. Leonard, "Being Baptist," 87–88.

7. Church meeting minutes, June 24, 2002, box 6196, Newton Abbot Baptist Church, DHC.

8. Arthur Gabb, "Short History of the Baptist Cause," 15, 6916D/67, Newton Abbot Baptist Church, 1947, DHC.

9. Gabb, "Short History of the Baptist Cause," 15–16, 6916D/67, 1947, DHC.

since 1863.[10] In view of this, while Gabb's comments express his opinion, they appear not to represent the theological position of the Newton Abbot Baptists during the 1940s.

Diverse Opinions

The fact that Gabb can express an opinion on communion that is not being shared by the wider membership of the Baptist church in Newton Abbot highlights the ability of Baptist congregations to hold together a group of people with differing viewpoints. Historically this ability to encompass a diversity of opinion and belief is encapsulated in the formation of the Baptist Union of Great Britain.

While the origins of the Union lie in a society of Particular Baptists dating from 1813, its scope was broadened in 1832 with the inclusion of the New Connexion of General Baptists.[11] The coming together of the Particular and New Connexion General Baptists created a Union out of two groups with diametrically opposed theological stances. According to Payne, while the Particular Baptists were Calvinistic and the New Connexion General Baptists were Arminian, they agreed that they shared an evangelical expression of Christian faith.[12] Thus, this commitment to evangelicalism formed a basis of agreement that enabled the theological divide to be overcome.

The fact that Baptists can hold together a polarity of theological belief within a single Union is a testimony to their ability to encompass a diversity of viewpoints while remaining able to express a single vocation. While this resonates with Wink's belief that there is often latitude within a denominational rubric for a variety of worship styles, it contrasts with his conviction that a denominational rubric restricts a congregation's theological stance. As the original churches that formed the Baptist Union of Great Britain came predominantly from two different streams

---

10. When the new building in East Street was opened in 1863 the Baptists who were committed to open communion were removed from membership of the church formed in 1819 and were sent to the new building. See Arthur Gabb, Extracts from the minutes of the Old Church, 40, 6916D/68, Newton Abbot Baptist Church, n.d., DHC. By 1947 there were seventy members at the new church in East Street with fifty-one children in the Sunday School. See *Baptist Handbook for 1947*, 37.

11. Payne, *Baptist Union*, 1, 3–5.

12. Payne, *Baptist Union*, 4.

of theological thought, the rubric that holds Baptists together errs on the side of liberty rather than constraint.

This liberty has already been referred to in chapter 5 in respect of the discussion the Newton Abbot Baptists held over the nature of Sunday evening worship services. In that context, the practical issues relating to how the meeting was structured and the use of voting to secure a decision were explored. However, the conversation recorded in the church minutes also considered how the Scriptures should influence their decision.[13] This suggests that, while concerned with the practical aspects of church life, they were also engaged in a process of applying Christ's laws to a contemporary situation.

According to Fiddes et al., the term "His Laws," used in the Declaration of Principle, refers to Christ's teaching as recorded by the gospel writers.[14] Reflecting on how this might be interpreted, Fiddes et al. note that Christ's teaching is usually a reinterpretation of an earlier understanding of what it meant to be the people of God.[15] Pursuing this line of thought, Fiddes et al. argue that, for laws to remain relevant, they must be continually updated. In view of this, while the Scriptures provide the basis upon which the life of faith is founded, the church has an ongoing role in interpreting the historical text in a contemporary context. According to this understanding, the first three points that form a Baptist denominational rubric not only grant each congregation the liberty to interpret the Scriptures but implore the church to understand how the Scriptures reveal the current will of Christ in their specific context.

Of course, this liberty has not always been sufficient to keep Baptist congregations within the Baptist Union of Great Britain, and on two notable occasions, Baptist churches have felt it necessary to leave the Union. These were during the downgrade controversy between 1887 and 1888 and following Michael Taylor's address to the Baptist Assembly in 1971. In each case, some Baptist churches felt that the liberty to express a theological position had been taken too far.

While individual congregations have decided to leave the Union, such is the liberty for theological interpretation that expulsion is a rare occurrence. Furthermore, in the case of Bugbrooke Baptist Church, which was expelled in 1986, the removal was due to the level of control

---

13. Church meeting minutes, June 24, 2002, box 6196, Newton Abbot Baptist Church, DHC.

14. Fiddes et al., *Something to Declare*, 32–33.

15. Fiddes et al., *Something to Declare*, 33.

exercised by church leaders over church members rather than the theological stance that they were taking.[16]

Baptists Together

Although there is an emphasis on liberty among Baptist congregations, this should not be confused with a commitment to the independence of the local church. Referring to a church as independent suggests that, as a congregation, the church acts as an island, unaffected by the decisions and actions of other churches holding the same doctrinal positions. This is not how Baptist ecclesiology should be understood. While the constraints of the denominational rubric allow each church the liberty to discern and express its understanding of Christ's will, it does so within the context of being part of a wider network of churches and the church universal. The 1948 paper *The Baptist Doctrine of the Church* highlights the need for interaction between other congregations by pointing out that although each local congregation is able, under Christ, to administer its own life, traditionally, Baptists have been aware of the dangers associated with isolation and individualism and have sought to mediate these by associating together.[17]

Early in their history, and in the face of persecution from local magistrates and bishops, Baptists found support in fellowship with other Baptists. The ties that bound these gatherings were sometimes strengthened by agreeing and publishing a confession of faith. Attesting to this, Ernest A. Payne describes the way thirty congregations from Leicestershire, Lincolnshire, and adjoining counties met in 1651 and drew up a confession of faith upon which they could all agree. Payne's narration develops further as he describes how the General Baptist's "standard Confession" emerged from a meeting in London of representatives from churches spread throughout England and Wales.[18] In 1678, a meeting of General Baptists from Buckinghamshire, Oxfordshire, and adjoining counties drew up what became known as the "Orthodox Crede."[19] Article 39 of this creed describes the forming of "general councils or assemblies" from representatives from the clergy, leaders, and brethren who have been

---

16. Betteridge, *Deep Roots, Living Branches*, 473.
17. *Baptist Doctrine of the Church*, 4.
18. Payne, *Fellowship of Believers*, 27.
19. Payne, *Fellowship of Believers*, 27.

appointed from a wider pool of churches. The aim of this gathering was to act in the name of Christ and in his authority to: "Preserve unity, to prevent heresy, and [provide] superintendence among or in any congregation whatsoever within its own limits or jurisdiction."[20]

The delegation of this authority represents a significant commitment to a group of churches who consider the local church sufficient unto itself, value their freedom to appoint their own leaders, and execute their own governance under the lordship of Christ. The significance of this willingness to submit to the authority of a wider gathering of Baptists is underlined by the latter part of article 39, where adherents agree to the assembly hearing appeals over injustice and heresy and subsequently having the "lawful power to determine [and] also to excommunicate."[21]

The ability to hold in tension the liberty to express Christ's will for the local congregation, as well as the willingness to share authority with a wider association, is equally evident among Particular Baptists. As with the General Baptists, Associations were quickly formed and confessions of faith produced, the first of these being written by seven London churches in 1644. Once again, there is an acknowledgment of the distinctiveness of a single congregation, coupled with the acceptance of the counsel of a wider group of Baptists. This willingness to accept outside counsel allows for the practice of the accepted outsider.

Earlier, in chapter 4, the role of the acceptable outsider was explored with respect to the minister, but representatives from other congregations can also adopt this role.

Inviting Assistance from the Acceptable Outsider

A Request for Assistance from the Baptists at South Street in Exeter

At the beginning of his ministry in the Baptist church at South Street in Exeter, the Rev. Brian Haymes noted that the church held a privileged geographical position and raised questions about the role and purpose of the church as the people of God meeting in the city center.[22] According to Trevor Gardner and Richard Frost, these questions

---

20. Lumpkin and Leonard, *Baptist Confessions of Faith*, 338.
21. Lumpkin and Leonard, *Baptist Confessions of Faith*, 338.
22. Gardner and Frost, *Faith in Exeter*, 6.

were prompted by a populous migration from the city center into new housing developments in the suburbs.[23] This conclusion is supported by Haymes's comments in *Multi-Voiced Church* by Stuart and Sian Murray Williams. Here, Haymes outlines the quandary faced by the church: Were they to sell their inner-city property and move to the suburbs or reinvent their ministry within the city center?[24]

As part of their decision-making process, the Baptists at South Street in Exeter invited the other local churches to pray for them and offer guidance. According to Haymes, the response to this invitation was mixed, with one church not replying, another stating that it was "none of their business," and a third suggesting they should stay. Following their deliberations, the members decided to remain in their city center premises. Gardner and Frost suggest that by inquiring the church's role in the city center, Haymes provided the catalyst from which the church developed a vision for serving the vulnerable adults who frequented the Exeter City Centre.[25]

Whether or not Haymes or Gardner and Frost are correct in their assessment of the actions of the Baptists at South Street in Exeter during the 1970s is open for debate. However, the responses described by Haymes to the invitation issued to the other local churches are interesting. Although the members of South Street Baptist Church in Exeter were willing to seek help from an acceptable outsider, the external help was not necessarily forthcoming. A similar reaction to this was encountered by the Baptists in Newton Abbot in early 2003.

A Request for Assistance from the Baptists in Newton Abbot

On February 10, 2003, the deacons of the Baptist church in Newton Abbot agreed that the minister should write to the leaders of the Baptist congregations in Barton, East Dartmoor, Hele, Teignmouth, and Upton Vale in Torquay.[26] The purpose of this approach was to encourage local fellowships to send families on secondment to the church in Newton Abbot for a two-year period and assist with developing the junior church.[27]

23. Gardner and Frost, *Faith in Exeter*, 6.
24. Williams and Williams, *Multi-Voiced Church*, 122.
25. Gardner and Frost, *Faith in Exeter*, 7.
26. Deacons meeting minutes, Feb. 2003, box 6196, Newton Abbot Baptist Church, DHC.
27. Deacons meeting minutes, Feb. 2003, box 6196, DHC.

The initial results of this request were discussed at the deacons meeting held on March 17, 2003. Here, the minister reported that their request for help had not been received enthusiastically, and very little help had been forthcoming. Reflecting on this, the deacons queried whether they should be more involved with their local "cluster," a small group of local, like-minded churches that were usually, but not necessarily, Baptist congregations. The deacons also considered organizing a visit to the Baptist Union Center in Didcot and approaching the regional minister to discover how Baptists operated outside of the local church.[28] This discussion suggests that, over time, the congregation had become isolated from other Baptist churches in the area. If this were the case, then it might explain the lack of confidence in the relationship between the local congregation in Newton Abbot and the wider circle of Baptists and possibly churches of other traditions. It might also explain why offers of help were not forthcoming. Despite this possible shortcoming, the deacons' comments also suggest that, while there was a lack of experience in seeking assistance from an external source, they and the minister were willing to explore how this might work.

By June 2003, the outlook was not very positive. Only one of the churches originally contacted had suggested that they might supply the help requested. This was the Baptist church at Upton Vale in Torquay, who agreed to send three people to meet with the deacons.[29] This meeting took place on July 14, 2003, and, according to the minutes, the deacons met with four delegates from Upton Vale Baptist Church. The discussion that followed appears to have been wide-ranging, with issues such as the current number of members and the plan to move from the chapel in East Street to Highweek School being addressed.[30] With the discussion encompassing such a wide range of aspects, it is possible that the delegates from Upton Vale had their reservations and were exploring what benefit their help would bring to the Baptist church in Newton Abbot. Although these reservations are not recorded by the Baptists in Newton Abbot, the events that eventually transpired appear to support this hypothesis, that while assistance might be sought from other Baptist congregations, the help required might not necessarily be forthcoming.

By October 2003, the planned move to Highweek School was underway. As part of the preparation for the move, concerns were raised

28. Deacons meeting minutes, Mar. 12, 2003, box 6196, DHC.
29. Deacons meeting minutes, June 16, 2003, box 6196, DHC.
30. Deacons meeting minutes, July 14, 2003, box 6196, DHC.

regarding how the church would cope if the relocation brought about an influx of children. The records show that the deacons were not sure how they would cope if no help were forthcoming from the Baptists at Upton Vale.[31] Clearly, following the initial contact, the relationship between the Baptists in Newton Abbot and Upton Vale had not progressed to the point where help was being received. As a result of the concerns raised in the deacons meeting, the minister agreed to write to the Baptists at Upton Vale. By the time the deacons at Newton Abbot met again on November 10, no reply had been received, and they agreed that a further reminder was required. On this occasion, the minutes suggest that the Baptists at Upton Vale had made a commitment to supply assistance.[32] By January 2004, the promised help by the Baptists at Upton Vale had not materialized. In view of this, the pastor agreed to write once more, only this time he would remind them of their commitment, quoting Luke 5:7.[33] This Bible text comes from Luke's account of the calling of the first disciples, and verse 7 relates to the request for the help of other fishermen following Peter's miraculous large catch of fish. Presumably, the implication in using this verse was to give a biblical imperative for the Baptists in Upton Vale to help fellow Baptists in their work.

From the church records, it seems that even reinforcing their request with scripture failed to generate the promised help as, by February 9, 2004, no assistance had been received from the Baptists at Upton Vale. However, the minutes of this meeting record that an email had been sent to the Baptists at Upton Vale and a reply had been received. Unfortunately, the nature of this reply is not recorded. All the minutes state is that one of the delegates from Upton Vale, who had previously met with the deacons at Newton Abbot, had been "designated to deal with this."[34] Following this notation, no further reference was made to receiving help from the Baptists at Upton Vale. In view of this, it can only be assumed that, for some undisclosed reason, the Baptists at Upton Vale decided not to make good on their offer of help.

Although it is impossible to build a hypothesis solely based on the experience of the Baptists at South Street in Exeter and Newton Abbot, it does appear that while there might be a commitment to seek help from an external source, the assistance required might not be forthcoming.

31. Deacons meeting minutes, Oct. 6, 2003, box 6196, DHC.
32. Deacons meeting minutes, Nov. 10, 2003, box 6196, DHC.
33. Deacons meeting minutes, Jan. 12, 2004, box 6196, DHC.
34. Deacons meeting minutes, Feb. 9, 2004, box 6196, DHC.

This, in turn, might suggest that Baptist congregations are reluctant to offer advice or assistance to other congregations and raises questions regarding the nature of associating among Baptist churches. It also suggests that, while representatives from the wider Union might articulate a commitment to associating among local churches, in practice, these congregations prefer to act autonomously. In the context of Wink's concept of the angel of the church, reluctance to offer advice to another congregation reduces the avenues through which the nature of the angel can be addressed and changed. As for the preference for acting autonomously, congregations that adopt this position reveal the inner reluctance of their angel to be addressed and possibly changed by external voices. The danger with a congregation whose angel exhibits this trait is that the church can become detached from the changing nature of their local community, which, in turn, can lead to their being unable to fulfill their God-given vocation. Although this process does not necessarily mean that the angel becomes demonic, it does mean that the gyroscopic effect of the angel might cause the church to hold on to and continue to practice outdated missiological concepts. This, in turn, might restrict the ability of a congregation to fulfill its vocation.

Midweek Activities

In his review of the relationship between theology, worship, and the angel of the church, Wink suggests that the educational program and the sort of organizations that a church is involved with will reveal the nature of the angel. In this respect, the records available from the churches in Budleigh Salterton, Newton Abbot, and South Street in Exeter offer little in the way of information. However, what records there are provide some insights into the nature of the angels of the churches. This is particularly the case in the Baptist churches at Budleigh Salterton and Newton Abbot.

Budleigh Salterton

Although the records kept by the Baptists at Budleigh Salterton are limited in respect of their educational program, some insights are available from the annual letter sent to the local Association. In their earliest minutes, the Baptists at Budleigh Salterton transcribed copies of these letters into the accounts of their church meetings. In addition to providing details of gains and losses to membership, many of these letters refer to attendance at the Sunday School or Bible Class. Thus, in the annual letter to the local Association, dated May 27, 1849, the Baptists at Budleigh Salterton announced the formation of a Sunday School. Then, in a similar letter dated May 19, 1884, they advised the Association that there had been a good attendance at the Bible Class.[35] While it is impossible to build a hypothesis on so little information, the formation of a Sunday School and the concern to report the number attending the Bible Class might suggest that the Budleigh Salterton Baptists were concerned that their members were familiar with the Scriptures. If this was the case, echoes of their concern might be seen in the financial contribution that they made to the Bible Society.[36]

Aside from the brief comments in letters to the Association, there is very little publicly available material that illustrates the nature of the midweek meeting in Budleigh Salterton and the sort of external organizations that the church was associated with. The exception to this are accounts from the 1940s and 1950s relating to the congregation's relationship with the Boys Brigade.

Budleigh Salterton and the Boys Brigade

In chapter 5, the relationship between Mr. Bulivant of Budleigh Salterton Baptist Church and Mr. Elston, the leader of the Boys Brigade Company linked to the congregation, was explored. This discussion revealed that during the 1940s, there was a clash of personalities between Mr. Bulivant, as minister, and Mr. Elston, as captain of the Boys Brigade. According to the later church records, these difficulties extended beyond a personality clash and resulted in the authorities who oversee the Boys Brigade as an organization investigating and eventually closing the Company linked to Budleigh Salterton Baptist Church. Details of this investigation were reported to the church by the Rev. Lane on June 18, 1958. At this meeting, the Rev. Lane advised the church that correspondence had been received from the Exeter and District Battalion of the Boys Brigade. The letter stated that the Boys Brigade executive, based

---

35. Minutes, May 27, 1849, 3548D M1, Budleigh Salterton Baptist Church minute book Oct. 1843–Apr. 1883, DHC; and minutes, May 19, 1884, 3548D M2, Budleigh Salterton Baptist Church minute book Aug. 1883–May 1902, DHC.

36. Minutes, Mar. 4, 1975, 3548D M8, Budleigh Salterton Baptist Church minute book Apr. 23, 1958–1975, DHC.

in London, had been made aware of irregularities in the finances of the Boys Brigade Company linked to the church. In addition to claiming that the Company was not being run on sound business lines, the letter also accused the organization of having a lack of discipline, little spiritual content, and only a loose association with the church.[37]

In the absence of Mr. Elston, Mr. Walters, the president of the Exeter and District Battalion of the Boys Brigade who had been invited to attend the meeting, addressed the church members. Mr. Walters explained that a meeting had taken place between representatives of the London executive, the local Boys Brigade leaders, and members of the church on June 10. Following this meeting, a letter had been received from the London executive stating that the Boys Brigade Company would have to close on August 31, 1958. The discussion that followed this announcement acknowledged two failures. The first concerned the lack of church oversight in the management of the Boys Brigade Company. The second was the failure by Mr. Elston to run the Company in accordance with the Boys Brigade Manual. Although Mr. Elston was not present at the meeting, the church members were advised that he had been requested to attend. In view of this and the seriousness of the accusations contained in the report, the church members accepted the information as it was presented to them and agreed that the Boys Brigade Company should close.

This episode in the life of Baptists at Budleigh Salterton is interesting, as operating the Boys Brigade Company might be seen as providing a contact point between the church and children and young people. Furthermore, as the Boys Brigade is an organization that operates with a Christian ethos and tradition, it might also be thought that hosting a Boys Brigade Company reflected the church's concern for the spiritual well-being of children and young people. If this were the case, it would support the suggestion that the congregation was committed to providing spiritual education for children. However, the accusation leveled by the London executive that the church had exercised a lack of oversight and provided little spiritual input suggests otherwise. Therefore, while the nineteenth-century letters to the local Association suggest that there was a concern for the spiritual instruction and oversight of children, by the twentieth century, the limitations of this concern are highlighted through their experience with the Boys Brigade. Although not sufficient to suggest that the angel of the church in Budleigh Salterton had become

---

37. Minutes, June 18, 1958, 3548D M8, DHC.

demonic, this episode in the life of the congregation does illustrate how a subtle shift in vocation can take place. It also suggests that, while in some areas of church life, the angel creates a gyroscopic effect, in others, it can be gradually redirected.

Newton Abbot

As for the educational program and relationship with other organizations in the Baptist church in Newton Abbot, their records reveal two interesting situations. The first relates to the focus of their church meetings, and the second reveals a willingness to share their building with an organization for which they have no oversight.

The Focus of the Church Meeting

The early records kept by the Baptists in Newton Abbot show that while they met monthly for a church meeting, this gathering was not always dedicated to discussing church business. This is evident from a decision taken on July 28, 1864. Here, the church members changed the focus of their church meetings. From this point forward, the Newton Abbot Baptists dedicated the monthly church meeting to discussing "spiritual things." As for the day-to-day business of church life, this would be reviewed at a quarterly meeting.[38]

The details of one of the church meetings where "spiritual things" were discussed are recorded on January 23, 1866. This was the format of the meeting:

- The minutes of the previous meeting were read and agreed.
- The pastor presented the claims of the Bible in Translation Society.
- An application for membership was dealt with.
- The pastor led a Bible study on chapters 9 and 10 of the book of Romans. The minutes also show that the focus of the pastor's address was to encourage God's people to reach out in mission as well as growing spiritually as individuals.
- Isaiah 66:1 was read and discussed.

---

38. Church meeting minutes, July 28, 1864, box 6916-1-1, Newton Abbot Baptist Church minute book Sept. 27, 1863–July 30, 1894, DHC.

- A church member read 1 Pet 4:1, commented on it, and led in prayer.
- Another member spoke on "engaging in prayer for the conversion of Souls."
- Communion was shared.
- The meeting ended with prayer.[39]

Even though the meeting was supposedly focused on "spiritual things," it is interesting to note that the minutes of the previous meeting were read and an application for membership was discussed. Aside from this, the schedule, with its multiple participants and focus on Bible study, preaching, prayer, and mission, shows a clear spiritual focus. It is also very similar to one of the earliest recorded patterns of Sunday worship attributed to Baptists. According to Christopher Ellis's research, the pattern of Bible study, where a text was read and members discussed its meaning, followed by sermons delivered by a number of individuals, is described in a letter dated 1609 by Hugh and Anne Bromhead in a letter to Sir William Hammerson.[40] Ellis suggests that this was a form of charismatic worship where the Scriptures were expounded and applied.[41] With this comment, Ellis is unlikely to be using the term "charismatic" to imply the use of the spiritual gifts. In a historic Baptist tradition, the term "charismatic" is likely to be used to describe the group leader being inspired by the Holy Spirit as they direct discussion of the Scriptures and their meaning. Alternatively, the term might also have been used to describe extemporary preaching or prayer.

The model of worship, where the Scriptures are interacted with and expounded, described by Ellis and echoed in the early records at Newton Abbot, is also an example of Baptist communities practicing theology together. This communal participation in forming theology to meet a current context is further illustrated in the twenty-first century in the discussion at Newton Abbot Baptist Church over what to do with Sunday evening services.

Within this discussion, the disagreements over how many times a week a worship service should be held and whether the cost of heating and lighting should be considered when making a decision on when

---

39. Church meeting minutes, July 28, 1864, box 6916-1-1, DHC.
40. Ellis, *Gathering*, 46, 264.
41. Ellis, *Gathering*, 47.

to hold worship services highlight the difficulties of applying a regulative principle to applying the laws of Christ. In Christian theology, the concept of a regulative principle often relates to the practice of worship. It insists that only those things included in the Bible should be used in a genuine expression of worship.[42]

The alternative to the regulative is the normative principle. This position accepts that not every aspect of life is referenced directly in the Bible; therefore, anything that is not directly prohibited by the Scriptures might be considered acceptable.[43] In the case of the discussion over Sunday evening worship services, the decisions over whether or not the cost of heating should be considered when discussing whether to continue the meeting would be covered by the normative principle. Likewise, the comment that there was not a biblical command to meet twice on a Sunday also falls into a normative principle.

Although the outcome of this discussion is not known, by raising the issues relating to the Sunday evening worship services, the Newton Abbot Baptists demonstrate a continued commitment to corporate theological reflection. Furthermore, this ability to engage with a theological reflection of a contemporary issue appears to be one of the positive aspects of the angel of the Baptist church in Newton Abbot. When the discussion over whether to continue with Sunday evening worship services is juxtaposed with the long-running debate over who should participate in the Lord's Supper, a pattern emerges. Although the indecision over whether or not the Lord's Table should be open or closed has been explored under the title of "Handling Conflict," at its heart, the dispute was a struggle to apply a theological principle to a contemporary issue.

Renting to an External Organization

Despite this commitment to applying theological debate to the day-to-day life of the church, the Newton Abbot Baptists appeared to act differently when it came to renting their premises to external organizations. This is highlighted by the records relating to the church's relationship with the Make a Life charity.

---

42. Owen, *Works of John Owen*, 464. Matthew Ward uses Owen's comments as the basis for his description of the regulative principle. See Ward, *Pure Worship*, 12, 126–27.

43. Ward, *Pure Worship*, 111–12, 26–27.

According to the records kept by the Baptists in Newton Abbot, it appears that during 2004 they had been allowing the charity to use their premises.[44] At the time of the meeting held on January 2, 2005, the charity had already been using the rooms for three days of the week, and at the church meeting, the deacons presented measures to formalize the arrangement. These included setting the level of rent and the installation of storage cupboards and a door lock. According to the church records, Make a Life was a relatively new charity whose aim was to encourage individuals who had recently recovered from mental illness to reintegrate into society.[45] In respect of Wink's comment relating to involvement with other organizations, the relationship with Make a Life illustrates that the Newton Abbot Baptists were willing to assist an organization that worked in an area that enhanced human life yet did not have an overtly Christian ethos. According to Wink's assessment, this sort of involvement may demonstrate a desire to reach the deeper needs of a community.[46] However, while making a room available might represent a desire to respond theologically to a need in the community, the rental income, realized by allowing the charity to use their premises, might also represent a form of pragmatism on the part of the Newton Abbot Baptists. If renting the premises to Make a Life represents an ingress of pragmatism in the twenty-first century, it marks a significant change in the nature of the church and its angel.

The Calvinistic Theology of the Newton Abbot Baptists

When the Baptist congregation at Newton Abbot was reformed in 1819, it was founded on a clear set of theological principles. In their foundational document, the Newton Abbot Baptists highlighted their Calvinistic stance:

> The important doctrine of the three equal persons in the Godhead: Eternal and Personal election: Original Sin: Particular redemption, Free justification by the imputation of Christ's righteousness: Efficacious Grace in Regeneration: The final perseverance of the saints: The resurrection of the dead: The day of judgment: The eternal blessedness of the saints: The eternal

---

44. Church meeting minutes, Jan. 2, 2005, box 6916, Newton Abbot Baptist Church minutes 2005, DHC.
45. Church meeting minutes, Jan. 2, 2005, box 6916, DHC.
46. Wink, *Unmasking the Powers*, 76.

misery of the wicked: with the congregational order of the church invisible...⁴⁷

The essence of this summary repudiates both the heterodoxy of Unitarianism and reducing the gospel message purely to moral behavior, all of which were prevalent among eighteenth-century General Baptists.[48] As for the issue of antinomianism, this is dealt with later in a procedure for addressing criminality and disorderly or reproachful speech.[49] Referencing both "Eternal and Personal election" suggests that the Newton Abbot Baptists practiced a moderate form of Calvinism.[50] This is unsurprising in the light of Roger Hayden's research on the nature of Calvinism at the Bristol Academy and within the Western Association during the eighteenth century.

The Bristol Academy and the Western Association

Hayden's published doctoral thesis challenges the perception that eighteenth-century Particular Baptists were predominantly high Calvinists.[51] He argues that through the ministry of Bernard Fosket and Hugh and Caleb Evans at the Bristol Academy, evangelical Calvinism had a significant impact on ministerial formation and, by association, the lives of local churches throughout the Particular Baptist Western Association.[52]

Pointing to the founding of the Western Association and the Somerset Confession of 1656, Norman Moon's history of the Bristol Baptist College presents a similar argument to Hayden's, contending that the Association and the Academy were committed to encouraging an evangelical form of Calvinism.[53] Peter Morden also supports Hayden's assessment that, due to the influence of the Western Association and the Bristol Academy, the first half of the nineteenth century was not totally dominated by high Calvinism.[54] However, having commended Hayden's

47. Gabb, Extracts, 2–3, 6916D/68, DHC.
48. Brown, *English Baptists of the Eighteenth Century*, 5–7.
49. Gabb, Extracts, 4–5, 6916D/68, DHC.
50. Gabb, "Short History of the Baptist Cause," 5, 6916D/67, Newton Abbot Baptist Church, 1947, DHC.
51. Hayden, *Continuity and Change*, xi.
52. Hayden, *Continuity and Change*, xi–xii.
53. Moon, *Education for Ministry*, 19.
54. Morden, *Offering Christ to the World*, 9.

work, Morden suggests that Hayden may have been over-optimistic in his assessment of the Academy's impact.[55]

In the context of this study, Hayden's hypothesis that the Western Association and Bristol Academy tempered the influence of high Calvinism is significant. According to Gabb's handwritten version of "A Short History of the Baptist Cause in Newton Abbot," between the years 1780 and 1786, the Baptist churches at Newton Abbot and Bovey Tracey went through a period of unsettled ministry.[56] During this episode, Caleb Evans, tutor and principal of the Bristol Academy,[57] had assisted with ministerial oversight of both churches.[58] Based on Hayden's argument for the tempering influence of the Bristol Academy and Caleb Evans's association with the churches at Bovey Tracey and the earliest Baptist congregation in Newton Abbot, it is safe to assume that both congregations practiced an evangelical, rather than high, form of Calvinism.

The Contrast Between the Baptists at Newton Abbot and Bovey Tracey

While the origins of the first Baptist church in Newton Abbot are unclear, the congregation formed in 1819 began when John Branscombe and six others left Bovey Tracey Baptist Church.[59] By stating their allegiance to the Particular form of Baptist ecclesiology and stating clearly their strict view of communion,[60] the founding members of the Baptist church in Newton Abbot made a statement of identity that distinguished them from the Baptists in Bovey Tracey.

The earliest records of the Baptist church at Bovey Tracey are contained in their church book. This covers the period 1773 to 1875 and provides records of new members, dismissals, and deaths. It also provides an important insight into the church's theology in respect of election and

---

55. Morden, *Offering Christ to the World*, 11.

56. Gabb, "Short History of the Baptist Cause," 4–5, 6916D/67, Newton Abbot Baptist Church, 1947, DHC.

57. Caleb Evans was a tutor at the Bristol Academy from 1758 and became principal in 1781. Moon, *Education for Ministry*, 140.

58. Gabb, "Short History of the Baptist Cause," 5, 6916D/67, 1947, DHC.

59. Bovey Tracey Baptist Church minute book, 1819 (the exact date is unreadable), 5547-0 3573, box 1400, East Dartmoor Baptist Church minutes 1795–1915, DHC.

60. Gabb, Extracts, 2, 6916D/68, DHC.

its stance on communion at the time of its formation. These are summarized in two key statements:

> We whose names are underwritten professing repentance towards God and faith towards the Lord Jesus Christ of different opinions respecting the subject and modes of baptism but our hope heartily united in the great essentials of Christianity...[61]

> ...to provoke one another unto love and good works and in the humble dependence upon the Holy Spirit's aid and influence to adorn the doctrine of God our savior, hoping and trusting that when we are removed from this Church militant on earth, we shall be received into the general assembly and Church triumphant in Heaven[62]

The lack of reference to election and predestination in the second of these extracts and the rest of the statement might suggest that the congregation at Bovey Tracey was formed as a General Baptist church. However, a lease agreement dated 1835 describes the church as being a Particular Baptist congregation.[63] This lack of clarity is further emphasized in the above statement regarding baptism and its relationship to church membership.

By stating that the church agrees to recognize differing positions on baptism, the Bovey Tracey Baptists appear to have formed a church with an open membership policy. If the opening statement was written when the church was formed, and there is no reason to suggest otherwise, adopting an open membership policy as early as 1773 is unusual. According to B. R. White, both the General Baptists and the New Connexion General Baptists maintained the policy and practice of closed membership until their inclusion in the Baptist Union in 1891.[64] As for the Particular Baptists, White suggests that while there are instances of Particular Baptist churches with open membership, their importance has been exaggerated by their interest to historians. He argues that following the Assembly of 1689, most Particular Baptist churches maintained a closed membership for a further one hundred and fifty years and, in

---

61. Dissenting Baptist's Church Year Book Bovey Tracey, July 22, 1773, front cover, 5447D add. 1, Bovey Tracey Baptist Church, DHC.

62. Dissenting Baptist's Church Year Book Bovey Tracey, July 22, 1773, front cover, 5447D add. 1, DHC.

63. D. Drew, The Revd Joseph L. Sprange and Mr William Tucker to Mr. William Bastow and others Lease for a Year, Dec. 6, 1839, 5547 D-0 3576, box 1404, DHC.

64. White, "Open and Closed Communion," 330.

some cases, longer.⁶⁵ In light of these comments, even if Bovey Tracey was formed as a Particular Baptist church, it is unusual in adopting an open membership policy. With a lack of clarity over whether the Baptists at Bovey Tracey were General or Particular Baptists and their uncommon position on church membership, it is perhaps unsurprising that the members who left to form a new church in Newton Abbot were concerned with defining their identity. This desire to define themselves is illustrated clearly in their theological stance and their views on who should be granted access to the Lord's Supper.

Church Membership and Sharing the Lord's Supper

At its heart, the debate over who should be allowed to participate at the Lord's Table is equally a dispute over ecclesiology and theology. In the new church at Newton Abbot, eligibility for membership is outlined in the first of their fifteen articles of faith:

> No person shall be admitted a member of this church, who does not contentiously believe the above doctrines [Personal election, Particular redemption, Free justification by the imputation of Christ's righteousness, Efficacious grace in regeneration, the final perseverance of the saints], and in a confession of his or her faith and experience before the Church, and if approved of by the whole membership then present, on his or her being baptised, shall be taken into full communion according to Regular Order.⁶⁶

By detailing a series of Calvinistic principles and placing them above a confession of faith and baptism, these Newton Abbot Baptists were making a clear statement of intent. Their church was to be thoroughly Calvinist in theology. Furthermore, by insisting on belief in their principles prior to baptism and acceptance by the present members, the church was demonstrating a desire to keep its Calvinistic principles pure.

This statement is also constructed in such a way as to suggest that baptism is the act of sealing belief. By placing baptism after the acceptance of specific doctrines and confession of a personal faith in Christ, baptism acts as a final step prior to commendation to the current membership. Therefore, baptism is viewed as a testimony not only

---

65. White, "Open and Closed Communion," 332.
66. Gabb, Extracts, 2–3, 6916D/68, DHC.

of personal faith but also of correct doctrine and thus provides an important line of demarcation.

In view of this, the desire expressed by the townsfolk to share the Lord's Supper with those with whom they were already sharing worship is understandable. However, it is also evident that allowing non-members to share in the Lord's Supper invites questions regarding the relationship between Christian faith and baptism and whether a person has to be baptized as a believer to be accepted as a church member. In view of the complexity of these questions, it is perhaps unsurprising that the Baptists at Newton Abbot vacillated over whether the Lord's Table should be open or closed. However, in their inability to settle on a fixed position, the Baptists at Newton Abbot exhibited a desire to create a theology that was both orthodox and relevant to their situation. They also demonstrated a commitment to creating this theology through conversation at the church meeting. This, in turn, marks the Newton Abbot Baptists out as a church that is willing to practice theological reflection as a community.

Reflecting Theologically as a Community

Haymes discusses communal theological reflection as he explores the relationship between theology and identity in *Doing Theology in a Baptist Way*. He concludes that if Baptists have a specific way of practicing theology, it is related to their understanding of the church as a gathered community. Furthermore, as Baptists have traditionally rejected the idea of giving authority to creeds, they have needed to continually renew their theology. This requirement to adapt their theology in response to the challenges of the current generation is also linked to the liberty of each church to discern the will and purpose of God for their congregation.[67] If this is the case, the continual renewal and application of theological principles poses a considerable challenge to Wink's thesis that the spirit of an organization changes little from generation to generation.[68] Of course, just because Haymes believes that a congregation should be involved in remaking its theology in each generation, this does not mean that this is the usual practice among Baptist churches. Therefore, if there is a discontinuity between theory and practice among Baptists, Wink's thesis that the internal nature of an organization transcends its current

67. Haymes, "Theology and Baptist Identity," 3–5.
68. Wink, *Unmasking the Powers*, 79.

generation will be proven correct in substance, even if it is incorrect in theory.[69] Furthermore, a situation where Baptists fail to remake their theology in each generation might also reveal the resilience of the angel of the church implied in Wink's concept.

Worship

In the final section of Wink's statement on denominational rubrics, theology, and worship, he argues that there is a paradox in worship and believes that while the influence of the angel of the church is experienced most acutely in worship, it remains predominantly hidden. In this respect, the act of preaching among Baptists simultaneously reveals a commitment to being a people whose theology is shaped by the Scriptures while also being pragmatic in their use when discerning and applying Christ's laws. This tension between spiritual discernment and pragmatism is evident in the relationship Baptists have with preaching, and specifically how they use preaching as a method of discerning the call of a new minister.

Preaching

If theology is a corporate act among Baptists, and their vocation is the application of the laws of Christ in a current generation and social context, then the preached word has, for Baptists, historically played a significant role in the act of worship.

In 1734, John Gill used 1 Tim 4:16 as the basis for his sermon "The Mutual Duty of Pastor and People." The sermon was preached at the ordination of George Braithwaite and urged the newly ordained minister to spend time each day meditating on the Scriptures and in prayer. What is more, Gill also suggests that, in addition to reading the Scriptures each day, ministers should read widely from other published works.[70]

Similarly, in 2008, as part of his address to the twenty-second Lester C. Randall Preaching Fellowship Lecture, Haymes states:

> The preacher is not in the pulpit to announce his or her own views, as if the task is to match the Sunday newspaper columnists for entertainment or influence. The preacher has a responsibility to expound and proclaim the Christian Faith, the

---

69. Wink, *Unmasking the Powers*, 79.
70. Gill, "Mutual Duty of Pastor and People," 9.

> God centered interpretation of life and history. It is why the church properly requires those years of preparation, of study of the Scriptures, and the story of the church's reflection through the generations on the Scriptures.[71]

Although these quotations are taken from a different era, they both reveal a commitment to seeking the will of God through interacting with the Scriptures. There is also an indication that the Scriptures need to be reflected upon in light of current events. Thus, while the biblical text is the basis from which the sermon begins, the preaching event places the sermon in the context of the ongoing story of God and his relationship with the church. This is not to say that the biblical text acts as a pretext upon which contemporary events are spoken of, but rather that the principles drawn from Scripture should form the basis for the congregation's response to current events. This interplay between the biblical text and the current situation is also necessary to encourage a faith that is relevant both in the time that it is preached and the context into which the sermon is delivered. This correlation between the ancient text and the contemporary context fulfills Judith Lieu's understanding of a textual community. In Lieu's opinion, a textual community is a place where the people are shaped by the text and reshape it as they live together.[72]

Lieu's concept of a community being shaped by a text while simultaneously reshaping its meaning for the current generation resonates with Haymes's understanding of how Baptists practice their theology. However, when it comes to the relationship between preaching and the appointment of a new minister, it might be argued that Baptists act more pragmatically than theologically.

Preaching and the Appointment of a New Minister

After preliminary meetings with the church leadership or search committee, the prospective candidate is invited to preach with a view to the pastorate.[73] This process, often shortened to "preach with a view," allows the wider church, through the sermon, to interact with the text and discern whether God is calling the candidate to be their pastor.

---

71. Haymes, "Integrity in Preaching Lecture," 5. Also Haymes, "Integrity in Preaching," 7.

72. Lieu, *Christian Identity*, 27.

73. Ministry Department of the Baptist Union, *Facing a Pastoral Vacancy*, 17.

While not dismissing this process, Michael Quicke is critical of it on the grounds that congregations are seldom offered guidance on how to interact with the sermon as a means of discernment. Furthermore, most preachers are assessed according to pragmatism and personal preference.[74] Quicke's critique is supported by four of the major publications dealing with church administration and dealing with a pastoral vacancy: *The Order and Administration of a Baptist Church*,[75] *Church Administration*,[76] *Guidelines for Churches Seeking Full-Time Ministers*,[77] and *Facing a Pastoral Vacancy*.[78] While J. R. Wood and Samuel Chick suggest that church members devote themselves to prayer both as individuals and corporately,[79] and *Facing a Pastoral Vacancy* supplies a list of possible questions to ask a prospective minister,[80] neither provides guidance on how the church should approach the preach with a view event. Likewise, the extent of the advice given in *Guidelines for Churches Seeking Full-Time Ministers* is that members should be encouraged to attend the worship service where the candidate will preach, not make hasty decisions, and that the name of the prospective minister should not be published in the church magazine without consent.[81]

Appointing a Minister at Budleigh Salterton

Pragmatism certainly played a role in the ministerial appointment process at Budleigh Salterton Baptist Church. This is particularly evident in the 1960s when the congregation sought to appoint a replacement for the Rev. Lance.

At a church meeting held on October 5, 1960, Mr. McLeod was rejected on the basis that it might cause the church financial hardship, as he was not accredited with the Baptist Union. The Rev. W. D. Edwards was rejected because he was unmarried, as the meeting believed "a wife would be an asset to the church." What is more, the Rev. Edwards's age also

---

74. Quicke, "Further Reflections," 18–19.
75. Wood and Chick, *Manual of the Order*, 19–24.
76. Bacon, *Church Administration*, 11–18.
77. General Superintendents of the Baptist Union, *Guidelines for Churches*, 9.
78. Ministry Department of the Baptist Union, *Facing a Pastoral Vacancy*, 16–17.
79. Wood and Chick, *Manual of the Order*, 20.
80. Ministry Department of the Baptist Union, *Facing a Pastoral Vacancy*, 32–33.
81. General Superintendents of the Baptist Union, *Guidelines for Churches Seeking Full-Time Ministers*, 9.

factored against him as the meeting thought that they should appoint an experienced minister.[82] Later, on December 13, 1960, the Rev. S. W. Cowley was also rejected because he was not accredited by the Baptist Union,[83] and the Rev. Lawrence because of his poor health.[84] In each of these cases, the potential minister appears to have been rejected for purely practical reasons. Although this does not rule out the possibility that God was not calling any of these candidates to the pastorate at Budleigh Salterton, it does appear that the congregation made their decision based on personal preference rather than theological discussion.

Appointing a Minister at Newton Abbot

Likewise, the records kept by the Baptists in Newton Abbot also hint at personal preference playing a role in bringing a ministerial candidate to the church meeting. Meeting with the regional minister on August 7, 1984, the deacons of Newton Abbot Baptist Church expressed their preference for "a pastor showing spiritual excitement and openness," while cautious of "a particular brand of charismatic experience."[85]

The issue of caution over "a particular brand of charismatic experience" suggests that there is a reticence, either among the leaders or the wider church, to engage with the resurgence of the charismatic experience promoted by the Charismatic Movement. This movement became prominent during the 1980s. Unfortunately, the records do not show if this reticence was the voice of an individual or a group of leaders. Neither do they reveal whether their concern was shared by a portion of, or the whole church. All that the records actually show is that following their discussion with the regional minister, a candidate was invited to meet the deacons. He subsequently met with the church, preached with a view, and was called to the pastorate. However, even here, the records lack clarity as the details of the candidate's conversation with the deacons are not recorded.

While twentieth-century theologians such as Haymes, Quicke, and Ellis speak of the importance of preaching to the lives of Baptist

---

82. Minutes, Oct. 5, 1960, 3548D M8, Budleigh Salterton Baptist Church minute book Apr. 23, 1958–1975, DHC.

83. Minutes, Dec. 13, 1960, 3548D M8, DHC.

84. Minutes, Dec. 1960, 3548D M8, DHC.

85. Deacons meeting minutes, p. 79, box 6916-1-8, Newton Abbot Baptist Church minute book Aug. 7, 1984–June 5, 1995, DHC.

churches, when it comes to recording the outcome of a preach with a view, very little comment is made. Furthermore, what records there are err toward Quicke's assumption that personal preference and pragmatism play a significant part in the discernment process. Of the three churches that are the focus of this dissertation, only the records of South Street in Exeter hint that the preach with a view process is anything but a process ruled by pragmatism and personal preference. Recording the process of calling the Rev. Haymes to the pastorate in 1968, the church meeting first enters into a long conversation on the percentage of votes necessary to issue a call to the pastorate before finally deciding to extend the call to the Rev. Haymes.[86] Although the presenting issue here is one of constitutional order, the need for a "lengthy discussion" suggests that the fellowship was keen to ensure that the process of calling a minister was correct. It also suggests that there had been some form of engagement with the earlier preach with a view that required expression through the voting system at the church meeting.

As with the discussion over the nature of the angel in respect of a Baptist church using a purely democratic decision-making process, the spiritual nature of the angel of the church might also be questioned if pragmatism and personal preference were the only reasons for calling a minister to the pastorate. The link between pragmatism and the nature of the angel is also significant as it is likely that it will be the pastor who will both recognize the flaws in the angel's nature and seek to address them. Furthermore, because the nature of the angel is transcendent, it is usually addressed through the spiritual disciplines of prayer and preaching. In view of this, if a church is unable to engage with the process of preaching with a view to the pastorate as a means of discerning the divine will, it is unlikely to be able to engage with preaching as a method of transforming their angel.

Despite the obvious pragmatism surrounding the preach with a view process, the very fact that a prospective minister is expected to preach as part of the discernment process is a tribute to the church's desire to engage with the text as well as the preacher. It also adds credence to the argument that the interaction with Scripture, as an attempt to discern and apply Christ's laws, plays a significant role in understanding Baptist congregations.

---

86. Minutes, p. 119, 75-9 add. 1-1, South Street Baptist Church, Exeter, minute book Mar. 11, 1964–May 14, 1974, DHC.

While there might be an argument that the process of preaching with a view to the pastorate reflects a pragmatic approach to theology rather than the exercise of a robust theological debate, the seventeenth-century debate among Particular Baptists over hymn singing was very different. According to Matthew Ward, the seriousness with which the early Baptists approached the subject of worship was more significant than any other subject in highlighting how they interacted with Scripture.[87] Furthermore, such was the enthusiasm of the debate that Ward considers the debate over hymn singing to have been seriously damaging among Particular Baptists.[88]

Hymn Singing

The introduction of hymns to the pattern of reading Scripture, prayer, and preaching was relatively early in Baptist history. John Briggs argues that while congregational singing was initially forbidden from communal worship, things began to change during the years of the Commonwealth.[89] However, he also contends that it was the loss of hymn writers to the Fifth Monarchists and the Quakers that led Baptists to reshape their liturgy.[90] This appears to concur with Ward's conclusion that, for some, singing should form part of the universal recognition that praising God was central to Christian worship.[91]

However, in the light of Briggs's comment, the reshaping of worship among Baptists is most evident through the ministry and leadership of Benjamin Keach. Keach began his ministry in the 1650s as a General Baptist; however, acting on a conviction that an Arminian understanding of Christ's atonement was incorrect, he later became a Calvinist.[92]

The process by which Keach introduced congregational hymn singing was a protracted one and is described in detail by his son-in-law, Thomas Crosby.[93] Crosby explains that Keach first introduced the

---

87. Ward, *Pure Worship*, 119.
88. Ward, *Pure Worship*, 175.
89. Briggs, "English Baptists and Their Hymnody," 153.
90. Briggs, "English Baptists and Their Hymnody," 153.
91. Ward, *Pure Worship*, 175.
92. Copeland, *Benjamin Keach*, 3.
93. Underwood, *History of the English Baptists*, 132.

singing of a hymn at the end of the communion service.⁹⁴ In the light of the commitment of early Baptists to shaping their worship on the basis of the Scriptures, this makes perfect sense as it echoes the practice recorded in Matt 26:30 and Mark 14:26. However, according to Crosby, the process of moving the church from singing a single hymn at the end of the communion service toward regularly singing hymns as part of worship was a long one and was not without its critics. It was six years before Keach introduced hymns to the celebration of notable thanksgiving services and a further fourteen years before congregational singing became a regular part of Sunday worship.⁹⁵

Despite the patient, pastoral concern that Keach demonstrates by introducing change over such a protracted period and the fellowship's willingness to follow his leadership, not all Baptists accepted congregational singing as part of their worship. In 1678, the "influential General Baptist Layman" Thomas Grantham published *Christianismus Primitivus*, critiquing congregational singing, claiming that it was unbiblical.⁹⁶ Grantham referred back to John Smyth's belief that if songs could take place in worship, something Smyth doubted, they should be similar to the examples found in the Psalms and other parts of Scripture.⁹⁷ Therefore, if congregational singing did not fit within these stringent criteria, it should be considered simply a form of art and, as such, not a true expression of worship.⁹⁸

In addition to his argument that singing should be only considered to be a form of art, Grantham was also concerned that singing written songs was no different than reading set prayers,⁹⁹ something that early Baptists had earnestly resisted. The issue here was two-fold: firstly, with the whole congregation singing a pre-composed song, the same words would come from the mouths of both believers and unbelievers, which was a promiscuous use of language.¹⁰⁰ Additionally, the use of set songs restricted the spontaneous movement of the Spirit in worship.

---

94. Crosby, *History of the English Baptists*, 298.

95. Crosby, *History of the English Baptists*, 299.

96. Briggs, "English Baptists and Their Hymnody," 154.

97. John Smyth, *Differences of the Churches of the Separation* (1605), cited in Copeland, *Benjamin Keach*, 118.

98. Thomas Grantham, *Christianismus Primitivus* (1678), cited in Copeland, *Benjamin Keach*, 118.

99. Briggs, "English Baptists and Their Hymnody," 154.

100. Briggs, "English Baptists and Their Hymnody," 154.

Keach countered the argument over spontaneity, claiming that, just as the Spirit was at work in the preparation of his sermons, the Spirit was equally capable of working through set hymns. The question of promiscuity was more serious and, among Particular Baptists, led to a heated discussion at the 1692 Assembly. According to Briggs, both sides in the debate were censured by the Assembly for a lack of self-control and infighting.[101] While Briggs notes that the promiscuous use of language formed part of the Assembly's deliberation, he does not say how the argument was resolved.[102] However, despite the debates over the legitimacy of congregational hymn singing, the number of participating churches continued to increase.[103]

Alongside the questions of spiritual inspiration and the promiscuous use of language, consideration was also given to the scriptural foundation for congregational singing. In the case of early Baptists, this is a further example of the liberty of Baptist congregations to interpret and apply the Scriptures to their situation and life together. Of course, as has been previously mentioned, this liberty also means that there will be differing opinions within and without a congregation. In respect of Keach's introduction of hymns to public worship, the debate with the London button-maker Isaac Marlow was significant. This debate became public when, in 1690, Marlow published *A Discourse Concerning Singing in the Publick Worship of God in the Gospel Church*.[104] According to Copeland, the essence of Marlow's argument was that prayer and praise were an experience of the inner self.[105] Therefore, just as there was unspoken prayer and "unspeakable joy," so rejoicing was an "inward Glory and Melody of the heart."[106] Copeland points out that Marlow supports his argument by referencing Eph 5:19–20 and Col 3:16, both of which speak of singing and making music "in your heart/s."[107] Ironically, these are the same verses used by Keach to support his argument for outward, vocal, congregational singing. When it came to singing Psalms, as opposed to hymns, Marlow pointed to the opening verses

---

101. Briggs, "English Baptists and Their Hymnody," 154.
102. Briggs, "English Baptists and Their Hymnody," 154.
103. Briggs, "English Baptists and Their Hymnody," 155.
104. Copeland, *Benjamin Keach*, 124.
105. Copeland, *Benjamin Keach*, 128.
106. Isaac Marlow, *A Brief Discourse Concerning Singing* (1690), 8, cited in Copeland, *Benjamin Keach*, 128.
107. Copeland, *Benjamin Keach*, 125.

of Ps 137 and argued that there was no congregational singing prior to the time of King David and, following that, singing only took place on joyous occasions.[108] Copeland suggests that, for Marlow, if there were to be singing, it should be a solo presented by the priest. Finally, Marlow concluded that there was no evidence from the Davidic psalms that the church should be involved in corporate singing.[109]

In a contemporary context, Marlow's arguments may appear somewhat obscure; however, they do provide an insight into the struggle to apply the Scriptures to a contemporary discussion. The debate with Keach also illustrates a genuine desire that worship be a fitting tribute offered to God. Arguing from this perspective, Ward contends that the disagreement over hymn singing was, at its root, a desire that the correct criteria be set for God to be praised in song.[110]

Choosing Hymn Books

The question of what is, or is not, a fitting tribute to God and thus acceptable in worship does not appear to have received the same scrutiny among the congregations at Newton Abbot and Budleigh Salterton during the eighteenth, nineteenth, and twentieth centuries. However, equipping the congregation for worship, particularly with respect to singing and the types of songs used, is discussed by the Baptists at Newton Abbot on September 25, 2000:

> G reported that the group who had asked to come to a conclusion concerning the choice of hymn books recommended that it should be the Complete Mission Praise. A list of prices were presented and it would appear that 60 word copies, 10 large print copies, and 2 music copies would amount to just over £800. We will commence using them on the last Sunday in October, which would be our Minister's anniversary. We will be opening an appeal for pledges immediately. We will dispose of the existing Let's Praise and Mission Praise books either to individuals or groups who need them.[111]

---

108. Copeland, *Benjamin Keach*, 125.

109. Isaac Marlow, *A Brief Discourse Concerning Singing* (1690), 14, cited in Copeland, *Benjamin Keach*, 129.

110. Ward, *Pure Worship*, 176.

111. Church meeting minutes, Sept. 25, 2000, box 6916, Newton Abbot Baptist Church minute book 2000, DHC.

Three key issues arise from this report. The first is that the choice of a replacement hymn book was delegated to a small group. This suggests that the members selected to form the small group were trusted by the church members. It also indicates that the decision made by the group would be sympathetic to the types of songs that were currently being used while open to those that might form a part of future worship services. Based on the broader scope, the records kept by the Newton Abbot Baptists during this period, delegating the choice of hymn book to a small group suggests that there was no real dissension over the types of songs the church might use during their worship services.

The second notable point arising from this report is the intention to mark the minister's anniversary by introducing the new hymn book. Considering the tension that arose over the move to Highweek School, this action suggests a degree of warmth and respect toward the minister was present in 2000.

Perhaps the most significant issue arising from the choice of new hymn books relates to the request that church members pledge money for their purchase. By calling for individuals to contribute toward the cost of hymn books, it appears that there was an expectation that the financial burden would not be borne purely by the church budget. This record echoes a similar episode noted in the church minutes for 1952. Here, on September 10, the church meeting was informed that new hymn books were being purchased, and individuals were given the opportunity to purchase a copy.[112] This repetition, if only once in a generation, suggests that within the nature of the angel of the Baptist church at Newton Abbot lies an expectation that the church members will equip themselves to participate in sung worship.

The Practicalities of Worship

Although the decision to renew hymn books is not frequently recorded in the minute books at either Newton Abbot or Budleigh Salterton, the practicalities of the worship are often discussed. This extract from the records kept by the Baptists at Budleigh Salterton illustrates the sort of conversation that takes place:

---

112. Minutes, p. 22, 6916D-1-9, Newton Abbot Baptist Church minute book Oct. 10, 1951–Dec. 18, 1963, DHC.

> The question for discussion came re. time of evening services during winter months, many elder members were in favour of 4pm as last year.
>
> A vote was taken 10 for it was decided to commence Jan. 5 until Feb 23, then return to the usual 6.30 time. Rev . . . . said he would try and obtain some literature on Operation Agri, as a Church we had shown much interest in this work. Sunday Jan 26 was to be leprosy Sunday and members left it to the deacons to decide if [the] loose collection this day could be for this work.[113]

This passage provides a digest of a wide-ranging discussion that not only covers the practicalities of the Sunday worship service but also its content. During the conversation, the church members affirm their commitment to worshiping on Sunday evening but recognize the pastoral issues associated with the winter months. Although the above excerpt addresses the issue of attending evening services on a winter's night, it does not accurately reflect the level of commitment to the temporary change in time. While the minutes show that ten members voted in favor, they do not record the number who voted against or abstained. A closer inspection of the records reveals that fifteen members attended the meeting. In view of this, it appears that a third of the members present either voted against the motion or abstained. Although the concerns of those against the motion are not recorded, the fact that such a large minority failed to support the temporary change to the time of the evening service suggests that the time of a worship service was a sensitive subject among the Baptists in Budleigh Salterton.

The reference to Operation Agri and the Leprosy Mission highlights two aspects of worship at Budleigh Salterton Baptist Church. First, it appears that introducing the work of missionary organizations was an accepted part of the Sunday service. What is more, the way the record is framed, it appears that Operation Agri had recently been introduced to the congregation, whereas the Leprosy Mission had received previous interest and support. This suggests that not only were new missionary causes regularly introduced to the church, but the congregation's interest encompassed both Baptist and non-Baptist causes.[114]

---

113. Minutes, Nov. 27, 1974, 3548D M8, Budleigh Salterton Baptist Church minute book Apr. 23, 1958–1975, DHC.

114. Operation Agri is an overseas, Baptist, urban development project. The Leprosy Mission is a non-denominational charitable organization working worldwide to alleviate the suffering caused by leprosy.

Finally, it could be argued that delegating the decision to financially support the Leprosy Mission is likely to be because the deacons have a better grasp of the church's current financial position. If this was the case, this may reflect the congregation's concern for the level of church finances. Therefore, it is to be expected that the deacons would be able to determine whether the church could afford to pass on the loose offering.

Although this section from the records kept by the Budleigh Salterton Baptists appears to discuss the practicalities of Sunday worship, it also provides an insight into the strengths and weaknesses of the church and its angel. With regard to the times that worship should be held, there is an inner resistance to change tempered by the practicalities of pastoral concern. Likewise, in the case of supporting external organizations, while there appears to be a genuine interest in the work of overseas missions, there may be a lingering concern about the church's ability to contribute financially.

Summary

Exploring Wink's reference to denominational rubrics, theology and worship in respect of the angel of the church reveals some important indicators in the quest to discover the nature and vocation of a congregation's angel. Among Baptists, the liberty of a local congregation to interpret and apply the laws of Christ to their context is important. However, this liberty does not come without its dangers. By allowing each church the freedom to discern and apply the laws of Christ to their situation, Baptists create an opportunity for the church to act without reference to other congregations or the local Association. While Baptist commentators reject the concept of individual self-sufficiency in favor of association, the experiences of the Newton Abbot congregation suggest isolation still takes place. What is more, the poor response to the request for help issued by the Baptist at Newton Abbots and South Street in Exeter implies that even when a church invites help from other congregations, the assistance may not be forthcoming.

Although isolation is a danger for Baptists, the emphasis on the liberty to express the will and purpose of God in a local context enables the Baptist Union of Great Britain and local Associations to exercise oversight with a light touch. While this corresponds with Wink's belief that denominational rubrics allow for the use of a variety of forms of liturgy in worship, it also contrasts with his belief that theological focus is set by the denomination. Of course, the control exercised by a denominational rubric may reflect Wink's Methodist tradition rather than the experience of Baptists. Furthermore, the liberty to express the laws of Christ by a congregation within a specific place and time allows each church the opportunity to continually review its theology. In the case of the Newton Abbot Baptists, this appears to have become part of their tradition. Even when internal tensions are present within the congregation, the church meeting continues to enter into a debate over how to apply theology to a contemporary problem.

Vocation and the Nature of the Angel

Although the records from the Baptist churches at Budleigh Salterton and Newton Abbot supplied very little information on the sort of midweek meetings held by the congregations, they did offer an insight into some of the issues that shape their vocation.

At Budleigh Salterton, the difficulties experienced with respect to the Boys Brigade may have revealed more than a clash of personalities between the leaders of the church and the organization. The lack of spiritual oversight highlighted by the London executive of the Boys Brigade might also suggest a tension between the desire to offer spiritual guidance to children and young people and an inability to work effectively with an external organization.

In Newton Abbot, the willingness to rent a room to the Make a Life charity appears to fulfill Wink's belief that links with external organizations can be a method by which the church expresses its concerns for some of the deep issues of society. However, the fact that the room was let to the charity for rent also raises the question of pragmatism. In light of Wink's belief that a congregation's vocation plays a significant part in forming its angel, the ingress of pragmatism poses a significant danger to the church. While pragmatism might assist the church in fulfilling its vocation, there is always a possibility that it will lead the church in a different direction. According to Wink, if this were to happen, the angel of the church would become demonic.

Pragmatism

This issue of pragmatism was particularly evident in the churches at Newton Abbot and Budleigh Salterton when they sought to discern the call of prospective ministerial candidates. Although Baptists have historically placed a high value on the preached word, when examined in relation to their discerning the call of a new pastor, the process of preaching with a view appears to be as much a pragmatic exercise as it is one of spiritual discernment. If this is the case, the possibility of appointing a person with a similar outlook and values is increased. This, in turn, may limit the ability of the appointee to address the nature of the angel and ensure that the church continues to concentrate on its vocation.

Worship

If the question of pragmatism lies at the heart of the process of discerning the call of a new pastor, it does not seem to be as prevalent when it comes to discussing worship. Although the church meetings at both Newton Abbot and Budleigh Salterton Baptists appear only to discuss the practicalities of Sunday worship, these discussions reveal a great deal about the underlying nature of the church and its angel. In Newton Abbot, there appears to be an understanding within the church that members will equip themselves for worship by paying for their own copies of the church hymn book. In respect of the Baptists at Budleigh Salterton, the practicalities of Sunday worship appear to reveal a commitment to overseas mission. However, the records at Budleigh Salterton also hint at tension over changing the times of regular worship services.

If, as Wink suggests, the worship is where the nature of the angel of the church is most acutely experienced, the fact that, in the twentieth and twenty-first centuries, church records reveal so little theological reflection on the weekly worship service is disappointing. However, within the discussions over the practicalities of church worship some issues of theology are exposed.

Theology

Although Baptist scholars such as Bacon, Haymes, and Holmes contend that the church meeting is a place where God's will is discerned, it is often treated as a business meeting. Even so, there are occasions when a theological position is both discussed and either upheld or rejected within a church meeting. This is particularly evident in the early life of the Newton Abbot Baptists. Between 1819 and 1863, the congregation struggled with their decision to follow a Calvinistic form of theology coupled with a strict view of communion. The church wrestled with the theological consequences of their actions as they both opened and then subsequently closed the table. The dispute was eventually settled by the church dividing and with those members advocating open communion being sent to the new building in East Street.

The Limitations of Church Records

It is evident that Wink's contention that denominational rubrics, the nature of midweek meetings, theology, and worship all contribute to the nature of the angel of the church is validated by records kept by Baptist congregations. However, it is not clear from this exploration whether there is sufficient information in the records kept by Baptist churches to assess the degree to which these aspects of church life influence the nature of a particular angel. In this respect, discerning the facet of the angel's nature that is formed by a congregation's theology might require being present within the worshiping community rather than simply reviewing their historical records.

The next chapter will explore how a church understands itself. This is the last facet of church life that Wink refers to with respect to observing the nature of the angel of the church.

7

Self-Understanding

WINK'S FINAL SUGGESTION FOR discerning the angel of the church is self-understanding. He introduces this section by asking the following questions:

> How does a congregation see itself? How do others see it? Does the membership confer status, or does it indicate a high level of commitment to mission? Is the church inner- or outer-directed? Is it related to its neighborhood or the larger community? Is it self-engrossed, or engaged in struggles for social justice and global peace? Is it evangelistic or nurturing, or both? Is it on speaking terms with its angel, and fired by a sense of divine vocation, or is it a country club or haven against the chill of rapid social change? What is the place of spirituality, or prayer and meditation, of the inner journey? Is it easy to "get on board," to become drawn into the life of the group? What about its history, its traditions, its annual celebrations, its invariant money-raisers and teas? Who have been its heroes and villains, and what are the skeletons in its closet?[1]

Summarizing these twelve questions, Wink tells the story of two English churches that had persistently resisted the efforts of a new rector to unite them. According to Wink, the reason for this resistance was that one church had failed to warn the other of an invasion by the Vikings in the ninth century.[2]

1. Wink, *Unmasking the Powers*, 77.
2. Wink, *Unmasking the Powers*, 77.

In addition to including a section on self-understanding, Wink also explores the corporate spirit of an organization using the motor manufacturer General Motors as an illustration. According to Wink:

> General Motors has its own unique spirit that sets it apart from every other corporation. . . . Corporate structures have a remarkable resilience through time. Change all the employees at General Motors and replace them with new ones the next day, and GM would probably go right on doing the same kinds of things it has always done and in something of the same manner. Like a river which is never made up of the same water molecules, yet remains the same river from one moment to the next, or the human body, which changes all its cells over a period of seven years, institutions also undergo the perpetual turnover of their employees without necessarily changing their essential nature.[3]

The combination of questions that Wink asks, along with the illustrations of the Viking invasion and the manufacturing process of General Motors, introduces a number of concepts that might assist the observer to understand the nature of the angel of the church. While the Viking story might be explored by examining its collective memory, the General Motors illustration lends itself to being assessed using theories of emergence and transition. Furthermore, how a church functions might also be studied using family systems theory. Finally, as Wink believes that vocation provides a significant key to understanding the nature of the angel of the church, this chapter will suggest where the basis of a congregation's vocation might be found.

Collective Memory

According to Maurice Halbwachs, memories are created and stored through social interaction. He contends that, throughout a typical day, memories are most often recalled in response to a question from another person.[4] However, these recollections are not accounts of a historical event as, rather than preserving a past event with all its contextual nuances, memory represents a reconstructed image of the event in a new, present context.[5] Peter Novick illustrates this phenomenon in his work

---

3. Wink, *Unmasking the Powers*, 79.
4. Halbwachs, *On Collective Memory*, 38.
5. Halbwachs, *On Collective Memory*, 40.

The Holocaust in American Life. Novick is intrigued by the way Americans have been unsettled by the Holocaust. He argues that while many Americans have not personally experienced the Holocaust or encountered its survivors since the 1970s, the subject has taken an increasingly prominent place in American culture.[6] For Novick, this is an example of Halbwachs's contention that a collective memory is an imposition of the present on the past. Thus, the growing concern for the perpetrators, survivors, and repercussions of the Holocaust are a present concern rather than the manifestation of a repressed emotion.[7] Therefore, in this context, collective memory provides a framework within which a number of reconstructed images, each belonging to a group member, are fused together to form a present response to a past event. Therefore, Wink's story of the church that refuses to forgive their neighbor as a result of the Viking invasion illustrates how a collective memory defined one congregation in respect of another. Furthermore, if Wink's illustration is based on a true story, the relationship between the two churches appears to have been blighted by the collective memory of the offended church over hundreds of years. Although none of the churches in this study have the extended collective memory of the two churches in Wink's illustration, there are hints to how resilient a collective memory can become.

Collective Memory Among the Newton Abbot Baptists

At several points in this study, reference has been made to the relationship between the Baptists in Newton Abbot and their building on East Street. In the chapter on architecture and ambience, it was suggested that when the new chapel in East Street was opened it gave the Newton Abbot church a significant status among West Country Baptists. Thus, when, in the early twenty-first century, the number of members had fallen to such a level that they could no longer maintain the building, the congregation found it very difficult to move to a new set of premises. If the theory of collective memory is used to interpret this move, the anxiety in the church meetings prior to leaving the East Street building would have been intensified by the fact that the new premises, in Highweek School, did not belong to the congregation. Furthermore, based on the importance placed on the building at the opening ceremony, moving from their

---

6. Novick, *Holocaust in American Life*, 2.
7. Novick, *Holocaust in American Life*, 3.

own building to premises owned by the local authority might suggest that the Baptists at Newton Abbot gave up their status symbol.

Emergence

According to Philip Clayton, contemporary theories of emergence have developed in response to the failure of science to explain all aspects of the natural world in terms of physical laws and objects.[8] In view of this, emergence theories provide a philosophical alternative to an empirical explanation by physical observation. Exploring this concept in relation to theology, Niels Henrik Gregersen begins by suggesting that the way water crystallizes as temperature falls; fire and gunpowder interact, causing explosions; birds flock; languages change with the addition of new words, and their reinterpretation, are examples of the sort of phenomena that emergence theories might explain.[9] Obviously, these examples are drawn from the physical sciences and linguistics; however, as Gregersen's contribution to *The Re-Emergence of Emergence* suggests, there is a metaphysical dimension to emergence theory that impacts religious experience and, therefore, on the nature and function of the church.

Reflecting on emergence from philosophical and theological perspectives, Gregersen suggests that there are five ways that emergence theory can be understood theologically: "flat religious naturalism," "evolving theistic naturalism," "atemporal theism," "temporal theism," and "eschatological theism."[10]

Flat Religious Naturalism

Flat religious naturalism views creation as it is. Thus, the emergence of novelty and diversity is seen as the product of a straightforward development in physical and chemical structure.[11] From an anthropological perspective, this viewpoint is supported through observing the differing challenges faced by individual churches as a result of their geographical locations and social demographics. Thus, each of the seven letters to the churches in Revelation addresses different issues, each of which

8. Clayton, "Conceptual Foundations of Emergence Theory," 1.
9. Gregersen, "Emergence," 279.
10. Gregersen, "Emergence," 281.
11. Gregersen, "Emergence," 287.

have arisen because of the context within which the church seeks to fulfill its vocation. Likewise, the Baptist church in Budleigh Salterton will be different from the one in Newton Abbot simply because of the topography of their geographical location. The critique of flat religious naturalism is that it makes no provision for a transcendent nature and the way heavenly/earthly relationships might instigate creative and unforeseeable responses to the challenges presented by geography and social demographics. Gregersen acknowledges this and argues that while flat religious naturalism might express a deep sense of the inner characteristics of natural phenomena, it remains committed to describing elements of emergence as the fulfillment of a natural process.[12] Thus, citing Ursula Goodenough, Gregersen suggests that while the Gospel stories of Jesus transforming water into wine might be interpreted as a miracle confirming Jesus' divinity, it can equally be interpreted as the result of an interaction between chemicals and temperature.[13]

Evolving Theistic Naturalism

Evolving theistic naturalism views God as emerging from a process of natural development.[14] From a theological perspective, this concept is the most difficult to equate to the vocation of a local church. While the emergence of God as a process of the interrelation between individual human beings, their environment, and circumstances might be a credible anthropological or sociological concept, it falters when placed within an orthodox theological matrix. The reason for this faltering is that, by its nature, evolving theistic naturalism roots the existence of God in the inter-reaction of human beings, thus ruling out the concept of a pre-existent God. While this resonates with the religious rationalism of Wink's early theological training, his experience and subsequent work on the angel of the church has led him away from this standpoint.

Atemporal Theism

Atemporal theism views the relationship between creation and God as interactive. Thus, in atemporal theism, God is connected to, and yet

---

12. Gregersen, "Emergence," 288.
13. Gregersen cites Goodenough, *Sacred Depths of Nature*, 28–29.
14. Gregersen, "Emergence," 287.

remains distinct from, the emergence of novelty and diversity.[15] Describing this as "the classic philosophical theology," it is unsurprising that Gregersen considers this position as central to both Judaism and Christianity.[16] Therefore, as a theological hermeneutic for use in the study of congregations, atemporal theism has more to commend it than either flat religious naturalism or evolving theistic naturalism. Adopting an atemporal theistic view of church life allows for God to engage with his people and offer direction as they seek to fulfill their vocation while simultaneously allowing the congregation the freedom to decide whether to accept guidance and determine the way it is subsequently applied. This is the process described in the letters to the churches in the second and third chapters of Revelation. While the angel is addressed and, through it, the local congregation, with its strengths and weaknesses, the responses are left to the church members who receive the letter and hear the commendation and rebuke.

Temporal Theism

Temporal theism is similar to atemporal theism but allows for God to receive from the creation process as well as creating an environment in which novelty can develop.[17] According to Gregersen, while the concept of temporal theism holds a prominent position within contemporary philosophical and systematic theology, it is, nevertheless, a twentieth-century construct.[18] If Gregersen is correct, and a temporal theistic view is not articulated in the vocabulary of the early and medieval church, there is a question of relevance and connectedness to Wink's position. If, as he claims, Wink is committed to rediscovering and reapplying the language of the early church, the theory of temporal theism has nothing to offer to his concept of the angel of the church. However, the way that the letters to the seven angels and their respective churches in the book of Revelation are individualized suggests a process of divine interaction with a developing community. Furthermore, the fact that God calls upon a human being to address the spiritual angel and call to account the earthly church points to an interaction between the physical and transcendent realms.

15. Gregersen, "Emergence," 287.
16. Gregersen, "Emergence," 290.
17. Gregersen, "Emergence," 287.
18. Gregersen, "Emergence," 293.

Therefore, while the process of temporal theism may be a twentieth-century philosophical construct, it is possible to read this form of emergence back into the ancient text and, thus, to the relationship between God, a local church, and its angel of the church.

Eschatological Theism

Eschatological theism attributes all forms of emergence to the intervention of God.[19] Developing this model of emergence, Gregersen draws heavily on the work of Wolfhart Pannenberg.[20] In *Toward a Theology of Nature: Essays on Science and Faith*, Pannenberg describes how the past is understood through the unfolding of the future.[21] Reflecting on "Contingency and Natural Law,"[22] Pannenberg argues that the Israelites viewed their history and their ongoing life as a people as evidence of God at work.[23] Thus, inspirational and transformational decisions that a faith community makes in the present will only be fully understood when reflected upon as events in the past.[24] This contention is significant as it suggests that a review of the stories and bureaucratic processes recorded by local Baptist congregations will reveal features of the angel's nature. It also acts as a counterargument to the critique raised in chapter 5, where it was suggested that church records provide insufficient information to discern the emotion present within a church meeting. While it is difficult to ascertain the emotion expressed within a specific church meeting by simply reading a written record, the theory of eschatological theism suggests that reading back through church records can reveal an interaction between God and his people. This interaction is implied through the conclusions drawn and decisions made within the meetings. Of course, there is the question of whether the action of God might be read into the records of board meetings held at General Motors. The answer to this question is found in how a board meeting and a Baptist church meeting are interpreted. While some Baptists refer to the church meeting as "the Church Business Meeting," as the day-to-day

---

19. Gregersen, "Emergence," 287.
20. Gregersen, "Emergence," 298–99.
21. Pannenberg, *Toward a Theology of Nature*, 83.
22. Pannenberg, *Toward a Theology of Nature*, 72–122.
23. Pannenberg, *Toward a Theology of Nature*, 82.
24. Pannenberg, *Toward a Theology of Nature*, 83.

business of church life is discussed, in Baptist ecclesiology, the church meeting is a place where the will and purpose of God are discerned. Thus, while there are similarities between a secular business meeting and a Baptist church meeting, the focus is different.

The Embedded Spirit

Aside from evolving theistic naturalism, each of Gregerson's models of emergence offers insights into the way the resident spirit produces diversity within a church and provides a means of observing the action of God. However, if Wink is correct in attributing an angel to the spirit of General Motors. In that case, his contention that the spirit of the company is embedded in the organization and is not dependent on the nature of the employees is questionable.[25] If all the employees of General Motors were changed overnight and the company's ethos remained unchanged, the spirit of General Motors could be described as being embedded in the company or its transcendent counterpart. Similarly, Wink's contention that the nature of a company is embedded in a spiritual nature that is separate from its employees would also be justified if the new workforce, having begun work in a new field of industry, subsequently reverted to constructing motor vehicles and retained the ethos of the company that predated their employment. Here, the embedded spirituality reveals itself as the decision to construct something other than motor vehicles is reversed. This form of embedded spirituality might be observed among Baptists if their desire to practice one form of Baptist ecclesiology changes in response to an internal desire or spiritual pressure and subsequently reverts to the original form of churchmanship. Arguably, this is what happened among the Baptists in Newton Abbot between 1819 and 1863 as they vacillated over who should be allowed to share the Lord's Supper.[26]

Transference

Despite the apparent support that emergence theories offer Wink's thesis on self-understanding, his illustration from General Motors does not necessarily imply the presence of an emerged and embedded spirituality.

25. Gregersen, "Emergence," 297.
26. See Arthur Gabb, Extracts from the minutes of the Old Church, 6916D/68, Newton Abbot Baptist Church, n.d., DHC.

If General Motors, having completely changed its workforce, continued to manufacture cars and based their production methods on the procedures left behind by the previous employees, then evidence of a similar ethos or spirit would represent an act of transference rather than emergence. This form of transference also occurs when a group of people move from a congregation to start a new church in a different location, such as when a small group of Baptists left the church in Bovey Tracey to restart the cause in Newton Abbot.

From a historical perspective, an act of transference can be described as a corporate narrative or an organization's tradition. According to Alexander Lucie-Smith, "Tradition can be understood as the furniture of the mind that is shared by a community that makes their conversation possible."[27] Thus, it might be argued that the ongoing development of the community is restricted by the sort of conversation that can be held within the parameters set by the shape of its furniture. Therefore, within this metaphor, substantive change takes place through subtle shifts in the way the shared language of a community understands the words it uses and reshapes the furniture. In the case of Gregerson's illustrations, the creation of new words represents the introduction of new furniture which, in turn, allows for the way a language changes. Likewise, small changes introduced to the church might eventually reorient a congregation and change the nature of its vocation.[28] Furthermore, Lucie-Smith argues that tradition need not be a barrier to change, contending that new concepts can be built upon the confluence of old traditions. Illustrating this, he points to the way Augustine built his theology upon a classical education that enabled him to engage with Porphyry and Cicero and use their concepts to carry his thinking beyond that of both original authors.[29] From a church perspective, this might be apparent as a fellowship explores new theological concepts and applies them to their current ecclesial practice.

For Wink, the continuity expressed through tradition is a restrictive, rather than creative, force. To illustrate this, he uses the life of a river and the renewing of the cells within a human body, referenced earlier.[30] He argues that while the molecules of a river might change and the cells within the human body are renewed, the river and body

---

27. Lucie-Smith, *Narrative Theology and Moral Theology*, 3–4.
28. Gregersen, "Emergence," 279.
29. Lucie-Smith, *Narrative Theology and Moral Theology*, 4.
30. Wink, *Unmasking the Powers*, 79.

remain substantively the same.³¹ The weakness in this argument is that by using the river and human body as metaphors for continuity and resilience within a group such as the church, Wink does not mention the subtle changes that take place in both the river and the human body. During a river's journey to the sea, not only are some of the water molecules replaced by the hydrologic cycle, but these new molecules also progress along at least part of the watercourse. Furthermore, over a protracted period, the watercourse itself changes as the process of silting and erosion shapes it. These changes are very subtle and are often only recognizable when the dimensions of the riverbanks are taken over an extended period. Likewise, while Wink is correct that the cells in a human body are replaced every seven years, this renewal of cells takes place within the context of the changes associated with the growth and maturing of the body, as well as the aging process. These changes in the river and the human body suggest Wink's argument that the underlying ethos of an organization is robust may only be part of the story. Over time, subtle changes to that ethos will take place as one generation gives way to another, and the church simultaneously adapts to the new challenges presented by their situation in society and the local community. Furthermore, over time, the change of personnel within a congregation will also introduce subtle changes in how a church functions, which will, in turn, change its nature and how it approaches its vocation.

Church Membership and Transference

According to the organizational psychologists Howard Schwartz and Stan Davis, an organization's culture can be described as a set of beliefs and expectations that shape the way both individuals and organizations function.³² While not specifically aimed at describing a church, Schwartz and Davis's description is apt. In a Baptist context, where the congregation believes that the church is a gathering of believers, certain expectations are held over how individuals might live both within and without the community of faith. Therefore, it is normal practice among Baptist congregations to interview a potential member before admitting them to the fellowship. However, as commonplace as it is for church

---

31. Wink, *Unmasking the Powers*, 79.

32. O'Reilly, "Corporations, Culture, and Commitment," 318, citing Schwartz and Davis, "Matching Corporate Culture and Business Strategy."

records to note that a church member has been interviewed, reception into membership does not mark the end of the expectation placed on the member by the community of faith.

Charles O'Reilly develops Schwartz and Davis's definition further by suggesting that the norms expressed within an organization are reinforced by attaching an unwritten approval or disapproval rating.[33] This rating is linked to the way certain corporately held attitudes and beliefs are expressed. The case of Annie Besly, a member of the Baptist church in Newton Abbot, provides an example of how the corporate body of the church expects a certain type of lifestyle from its members. At a special church meeting held on September 5, 1867, the pastor opened with a prayer for wisdom before explaining to the church that:

> Having heard numerous reports of [Annie's] moral character, Brother Nicholson and himself visited her mother with a view to ascertaining the true picture. . . . It was found that she had married Wm. Penfound (who was at the time under the discipline of the church) and that there had been a necessity of a speedy marriage, the act of fornication having been committed by them.[34]

Having outlined the facts, Brother Nicholson described how these actions are contrary to the word of God and recommended to the church that the name of Annie Besly be removed from membership. This recommendation was seconded by Brother Welford and carried unanimously. Likewise, because of Penfound's involvement in an "act of fornication," his removal from membership was proposed by Brother Nicholson, seconded by Brother Davie, and carried unanimously.[35]

Records such as these illustrate how the culture of a congregation is defined. By interviewing applicants for membership, the community ensures that their foundational principles are retained. Furthermore, when the boundaries that define their culture are transgressed, the church expresses its disapproval by removing the rights of membership and expelling the person from their community. This sort of action reinforces the expectations and beliefs held by the community. It also ensures a continuity of culture within the fellowship. However, while a church might appear to perpetuate its ethos through the membership

---

33. O'Reilly, "Corporations, Culture, and Commitment," 318-19.

34. Church meeting minutes, p. 45, 6916-1-1, Newton Abbot Baptist Church minutes Sept. 27, 1863–July 30, 1894, DHC.

35. Church meeting minutes, p. 45, 6916-1-1, DHC.

approval process, subtle changes are inevitable. These changes are evident in the way churches such as those at Bovey Tracey, Budleigh Salterton, and Newton Abbot periodically update their church rules or even their constitution.[36]

The question raised by the way a congregation's culture is perpetuated through the membership process is, "To what effect does the underlying ethos of a church affect its ability to adapt to a changing environment?" Lucie-Smith's view is that, while the past traditions help to form the way a group functions in the present, they are not necessarily a barrier to change in the future. In his opinion, tradition acts as a set of shared presuppositions that bind a group together within its ongoing narrative.[37] Within Lucie-Smith's paradigm, a dialogue with past traditions provides a resource from which new understanding can develop and thus create the possibility of progress in the future.[38] Therefore, the narrative that the Baptists in Budleigh Salterton, Newton Abbot, and South Street in Exeter articulate should not necessarily restrict their ability to adapt to new challenges and thus continue with their vocation. However, if the congregation's tradition becomes unable to adapt to the surrounding culture, then their ability to fulfill their vocation becomes impeded.

The unacknowledged changes within Wink's metaphors of the river and human body constitute a maturing and/or aging process that can equally be replicated within a group. Just as in the course of a river, it broadens and meanders, causing the phenomena of oxbow lakes, so a church might separate over issues of theology and leave aside a small group of

---

36. The earliest example of the church rules at Bovey Tracey Baptist Church date from August 20, 1891. These were revised on March 26, 1906. Minutes, 5545D-0 3576, box 12400, East Dartmore Baptist Church minute book Jan. 16, 1899–Aug. 31, 1908, DHC. These rules were further revised on March 25, 1924; minutes, 5545D-0 3576, box 12400, East Dartmore Baptist Church minute book July 1917–Aug. 26, 1924, DHC.

The earliest example of the church rules at Budleigh Salterton Baptist date from 1843. Minute book, 3548D M1, Budleigh Salterton Baptist Church, Oct. 1843–Apr. 1883, DHC. These rules are articulated again in the minute book of 1883. Minute book, 3548D M2, Budleigh Salterton Baptist Church, Aug. 1883–May 1902, DHC.

The first rules formed by the Baptists in Newton Abbot date from 1819. Gabb, Extracts, 6916D/68, DHC. There are also updated rules dating from March 16, 1960, and September 28, 1977. Minutes, 6916-1-5, Newton Abbot Baptist Church minute book Jan. 15, 1954–July 27, 1988, DHC. These rules are changed again in 2002. Church rules, box 6916, Newton Abbot Baptist Church, 2002, DHC.

The records of the Baptist church at South Street in Exeter do not contain copies of the church rules in the same way as those at Budleigh Salterton and Newton Abbot.

37. Lucie-Smith, *Narrative Theology and Moral Theology*, 4–5.
38. Lucie-Smith, *Narrative Theology and Moral Theology*, 5.

dissenters as the main body of the church progresses with a subtle change of direction. If evident in the lives of local congregations, these changes support Lucie-Smith's contention that a continuing ethos, or tradition, does not necessarily represent stagnation within an organization.

Organizational, or Family, Systems

According to Helen Cameron, churches are often suspicious of organizational studies due to their links with a managerial ethos.[39] However, as Wink himself notes, the way the church is structured, particularly in relation to leadership and the dissemination of power, has a significant impact on the way a church functions.[40] Edwin Friedman, an organizational systems specialist, describes a family system as a method of understanding how a group of human personalities interact.[41] In relation to Wink's illustration, yet without reference to the spiritual, Friedman also contends that the nature of the organization is able to transcend the lifespan of its members. He argues that despite the members of an organization changing more frequently than those of a family, the principles that form their organizational structure are the same.[42] In this respect, Friedman agrees with Wink that the essence of an organization is extremely resilient. However, Friedman differs from Wink in that Friedman's thesis is based on the transference of organizational principles rather than their embedded existence.

The similarity between family systems theory and how Wink interprets the way a church understands itself is also evident when his work is compared with that of Steinke. Steinke's exploration of the nature of a church has already been explored with respect to anxiety among church members. However, as an organizational, or family, systems specialist, the language Steinke uses to describe how a church functions is remarkably similar to Wink's.

Describing the angel of the church, Wink suggests that the personality of the angel of the church cannot be separated from the congregation. Equally, a congregation finds its corporate spiritual identity in the angel.

---

39. Cameron et al., *Studying Local Churches*, 15.
40. Wink, *Unmasking the Powers*, 74–75.
41. Friedman, *Generation to Generation*, 13.
42. Friedman, *Generation to Generation*, 198.

Effectively, the angel and the congregation are the internal and external expressions of the same entity.[43]

Peter Steinke's description of a family system resonates with Wink's description as he argues that a family system is:

> A fundamentally new way of thinking about relationships. It is based on the idea that relationship systems are not built up out of the personalities of those who belong to them but rather that the "personalities" in any institution express themselves according to forces within the system and their position within those forces.[44]

For both Wink and Steinke, the personality of the group, or church, is formed with the coming together of individual characters. However, the confluence of individual personalities forms a separate institutional identity that is distinct and different from those of the individuals from which the group is formed. Furthermore, Steinke believes that individual temperaments can change depending on the role they are asked to adopt within the group.[45] Therefore, if a person's role within a group is changed, the character they adopt will change accordingly. Wink describes a similar phenomenon in *Engaging the Powers*, where he asks the reader to consider how normally peaceful individuals can be caught up in acts of hooliganism at a football match.[46]

If Steinke and Wink are correct, and the temperaments of individuals are subverted by the personality or angel of the organization, it suggests that there is an intrinsic emotional tension within the life of a group. This tension has the capability of subverting a person's individual persona in favor of one that serves the objective of the group. This observation suggests that the presence of a latent spirit within an organization will influence not only how a church functions corporately but also how individuals function within a group. Thus, although Wink claims that the angel of the church is neutral, its very existence acts as a gyroscope that holds the church in specific equilibrium. While this equilibrium might be benign, it might equally be self-destructive. In the case of the Baptists in Newton Abbot, it appears that because their angel was shaped by a strong relationship between the people and their

---

43. Wink, *Unmasking the Powers*, 70.
44. Edwin H. Friedman, quoted in Steinke, *How Your Church Family Works*, vi.
45. Steinke, *Healthy Congregations*, 7–8.
46. Wink, *Engaging the Powers*, 9.

building, the decision to move to Highweek School in 2003 affected the angel to such an extent that the church never recovered.

Vocation

Throughout this book reference has been made to the relationship between aspects of church life and a congregation's vocation. This is because Wink believes that the confluence of a church's nature and its vocation forms the basis from which the angel of the church is formed. What is more, according to Wink, a congregation's vocation represents what a church might become in Christ, and this distinguishes a church from other organizations.

Of course, observing what a church might become in Christ is very difficult. However, while a congregation's vocation is ultimately held in the knowledge and purpose of a transcendent God, it might be possible to obtain a sense of the church's calling from the opening paragraphs of their records. Where these records exist, these introductions provide an insight into the intentions and ethos of the founding members. They may also set the basis from which a congregation's collective memory is drawn.

The Vocation at Newton Abbot

Earlier in this thesis, reference was made to the anxiety experienced by the Baptists in Newton Abbot as they moved from their premises in East Street to Highweek School. While this anxiety might simply be sociological in nature, it might also be linked to the congregation's vocation. Although not reflected in the minutes, it is possible that there was a collective memory of the remarks made when the building was opened in 1863. These comments bestowed a status on the Baptists at Newton Abbot that was lost when they moved to Highweek School:

> The importance and necessity of a new, enlarged, and commodious Baptist Chapel was long felt by the members of the Baptist congregation in Newton Abbot and also by the churches of the county. At length, the way was made plain, and the present building was erected & opened on Thursday, Sept 22nd, 1863.[47]

---

47. Church meeting minutes, p. 1, 6916-1-1, Newton Abbot Baptist Church minutes Sept. 27, 1863–July 30, 1894, DHC.

By recording these observations, the Newton Abbot Baptists created a link between their building and their status among their peers. This status arguably formed part of the church's vocation. What is more, the church's nature was formed by their experience of being removed from the Baptist church founded in 1819. On the day that the new building was opened, the Newton Abbot Baptists achieved recognition not only among the Baptists of South Devon but also among the members of the 1819 Baptist church in Newton Abbot, who had ejected them because of their views on open communion.[48]

Although this nature of the new congregation's theology was based on open communion, its vocation is encapsulated in the opening statement quoted above. With a large new building, the local Baptists clearly considered that the new church at Newton Abbot would become a major contributor to the Baptist cause in South Devon. This expectation is even more poignant in the light of the new church only consisting of twenty-five members.

To a large degree, the Baptists in Newton Abbot both pursued and fulfilled this vocation of prominence, and even in the 1970s, the church was considered significant among Baptist churches in the South West. Commenting on this, the Rev. Jeremy Brown[49] states that as a lay preacher during the 1970s, he always considered it to be a privilege to preach at Newton Abbot Baptist Church. However, he also notes that as time passed, despite the congregation's belief that they would remain numerically strong, the church dwindled. Brown attributes this decline to an unwillingness to change. He illustrates this by stating that when the church eventually moved to Highweek School, the members set up the furniture used in worship in a format similar to the layout in East Street Chapel. Although Brown attributes the decline of the Newton Abbot Baptists to a reluctance to change, he also recognizes that other "more outward-looking" churches had begun to occupy the theological ground previously held by the Newton Abbot Baptists.[50] Arguably, this

---

48. Gabb, Extracts, 40, 6916D/68, DHC.

49. The Rev. Jeremy (Jez) Brown was minister of Preston Baptist Church Paignton, South Devon, between 1997 and 2002. He then served as regional minister for the South West Baptist Association between September 1, 2002, and August 31, 2015. On September 1, 2015, the Rev. Brown returned to pastoral ministry at Paignton Baptist Church, South Devon.

50. Jeremy Brown, personal correspondence regarding Newton Abbot Baptist Church, 2017. The details contained in the correspondence have been used with the Rev. Brown's permission.

loss of theological position and the loss of status within a wider church community might constitute a loss of vocation. If this was the case, then the fact that the Baptist church declined to a point where it was no longer viable is unsurprising.

The Vocation at Budleigh Salterton

If a congregation's vocation is set out in the opening statement of their minute books or church rules. In that case, the first paragraph of the church records for Budleigh Salterton Baptist Church might explain the sense of calm presented throughout their history:

> If for the sake of peace and good order in society generally, men [sic] of the world are found adopting and employing means for promoting the same, surely those who are the professed followers of the King of Peace, and from whom alone true peace cometh, should not be negligent in the adoption of any measures, or backward in the employment of any measures, consistent with the Word of God, to promote that which may then in some degree to present comfort and prevention of what might disrupt the whole Church; a cause for, if not a direct necessity of an associated body of Christians having rules must appear evident to every partaker of divine Grace.[51]

At its heart, this is a missional statement. However, in advocating the use of any means to promote the gospel, the founding members of Budleigh Salterton Baptist church concentrated on the peace that comes from God. What is more, they believed that the peace that comes from God should be addressed to any potential disruption within the church. This commitment to promoting peace, as the divine grace associated with achieving a peaceful status within the congregation, might explain why the disagreements recorded in the minute books do not reflect the same degree of anxiety as those at Newton Abbot.

If creating a peaceful community that can overcome their disagreements and deal with the challenges of church life reflects their vocation, the Baptists at Budleigh Salterton appear to have retained their focus. While it is impossible to tell for certain, it is possible that part of their success has been achieved because of their tenacious nature. This tenacity

---

51. Minutes, 3548D M1, Budleigh Salterton Baptist Church minute book Oct. 1843–Apr. 1883, DHC.

was illustrated above by the congregation's commitment to employ a minister even though they might struggle to pay a stipend.

The Vocation of South Street in Exeter

The situation with the records at South Street in Exeter is different from that of Budleigh Salterton and Newton Abbot, as the earliest minute books were destroyed.[52] However, the earliest surviving minute book, dated 1746, begins by stating:

> With no certain account of the commencement of the Baptist Church at Exon or what minister or ministry they had till 1688 when from the Baptist register published in London, it appears that they had at that time Mr Phillips for their Pastor and Mr Sampson for an assisting minister.[53]

Following this introduction, there is an extensive list of the ministers and the dates they served at South Street Baptist Church Exeter. The last minister listed is Mr. Enoch Francis, who, according to the record, resigned his position on October 4, 1749. The date of Mr. Francis's resignation is significant, as it is later than the first recorded minute dated February 25, 1746. In view of this, it is safe to assume that when the minute book was started, space was allocated to reconstruct the list of previous ministers.[54]

Although the list of ministers appears to provide little insight into the nature of the congregation's vocation, the fact that space was allocated to this list at the beginning of the minute book indicates that ministry and its continuity are important to the way the Baptists in South Street understand themselves. It also suggests that whatever the church is called to be in Christ, pastoral ministry plays an important part in the congregation fulfilling its vocation.

Vocation and Subcultures

Reflecting on the way churches organize themselves and the cultures that this creates, Christopher Burkett argues that individual congregations

---

52. "MSS History of the Discenting Churches by Isaac James," insert, 75-9-1-1, South Street Baptist Church, Exeter, minute book 1749–Nov. 7, 1868, DHC.

53. Minutes, 75-9-1-1, South Street Baptist Church, Exeter, minute book 1749–Nov. 7, 1868, DHC.

54. Minutes, 75-9-1-1, DHC.

construct cultural matrices within which a distinctive sub-culture is allowed to flourish.[55] According to Burkett, these subcultures are specific to the locality and thus represent the specific nature of an individual congregation.[56] Therefore, in Wink's General Motors example, a distinctive subculture is generated through the interaction of human beings as they work together to make motor vehicles. This subculture will distinguish General Motors from other motor manufacturers. Furthermore, subcultures are contextual. Thus, a person's experience of working for General Motors in the United States of America will differ from what it would be if they worked at a factory in Europe or Asia. This form of subculture has become evident from the discussion above. Individual distinctiveness can be seen among Baptist congregations in their architecture, demographics, and theology. Furthermore, while Baptist churches share a vocation in Christ, the focus of their calling will differ according to the congregation's location.

Ethos

Although Wink's description of the angel of the church is multifaceted, his General Motors illustration might be interpreted as institutional ethos. According to the anthropologist Clifford Geertz, the ethos of a group of people is seen in how their character is expressed through their morals, lifestyle, and how they understand themselves.[57]

This definition aptly describes a church community whose character and collective understanding of the Christian faith shape the moral lifestyle of the individual members as well as their corporate identity. There is also a synergy between Geertz's statement and Wink's description of the angel of the church, as both Wink and Geertz state that the way a community understands itself plays an important part in the formation of a group ethos.[58] In the case of the two churches separated by their interpretation of the Viking raid, at least one of the two churches is defined by how it perceives it was treated by its neighboring church. Likewise, it might be argued that the workforce at General Motors defines itself by the procedures that it uses to make motor vehicles.

55. Burkett, "Organisational Culture in Congregations," 206.
56. Burkett, "Organisational Culture in Congregations," 206.
57. Geertz, *Interpretation of Cultures*, 127.
58. Wink, *Unmasking the Powers*, 76–77; and Geertz, *Interpretation of Cultures*, 127.

In this respect, Geertz's belief that the ethos of an organization is partly defined by their relationship with others suggests that the actions of the congregation who felt most affected by the Viking raid could be described as an anthropological rather than spiritual phenomenon. However, if this story were extended to include an attempt at reconciliation based on a scriptural mandate and thus an appeal to live up to the ethos of Christ, a transcendent link would have been established. Russ Parker illustrates this as he recounts his experience of leading a conference in preparation for an evangelistic endeavor in Warwick. Parker explains that the church leaders were keen that part of the preparation process should reflect on the story of the churches in the town.[59] As a result of their discussions, the leaders concluded that before their outreach program could commence, they must first hold a service of reconciliation, within which apologies would be made for the way different churches had treated each other.[60] The significance of Parker's story is that, recognizing that there were historical and unresolved issues in the relationships between their churches, the leaders sought to address the earthly tensions through an act of worship, thus engaging with the issue in both the earthly and heavenly realms.

Summary

In common with the rest of Wink's thesis, his exploration of the relationship between how a congregation understands itself and the nature of its angel is underdeveloped. However, unlike some of the facets discussed earlier in this study, Wink does at least illustrate his argument. Despite this, the illustration of the two East Anglican churches is ambiguous in its assumptions. While Wink may be correct in suggesting that the relationship between the two churches is defined by the Viking raid in the ninth century, he does not create a viable link between the earthly and heavenly identities. Even so, his illustration does highlight the longevity of a collective memory. It also indicates the role that a past event can have in shaping a congregation's ongoing life. According to Wink's thesis, this longevity presents a two-dimensional challenge to anyone wishing to address the relationship between the churches. Along with the sociological issues associated with two groups of people whose separation is based

---

59. Parker, *Healing Wounded History*, 48.
60. Parker, *Healing Wounded History*, 48–49.

upon a collective memory, the spiritual identity has also been formed and reinforced by the result of the Viking raid.

Emergence or Transference

Although Wink's General Motors illustration is not directly linked to his statement regarding self-understanding, the conclusions that he draws relate directly to a congregation's nature and how it functions. As discussed above, this illustration raises an interesting question in respect of how the angel of the church is formed. Although Wink appears to argue for a form of emergence, actually finding a congregation that has not experienced a form of transference may prove extremely difficult. This is especially the case among Baptist congregations as, historically, Baptists are dissenters and, therefore, have usually formed new churches by leaving existing congregations. In these cases, the founding members of the new church inadvertently carry with them identifying features or character traits from their previous congregation. While these traits may be repeated in the new church, they may also become the basis for a counter-reaction. As previously mentioned, this counter-reaction may have been the reason for the strong stance on Calvinistic theology and a closed communion table expressed by the Baptists who moved to Newton Abbot in 1819.

Identity and Vocation

While the embedded spirituality that Wink describes in the General Motors illustration is unlikely to exist in the way he describes, the work of Friedman and Steinke supports the contention that organizations have a defined identity. For Wink, this identity is intrinsically linked to a church's vocation. Therefore, once a church ceases to attempt to fulfill its vocation, the essence of the organization changes, and, arguably, it now becomes something other than a church. In these cases, Wink describes the angel of the church becoming demonic.

In view of this, knowing how a church understands itself, particularly with respect to its vocation, will be a significant factor in any attempt to transform the nature of the church and redeem the nature of its angel. While this will be the focus of the next chapter, Lucie-Smith's description of tradition as "furniture of the mind" and Wink's use of the human body and the river provide helpful insights into the nature of change within the nature of the angel of the church.

Nature

The idea that the traditions held as part of a congregation's collective memory might act as pieces of furniture that can be rearranged to give a room a different feel holds out the possibility that even the most entrenched congregation might be reshaped. Furthermore, Wink's use of the river and the human body to describe a congregation's resilience might also shed light on the ability of new members to bring subtle changes to church life, which could provide the capacity for a congregation to change its direction of travel without affecting its ethos and thus the nature of its angel.

In the final chapter of this thesis, the possibility of redeeming and transforming the angel of the church will be explored along with drawing conclusions from the discussions above. Finally, consideration will be given to how the work carried out in this thesis might be developed further.

8

Transforming the Angel and Drawing Conclusions

Reviewing the Methodology

THE MOTIVATION FOR THIS thesis, as noted in the introduction, came from a lecture on "The Angel of the Church" presented by David Runcorn to pastoral theology students. By encouraging his students to read the records kept by the churches within which they served as ministers, Runcorn also provided the methodology for this course of study. While he never advocated that church records were the only source from which the nature of the angel could be discerned, Runcorn did, nevertheless, suggest that church minute books provide a useful window through which the angel of the church can be observed. Although there are limitations to the records kept by the churches at Budleigh Salterton, Newton Abbot, and South Street in Exeter, there was still sufficient information to begin to understand the nature of the angel of each congregation. Indeed, with respect to the relationship between the Baptists at Newton Abbot and their building, and those at Budleigh Salterton and their finances, the records are extensive and insightful. However, having stated this, there were areas of Wink's rubric where it was difficult to fully evaluate what happened in the life of the church and, thus, how the nature of the angel might be affected. The reason for this is that some areas that Wink suggests for observing the angel require an experience rather than a written account. This is particularly true with respect to the way a congregation's theology is expressed in worship. It is also true of how architecture and the ambience of a building affect how a congregation functions within its premises. In view of this, an experience of a regular worship service would assist in providing a complete sense of the angel's nature.

A Broad Spectrum Approach

Wink's concept of the angel of the church is both illuminating and frustrating. While his chapter on "Angels of Churches" introduces the theological basis for the presence of an angel of the church, the areas of church life he suggests as a basis for revealing its nature are poorly developed and illustrated. Furthermore, the areas of church life that Wink suggests will reveal the nature of the angel cover a broad spectrum of academic disciplines. These include aspects of geography, history, sociology, and psychology. Thus, to grasp the full nature of the angel of a church, several skills are required. Despite this, Wink's work is important as it ensures that the visible aspects of church life are interpreted theologically.

In addition to using the work of scholars in the areas of geography, sociology, and psychology to explore the facets of church life listed by Wink, this thesis also assessed historical material relating to specific congregations. The primary documents used in this research were the publicly available records from the English Baptist churches in Budleigh Salterton, Newton Abbot, and South Street in Exeter. Secondary material was also gathered from journals and websites that illustrated certain facets of Wink's work. The weakness in this method is that the stories chosen were selected because of their relevance to the areas of church life that Wink explored. Therefore, while Wink's contention can be supported by stories from Baptist congregations, not all the aspects that Wink explores are illustrated from the records of a single congregation. In view of this, when it comes to describing the nature of the angel of the Baptist churches at Budleigh Salterton, Newton Abbot, and South Street in Exeter, the description can only represent a partial profile.

Understanding the Angel

As well as the gaps Wink leaves as he describes some areas of church life that reveal the nature of the angel of the church, his vacillation between seeing the angel as a transcendent being and a social construct is equally frustrating. The reasons behind this vacillation might be that his research into spiritual powers has caused him to embark on a journey of discovery. His statement that he was trained in a rational form of liberal theology, his experience in South America, subsequent illness, and his review of Wesley Carr's *Angels and Principalities* appear to have been the catalysts for a change of theological worldview.[1] Furthermore, according to Wink's own testimony, writing his first work, *Naming the Powers*, was a cathartic experience.[2] In view of this, while authors such as Clinton Arnold disagree with Wink's deductions, they do so presuming that Wink has a limited belief in the supernatural. This assumption appears to be unfair in the light of how Wink describes his experiences of the angel of the church. The story of the Bible study exploring the relationship between the wealthy and the kingdom of God in the home of the rich man reveals a belief in a supernatural dimension that belies Arnold's critique.[3]

The Biblical Basis for the Angel

Regardless of whether Wink's view of the supernatural actually changed during the writing of the Powers Trilogy, his exploration of the angel of the church referred to in the book of Revelation is limited. However, this limitation can be overcome by referring to Aune's investigation into what the Greek word *angelos* might mean with respect to the phrase "angel of the church."

Aune highlights a clear division of opinion over how the word *angelos* might be understood. The possibilities appear to be three-fold: a human messenger, a transcendent entity, and a literary construct.[4] Although it is a little dated, Aune's investigation, along with the work of Davidson and Newsom on the documents of Qumran, provides helpful insights into the concept of an angel of the church. Their research suggests that, during the intertestamental period, religious communities, such as the one at Qumran, developed an angelology that included an angelic priesthood that ministered before God in heavenly temples. Furthermore, the biblical and intertestamental literature also creates a link between nation-states and angelic overseers. It is this link that provides the basis upon

1. Wink, *Naming the Powers*, ix.
2. Wink, *Naming the Powers*, x.
3. Wink, *Unmasking the Powers*, 74.
4. Aune, *Revelation 1–5*, 108–12.

which Wink's concept of an angel of the church is built. This, along with Wink's argument for viewing the heavenly realms as an interior dimension rather than an external and elevated realm, adds support to his belief in the gyroscopic effect of the angel.[5]

The Nature of the Angel and an Evolving Theology

As has become evident, this thesis supports Wink's position that the angel is a transcendent entity that represents the interiority of an organization. However, adopting this position is not without its difficulties. For example, if Baptists acted in the way Haymes argues for and remade their theology in each generation, the resilience created by the presence of the angel would be open to question.[6] What is more, Haymes's position appears to be supported by the Baptists at Newton Abbot who appear to have reconsidered their theology in respect of communion and Sunday evening worship services. However, while the Newton Abbot Baptists appear to be able to remake their theology with respect to areas of worship, their relationship with the building in East Street resisted change.

Although Wink notes that the angel is neutral in its effect on a congregation, contending that the angel's nature will bring both positive and negative influence to bear, it does nevertheless have an effect on how a church functions. Acting like a keel or gyroscope, the angel of the church brings stability to a congregation, which in turn creates a resilience that is capable of both resisting and promoting change. Therefore, adopting a position in which the angel of the church is both transcendent and forms part of the interiority of a congregation allows for the resilience demonstrated by the Newton Abbot Baptists, both in their commitment to their building and ability to reinvent their theology in a new generation.

Transforming the Nature of the Angel

According to Wink, the role of human beings in the transformation of the transcendent angel is found in the instruction given to John in the second and third chapters of Revelation.[7] By commanding John to write to the angel of the church in a specific location, the transcendent

---

5. Aune, *Revelation 1–5*, 70, 80.
6. Haymes, "Theology and Baptist Identity," 3–5.
7. Wink, *Unmasking the Powers*, 80.

God is addressing spiritual entities through an earthly conduit. The reason for this convoluted approach to transforming the angelic entity is that the angelic nature cannot be changed unless the way the earthly congregation functions is also transformed. Citing Eusebius's *Homily on Ephesians*, Wink argues that the reason why God does not address the angels directly is that angels cannot prevent "the fall of humanity."[8] Therefore, if the nature of the angel is to be altered, it must be addressed by human beings who have themselves been transformed by the divine Christ. Wink develops this argument by suggesting that it is only as the earthly congregation encounters God in his transcendent nature and accepts the judgment which accompanies the encounter that they themselves are changed.[9]

For Wink, addressing the angel and thus reshaping its personality is the only sure way to bring lasting change to the way a congregation functions. He argues that while it is only Christ who can truly change the church, it is the clergy or dedicated laity that have an important role in discerning the nature of their church's angel and presenting this to Christ. Wink highlights this by telling the story of Melinda, a pastor of two churches in New England.[10]

Melinda's Story

Wink explains that while one of the churches under Melinda's charge flourished, the other stagnated.[11] Investigating the cause of the stagnation, Melinda discovered a series of behavior patterns:

i. A wealthy member of the community exercised power over the church leadership even though they were not a church member.

ii. Long-standing members quickly elected people new to the church into positions of leadership and then created an environment that would cause them to fail in their appointed tasks.

iii. Oppressed by their husbands, the frustration experienced by the women of the church was increased by the presence of a female minister.

---

8. Wink, *Unmasking the Powers*, 80.
9. Wink, *Unmasking the Powers*, 80.
10. Wink, *Unmasking the Powers*, 81–82.
11. Wink, *Unmasking the Powers*, 82.

iv. The emotional poverty and short life expectancy prevalent within the community were transferred into the church and resulted in a culture that emphasized survival over flourishing.[12]

When invited to make a three-dimensional model of what she thought the angel looked like, Melinda created a bowl-shaped structure that was unable to stand unaided.[13] Furthermore, the bowl's sides were filled with holes, and the top of the structure had an irregular shape.[14] Reflecting on this construction, Wink asked himself what vocation such a misshapen church could possibly fulfill.[15]

Reflecting further on the problems highlighted by Melinda, Wink concludes that the church experienced a deep self-loathing and desired atonement. However, it achieved this by scapegoating the most gifted among them, usually the minister.[16] Despite highlighting the issue, Wink only offers three tentative solutions that he admits involve a huge effort and yet only represent a partial solution.[17] He suggests that the first course of action would be to work with as many people as possible to discern the nature of the angel.[18] This action is echoed by Warren, who notes that while an individual can interpret a congregation's actions and thus discern the nature of the angel as it represents a community of believers, the angel's nature can be explored more fully by a larger segment of the congregation.[19]

Working with Others

Wink's and Warren's comments highlight an important part of the process of changing the nature of the angel. While the areas requiring adjustment are likely to be seen more clearly by an accepted outsider, the transformation will only take place when a significant number of the community accepts the need for change.

---

12. Wink, *Unmasking the Powers*, 82–83.
13. Wink, *Unmasking the Powers*, 84.
14. Wink, *Unmasking the Powers*, 84.
15. Wink, *Unmasking the Powers*, 84.
16. Wink, *Unmasking the Powers*, 84–85.
17. Wink, *Unmasking the Powers*, 85.
18. Wink, *Unmasking the Powers*, 84.
19. Warren, *Healthy Churches Handbook*, 96–97.

From a Baptist perspective, the ability of the church to undertake a process of consultation should be straightforward. Their tradition of calling an outsider to be their minister and seeking help from the local Association and national Union provides readily available opportunities for the congregation to enlist the help of an accepted outsider. Of course, there will be times, such as when the Baptists in Newton Abbot and at South Street in Exeter sought help from other local churches, that assistance from other congregations will not be forthcoming.

In addition to an ecclesial tradition that welcomes the advice of an accepted outsider, Baptists also have a history of conversing together. Gouldbourne highlights this in an article in *The Baptist Ministers' Journal*. Recounting an Anglican and Methodist critique of an ecumenical quiet day jointly hosted by three theological colleges, Gouldbourne notes that the Anglican and Methodist participants complained that the day contained too much talking and too little silence.[20] Reflecting on this, she suggests that while silence holds an important place in developing Christian spirituality, conversation has played, and continues to play, a significant part in the way Baptists express their particular form of Christian spirituality.[21] Furthermore, she notes that the spoken word not only plays an important part in the way Baptists worship but also in how they seek the will and purpose of God.[22] Gouldbourne argues that, throughout their history, Baptists have always held the expectation that God would speak through the gathered congregation.[23] This expectation underpins the practice of a Baptist church meeting, where the emphasis is as much on discerning the will of God as it is the practicalities of fulfilling the congregation's vocation.

While Wink's illustration does not state the type of ecclesial tradition that Melinda is working within, for Baptists, the act of employing the assistance of an outsider and discerning together the nature of the angel is an achievable proposition.

---

20. Gouldbourne, "Voices," 6.
21. Gouldbourne, "Voices," 7.
22. Gouldbourne, "Voices," 7.
23. Gouldbourne, "Voices," 6.

Breaking a Destructive Cycle

The second piece of advice that Wink offers Melinda is the need to break the cycle of gossip. He argues that all of those who are supporting Melinda in discerning the nature of the angel should be involved in breaking the "cycle of gossip, sniping, and underground recriminations."[24] Illustrating how this might be achieved, Wink cites how one church required all of their church officers to refuse to listen to conversations regarding a third party unless the person initiating the conversation could also confirm that the third party had been informed that their information was being passed on.[25] Alternatively, Wink suggests that the originator of each story could be confronted. While acknowledging that this would be a difficult task, he argues that taking this form of action would create an environment where the benefits to be gained from gossiping would become prohibitively expensive.[26]

While the issue in Newton Abbot Baptist church appears to be chronic anxiety rather than gossip, the result appears to be similar. The discussion over whether to continue with Sunday evening services revealed a lack of trust in the decision-making process. Furthermore, as previously mentioned, the minutes also hint at a fear that once the decision had been made, it would be overturned. As with Wink's advice regarding Melinda's church and the self-destructive cycle of gossip, Steinke argues that, for a church to overcome its chronic anxiety, the destructive cycles that lie at the core have to be exposed.[27] In the case of the Baptists at Newton Abbot, the cycle of overturning a decision not only predates the formation of the church that was currently meeting in the East Street Chapel, it also predates the eventual split in the congregation that led to the formation of the current church. In this situation, redeeming the past might prove impossible. Therefore, transforming the present might have proven to be a more effective option. If, instead of seeing the continual overturning of a decision as a negative personality trait, the Baptists at Newton Abbot had viewed their actions as remaking their theology in a current time and context, overturning the decision might be viewed as adapting to a current situation rather than a failure in sustaining the original decision. This reinterpretation

---

24. Wink, *Unmasking the Powers*, 84.
25. Wink, *Unmasking the Powers*, 84–85.
26. Wink, *Unmasking the Powers*, 85.
27. Steinke, *How Your Church Family Works*, 24.

of their actions might have provided the catalyst for a reduction in anxiety among the Newton Abbot Baptists.

Creating New Patterns

Wink's third piece of advice for Melinda involved creating new programs that did not involve the long-standing church leaders.[28] Wink explains that the reason for excluding those who had been in leadership for a long period was to create a new expression of the original church that was not tainted by the negativity of the historic leaders.[29] This would be a difficult process for Melinda as she would be deliberately creating a division within the leadership and possibly the church. However, as Wink observes, Melinda's central task was to break the cycle that searches for atonement and finds it through scapegoating their minister or gifted members of the congregation.[30]

Having outlined his advice, Wink admits that transforming the angel would be a huge undertaking. He argues that even if Melinda could find the energy necessary to deal with these three issues, dealing with the behavioral patterns that find atonement through scapegoating gifted leaders would be an extremely demanding task. In view of this, Wink argues that while knowing the problems might give Melinda a fresh impetus, the work of transformation might require more than one sustained ministry.[31]

In the illustration of Melinda's church, Wink expresses the opinion that the work of transforming that angel can be a complex and difficult task. Furthermore, even if an outsider can identify the cycles of behavior that require transformation, whether they have the ability to implement the necessary changes is another question. This is particularly poignant in Baptist ecclesiology for two reasons. Firstly, as became evident in chapter 4, within Baptist ecclesiology, the authority and power of a minister to bring about substantial change will be limited by the willingness of the church meeting to face the challenges of the transformation process. If Melinda's church was Baptist, it is doubtful that a leadership entrenched in a behavior cycle that finds atonement

28. Wink, *Unmasking the Powers*, 85.
29. Wink, *Unmasking the Powers*, 85.
30. Wink, *Unmasking the Powers*, 85.
31. Wink, *Unmasking the Powers*, 85.

through scapegoating its minister would grant sufficient authority to the minister to introduce the necessary changes. While the leaders in a Baptist context do not have the final authority, their words do carry influence within the church meeting. This is because they are usually chosen from the membership of the church and thus represent its history and tradition. This leads to the second reason why a Baptist minister might find the task of transforming the angel of Melinda's church extremely difficult. As Baptists employ a system of membership that requires an interview prior to acceptance, there is a possibility that church members will not only restrict membership to people like themselves but will also only appoint a minister whose values are similar to their own.

Therefore, while Wink's thesis is credible, and it is possible to see the indicators he uses within the records of Baptist congregations, discerning the nature of the angel and bringing about its transformation is an extremely complex process. Furthermore, as the focus of this thesis has been on observing the angel through the records kept by the Baptist churches in Newton Abbot, Budleigh Salterton, and South Street in Exeter, the descriptions below can only ever be partial representations of the angel's personality.

Three Profiles of an Angel of the Church

Newton Abbot

Of the three churches whose original records form the core of this research, the nature of the angel of the church at Newton Abbot is the easiest to describe. It has already been noted that throughout its history the church was willing to consider remaking its theology in the light of contemporary challenges. This has been illustrated in the indecision over who should share at the Lord's Table and, over one hundred and fifty years later, in the discussion over whether or not to continue with worship services on a Sunday evening.

On the negative side, the angel of the Baptist church in Newton Abbot became overly attached to the East Street Chapel. This may be due to the expectation placed upon them during the opening ceremony in 1863. The strength of the relationship that the church had with its building is highlighted by the long battle that the congregation engaged in as they attempted to deal with the decaying fabric of their premises. Despite the difficulties associated with the chapel in East Street, when the possibility of moving to Highweek School was discussed and eventually agreed upon, there continued to be a large minority of church members who felt the incorrect decision had been made.

In addition to the relationship with their building, in the latter stages of their history, the Baptists at Newton Abbot exhibit symptoms of being a chronically anxious church. This is revealed in the measures taken to ensure that a lasting decision was made over the continuation or cessation of Sunday evening worship services. There are also hints of the congregation's anxiety in its earlier concern over the ministry of their pastor. While calling the pastor to account was within the purview of the church meeting, the records show that the problems the church was experiencing may not have been completely of the pastor's making. In this respect, he became the scapegoat for the leadership, who were considered to be a law unto themselves.

While there are positive aspects to the angel of the church in Newton Abbot, the records reveal a growing anxiety within the congregation. Such was the level of this anxiety it is perhaps unsurprising that the nature of the angel became irredeemable, and the church closed in 2009. Taking Wink's thesis to its natural conclusion, with the closure of the church, the angel of the church ceased to exist. However, this was not the end of the story, as in 2010, This Hope Baptist Church was founded in Newton Abbot.[32] Of course, according to Wink's concept, the formation of a new church is accompanied by the birth of a new angel. In light of this, it might be argued that while the initial angel was irredeemable, a transformation has taken place with its death and the birth of the new angel.

Budleigh Salterton

The nature of the angel of the Baptist church in Budleigh Salterton is more at peace with itself than that of Newton Abbot. While it is true that disputes existed, and there are even records recounting public exhibitions of frustration, the church meeting appears to be able to approach the situation with a calm rationality.

In addition to an ability to deal calmly with instances of potential conflict, the angel of the church at Budleigh Salterton values its ministers and, when they are called to new pastorates, is tenacious in seeking

32. This Hope Baptist Church, Newton Abbot, "Home/Who Are We?"

out a replacement. According to the records available, it appears that this tenacity was born out of financial adversity. The minutes regarding the search for a successor to the Rev. Shaw suggest that the congregation's inability to offer a stipend similar to other Baptist churches may have led to some ministers turning down the opportunity to serve as pastor in Budleigh Salterton.

As there are no publicly available records for the Baptist church at Budleigh Salterton after 1975, there is a question as to whether the congregation continued to struggle financially. This is particularly pertinent as the contemporary reputation of Budleigh Salterton is of a small but relatively wealthy town. Furthermore, while the records suggest that the early congregation comprised members from the working-class community, there is also a question as to whether the current church continues to be working-class or reflects the current demographic of the town.[33]

Besides the effect a lack of money has in creating a tenacity among the Budleigh Salterton Baptists, the angel of this church also values the contribution that church members of both genders make to the life of the church. This is particularly evident in the appointment of Miss Cork as church treasurer in 1909. Although the appointment of Miss Cork as church treasurer is significant, it is interesting that, in the period covered by the records, the church did not take the step of appointing a female minister. Of course it might be argued that appointing a female minister would be a counter-cultural act in the period covered by the records. However, the same argument could be leveled with respect to the appointment of Miss Cork to such a senior position in 1909. This suggests that while the nature of the angel allows for some counter-cultural action in the appointment of leaders, there is a degree of cultural conservatism that influences the process of appointing a minister.

South Street in Exeter

Based on the extracts of the records used in this thesis, the angel of the Baptist church at South Street in Exeter is the least well-defined. However,

---

33. The Office of National Statistics records for the 2011 census reveal that 23.4 percent of the population of Budleigh Salterton declare themselves to be either managers, directors, senior officers, or in professional occupations, whereas only 12.8 percent of the population consider themselves to be process, plant, and machine operators or in elementary occupations. Office for National Statistics, "Neighbourhood Statistics: Budleigh Ward."

the small amount of material used to illustrate Wink's concept suggests that the angel of this church also values its ministers. This may be illustrated by the perceived depth of theological reflection that took place prior to the appointment of the Rev. Haymes. Furthermore, the secession in 1891 demonstrates a belief in the integrity of their minister. When the Rev. Pike failed to act on his belief that he was called to a new ministry elsewhere, some of the church members found this action intolerable. However, the significance of this action is not just in the willingness of some church members to secede when a ministry, such as that of the Rev. Pike, becomes stagnant, but that they were willing to return upon the appointment of a new minister.[34]

In addition to a commitment to that practice of Christian ministry, the angel of the Baptist church at South Street in Exeter also demonstrates a commitment to exploring and pursuing their vocation. This is evident not only in the frustration during the period between Rev. Pike's announcement of his belief that he had another ministry to fulfill and his eventual departure but also the interaction with other churches prior to the start of the Palace Gate Project in the 1970s. This commitment emphasizes the connection Wink makes between the people who make up a church and their vocation. Furthermore, by inviting the church to consider what it was to be a church in a city center, the Rev. Haymes uses the position of minister to keep the congregation focused on presenting the gospel to the local community. The fact that the church decided to remain in the city center suggests that their angel may be committed to a specific geographical location.

Further Research

The parameters of this research have been set by Wink's description of the angel of the church in *Unmasking the Powers*. In this respect, while this research has required an introduction to a number of academic disciplines it has, nevertheless, been focused on specific aspects of church life. This means that while Wink's approach to discerning the nature of the angel of the church is extensive, there is a great deal of scope for further research.

---

34. The records from the group that met in the Royal Public Rooms show that they rejoined the congregation at South Street in Exeter in 1893. Furthermore, the records from the church in South Street in Exeter show that, at this time, the Rev. D. P. McPherson was their pastor.

The Link Between Heaven and Earth

Although this thesis has explored the possible ways of understanding the term "angel of the church" and has noted the link between heaven and earth, there is further work to be done in this area. Bringing Wink's concept of the angel of the church into conversation with Newsom's translation and interpretation of the Sabbath Shirot and Davidson's exploration of how angels were understood in the Qumran community offers interesting possibilities. If, as this thesis has suggested, there is a link between the earthly function of the church and a transcendent angel, developing this link would provide the foundation for a new praxis for pastoral leadership. By exploring further the link between the way an earthly church functions and its transcendent counterpart, pastoral ministers could be encouraged to address a congregation's recurring behavior in a heavenly dimension as well as in the earthly realm.

A Wider Exploration of Church Records

Throughout this thesis, Wink's approach to understanding the angel of the church has, with a few exceptions, been illustrated using stories taken from the records of three English Baptist Churches. These records have been the churches at Budleigh Salterton, Newton Abbot, and South Street in Exeter, all of which are situated in the South West of England. While the records of each reveal aspects of the nature of the angel of the church, contrasting these stories with those contained in the records of other Baptist congregations would broaden the basis from which Wink's concept could be supported or critiqued. Furthermore, comparing the records of a set of churches in one part of England with another might also reveal similarities and differences in behavioral patterns. Extending this comparison still further and including churches from Scotland and Wales would offer additional insights into cultural differences that can be incorporated into Wink's concept.

The Use of Oral History

Based on Runcorn's encouragement to read church records as a method of discerning the angel of the church, this thesis has refrained from using other methods of gathering data that might reveal the nature of a congregation's angel. In this respect, oral history could provide a means by which a more expansive picture of the angel may possibly be developed.

The collection of oral history might provide greater insight into the nature of collective memory within a congregation. By exploring church members' recollections of a specific incident within a church's history, a congregation's strengths and weaknesses could be explored. If this data was then compared to the historical records kept by the church, the similarities and differences may reveal an extra dimension to the nature of the congregation's angel.

However, the difficulty with using oral history is highlighted by Wink's arguments regarding the complicit nature of a congregation and, on occasions, their minister. If oral history was only collected by members of the congregation, it might provide helpful and misleading information in equal quantities.

An Exploration of the Church in Relation to Its Topography

Although Wink suggests that the architecture and ambience of a church building can affect the nature of a congregation and its angel, he does not explore how the site of the building might have a similar effect. This question became apparent in a conversation with Runcorn that took place on February 11, 2014. During the conversation, Runcorn described how a pastor he had encountered was experiencing exhaustion in his ministry. Having questioned the minister regarding their church and congregation, it transpired that the church was situated in a mining village. Questioning more closely, Runcorn deduced that the church had adopted the nature of a mine shaft. As much as the pastor poured energy into the church, the congregation appeared to swallow it up and still required more.[35]

Although Wink does not explicitly suggest that topography can affect the nature of the angel of the church, his illustration of the Peruvian church built on the site of an Inca temple hints at this relationship.[36] Therefore, in view of Wink's experience and Runcorn's deductions, the site that a church occupies might be as important to the nature of the angel of the church as the architecture of the building.

---

35. Permission to use this story was given by Rev. David Runcorn on July 28, 2016.
36. Wink, *Unmasking the Powers*, 74.

The Influence of the Charismatic Renewal Movement

As this study has kept very closely to the format and content of Wink's chapter on the angel of the church, there are areas of theology that have not been explored. Among these, the most obvious would be the influence of the Charismatic Renewal Movement among Baptists.

Also known as neo-Pentecostalism, the Charismatic Renewal Movement's beginnings are dated by Ian Randall to the 1960s. He supports this argument by referring to the *Orders and Prayers for Church Worship*, written by the Baptist authors Ernest Payne and Stephen Winward and published in 1960.[37]

While, as Randall's research suggests, the Charismatic Renewal Movement had a significant impact among some Baptists throughout the 1960s, seventies, and eighties, this does not appear to have been the case in the Baptist churches at Budleigh Salterton, Newton Abbot, and South Street in Exeter. Of course, this is not to say that these congregations were not predisposed toward the Charismatic Renewal Movement. All that it is possible to say with certainty is that, according to the publicly available records from these three congregations, it cannot be determined to what level these congregations were influenced by the movement.

In view of this, any future research into the nature of the angel of the church among Baptists should include the study of a church that was significantly changed as a result of charismatic renewal.

Final Remarks

The question that sparked this research was formed of three parts. The first asked whether Wink's concept of an angel of the church was credible. The reply to this is yes. The biblical and intertestamental literature contains enough references to the concept of a transcendent entity that represents an earthly people group to support the idea that there is an angel for each congregation. Furthermore, Wink's description of the angel of the church having a gyroscopic effect on how a church functions goes some way to explaining how congregations repeat past mistakes or become obsessed with certain areas of their lives and ministry.

The answer to the second question, "Can Wink's concept can be seen in the lives of Baptist congregations?" is also yes. The records kept

---

37. Randall, *English Baptists of the Twentieth Century*, 324.

by the Baptists in Budleigh Salterton, Newton Abbot, and South Street in Exeter all reveal enough of the aspects highlighted by Wink as indicators of the angel's nature to describe at least part of the nature of each congregation's angel.

Answering the final question addressed by this thesis is less conclusive. While church records can provide useful insights into the nature of the angel of a church, they are not sufficient in themselves. In addition to reading the church records, pastors wishing to understand the nature of the angel of their church should also consider the setting and architecture of the church along with the sociological changes within the local community that have taken place during the life of the church. In view of this, the research required might need to be extensive in its scope and may require the use of a variety of academic disciplines. The complexity of the research required to construct a detailed profile of the angel of the church reveals just how difficult it is to understand the nature of an organization that exists in both the earthly and heavenly realms. Furthermore, while Wink argues that the influence the angel of the church exerts over a congregation is neutral, it does, nevertheless, create an inner resilience that restricts the level and speed of change that can be brought to a congregation.

At its heart, this thesis is a theological piece of work. It has sought to develop Wink's work and, thus, provide additional insight into the spiritual resilience that creates positive and negative character traits within a congregation. Furthermore, in addition to recognizing the areas of church life that create spiritual resilience, the possibility that an angel's nature might be transformed has also been suggested.

While it is true that the records used in this thesis have been insufficient to create a fully developed profile of the angel of the churches in Budleigh Salterton, Newton Abbot, and South Street in Exeter, they have been sufficient to begin the process. Therefore, while this thesis might not be able to fully describe the angel of a church, it has fulfilled its task in developing Wink's work and showing how its application can be seen in a Baptist context.

Bibliography

Arnold, Clinton E. *Powers of Darkness: A Thoughtful, Biblical, Look at the Urgent Challenge Facing the Church*. Leicester: Inter-Varsity Press, 1992.

Aune, David. *Revelation 1–5*. Dallas: Word Books, 1997.

Avery, W. J., ed. *The Baptist Handbook for 1900*. London: The Baptist Union of Great Britain and Ireland, 1900.

Bacon, Fred. *Church Administration: A Guide for Baptist Ministers and Church Officers*. Bristol: Bristol and District Association of Baptist Churches, 1981.

The Baptist Church, Little Knowle, Budleigh Salterton. Budleigh Salterton, 1993.

The Baptist Doctrine of the Church: A Statement Approved by the Council of the Baptist Union of Great Britain and Ireland, March 1948. London: Kingsgate, 1948.

The Baptist Handbook for 1940. London: The Baptist Union Publication Department, 1940.

The Baptist Handbook for 1947. London: The Baptist Union Publication Department, 1947.

The Baptist Handbook for 1971. London: The Baptist Union of Great Britain and Ireland, 1971.

Baptists Together. "Declaration of Principle." Accessed April 4, 2016. http://www.baptist.org.uk/Groups/220595/Declaration_of_Principle.aspx.

Barker, Margaret. *The Revelation of Jesus Christ Which God Gave to Him to Show His Servants What Must Soon Take Place (Revelation 1:1)*. Edinburgh: T&T Clark, 2000.

Beal, G. K. *The Book of Revelation: A Commentary on the Greek Text*. The New International Greek Testament Commentary. Carlisle: Paternoster, 1999.

Beasley-Murray, G. R. *The Book of Revelation*. New Century Bible. Rev. ed. London: Marshall, Morgan & Scott, 1978.

Beasley-Murray, Paul. *Power for God's Sake: Power and Abuse in the Local Church*. Carlisle: Paternoster, 1998.

Beaumont, Susan. *How to Lead When You Don't Know Where You're Going: Leading in a Liminal Season*. London: Rowman & Littlefield, 2019.

Bebbington, David W. *The Dominance of Evangelicalism: The Age of Spurgeon and Moody*. Leicester: Inter-Varsity Press, 2005.

———. *Evangelicalism in Modern Britain: A History from the 1730s to the 1980s*. London: Routledge, 2000.

Betteridge, Alan. *Deep Roots, Living Branches: A History of Baptists in the English West Midlands*. Kibworth Beauchamp: Matador, 2010.

Bickers, H. E. *A Brief History of the Baptist Church Now Meeting in South Street Chapel, Exeter, from the Year 1656*. Exeter: South Street Baptist Church, 1906.

Binfield, Clyde. "Nonconformist Architecture: A Representative Focus." In *T&T Clark Companion to Nonconformity*, edited by Robert Poole, 257–84. London: Bloomsbury, 2013.

Boring, M. Eugene. *Revelation*. Interpretation: A Bible Commentary for Teaching and Preaching. Louisville, KY: Westminster John Knox, 1989.

Bowers, Faith. "For God and the People: Baptist Deaconesses 1901–1905." *Baptist Quarterly* 43.8 (Oct. 2010) 473–93.

———. "Liberating Women for Baptist Ministry." *Baptist Quarterly* 45.8 (Oct. 2014) 456–64.

Boxall, Ian. *The Revelation of St John*. Black's New Testament Commentaries. London: Continuum, 2006.

Brierley, Peter. "The Elderly in the Church." *Future First* 82 (Aug. 2022) 5.

———. "Generations of Older People [Insert]." *Future First* 17 (Oct. 2011).

———. "Twenty Truths About Twenties." *Future First* 32 (Apr. 2014) 1–2.

Briggs, John H. Y. "English Baptists and Their Hymnody." In *Baptist Faith and Witness: The Papers of the Study and Research Division of the Baptist World Alliance 1990–1995*, edited by William H. Brackney and L. A. (Tony) Cupit, 152–59. Birmingham, AL: Samford University Press, 1995.

Briggs, Martin S. *Puritan Architecture and Its Future*. London: Lutterworth, 1946.

British Educational Research Association. "Ethical Guidelines for Educational Research." 2011. https://www.bera.ac.uk/wp-content/uploads/2014/02/BERA-Ethical-Guidelines-2011.pdf.

Brockett, Allan. *Nonconformity in Exeter 1650–1875*. Manchester: Manchester University Press, 1962.

Brown, Callum G. *The Death of Christian Britain: Understanding Secularisation 1800–2000*. 2nd ed. London: Routledge, 2009.

Brown, Kenneth K. D. *A Social History of the Nonconformist Ministry in England and Wales 1800–1930*. Oxford: Oxford University Press, 1998.

Brown, Raymond. *The English Baptists of the Eighteenth Century*. London: The Baptist Historical Society, 1986.

Burkett, Christopher. "Organisational Culture in Congregations." In *Leading, Managing, Ministering: Challenging Questions for Church and Society*, edited by John Nellson, 203–25. Bury St. Edmunds: Canterbury, 1999.

Cameron, Helen, et al., eds. *Studying Local Churches: A Handbook*. London: SCM, 2005.

Chardin, Pierre Teilhard de. *The Future of Man*. Translated by Norman Denny. London: Collins, 1969.

Clayton, Philip. "Conceptual Foundations of Emergence Theory." In *The Re-Emergence of Emergence*, edited by Philip Clayton and Paul Davies, 1–34. Oxford: Oxford University Press, 2006.

Collins, Peter. "Congregations, Narratives and Identity: A Quaker Case Study." In *Congregational Studies in the UK*, edited by Matthew Guest et al., 99–112. Aldershot: Ashgate, 2004.

Collis, Michael J. "Female Baptist Preachers and Ministers in Wales." *Baptist Quarterly* 45.8 (Oct. 2014) 465–84.

Colwell, John E. "The Sacramental Nature of Ordination: An Attempt to Re-Engage a Catholic Understanding and Practice." In *Baptist Sacramentalism*, edited by Anthony R. Cross and Philip E. Thompson, 228–46. Studies in Baptist History and Thought. Milton Keynes: Paternoster, 2003.

Copeland, David A. *Benjamin Keach and the Development of Baptist Traditions in Seventeenth-Century England*. Studies in Religion and Society. Lampeter: Edwin Mellen, 2001.

Cresswell, Julia. *The Watkins Dictionary of Angels*. London: Watkins, 2006. Kindle.

Creswell, Tim. *In Place/Out of Place: Geography, Ideology and Transgression*. London: University of Minnesota, 1996.

Crosby, Thomas. *The History of the English Baptists from the Reformation to the Beginning of the Reign of King George 1*. Vol 4. London: Theo. Crosby, 1740.

Currie, Robert, et al. *Churches and Chuchgoers: Patterns of Church Growth in the British Isles Since 1700*. Oxford: Clarendon, 1977.

Dakin, A. *The Baptist View of the Church and Ministry*. London: The Baptist Union Publication Department, 1944.

Dale, A. W. W. *The Life of R. W. Dale of Birmingham*. London: Hodder and Stoughton, 1898.

Daniélou, Jean. *According to the Fathers of the Church: The Angels and Their Mission*. Translated by David Heimann. Westminster, MD: Newman, 1957.

Davidson, Maxwell J. *Angels at Qumran*. Sheffield: Journal for the Study of the Pseudepigrapha, 1992.

Davies, Horton. *Worship and Theology in England from Andrews to Baxter and Fox, 1603–1690*. Princeton, NJ: Princeton University Press, 1975.

Devon Heritage Centre. Budleigh Salterton Baptist Church collection. Exeter, England.

———. East Dartmoor Baptist Church collection. Exeter, England.

———. Newton Abbot Baptist Church collection. Exeter, England.

———. South Street Baptist Church, Exeter collection. Exeter, England.

Dowley, T. "Baptists and Discipline in the 17th Century." *Baptist Quarterly* 24.4 (Oct. 1971) 157–66.

Egner, Malcolm J. "Re-Imagining the Covenant Community." Masters thesis, University of Wales, 2007.

Ellis, Christopher J. *Gathering: A Theology and Spirituality of Worship in Free Church Tradition*. London: SCM, 2004.

Ellis, Christopher John, and Myra Blyth, eds. *Gathering for Worship: Patterns and Prayers for the Community of Disciples*. Norwich: Canterbury, 2005.

Ellis, Robert A. "'The Leadership of Some . . .' Baptist Ministers as Leaders?" In *Challenging to Change: Dialogues with a Radical Baptist Theologian. Essays Presented to Dr Nigel G. Wright on His Sixtieth Birthday*, edited by Pieter J. Lalleman, 71–86. London: Spurgeon's College, 2009.

Enroth, Anne-Marit. "The Hearing Formula in the Book of Revelation." *New Testament Studies* 36.4 (Oct. 1990) 598–608.

Epp, Menno H. *The Pastor's Exit: The Dynamics of Involuntary Termination*. Manitoba: CMBC Publications, 1984.

Evangelical Alliance. "Basis of Faith." Accessed April 7, 2016. http://www.eauk.org/connect/about-us/basis-of-faith.cfm.

Fairbairn, Richard G., and Ronald W. Thomson. *The Church Secretary's Handbook*. London: The Baptist Union of Great Britain and Ireland, 1967.

Fee, Gordon D. *Revelation: A New Covenant Commentary*. Eugene, OR: Cascade, 2011.
Fiddes, Paul S. "Covenant—Old and New." In *Bound to Love: The Covenant Basis of Baptist Life and Mission*, by Keith Clements et al., 9–23. London: The Baptist Union, 1985.
———. *Tracks and Traces: Baptist Identity in Church and Theology*. Studies in Baptist History and Thought. Carlisle: Paternoster, 2003.
Fiddes, Paul, et al. *Something to Declare: A Study of the Declaration of Principle of the Baptist Union of Great Britain*. Edited by Richard Kidd. Oxford: Whitley Publications, 1996.
Finamore, Stephen. "Baptists in Covenant." In *Bound for Glory? God, Church and the World in Covenant*, edited by Anthony Clarke, 73–86. Oxford: Whitley Publications, 2002.
———. *God, Order and Chaos: René Girard and the Apocalypse*. Milton Keynes: Paternoster, 2009.
Fiorenza, Elisabeth Schüssler. *The Book of Revelation: Justice and Judgement*. Philadelphia: Fortress, 1985.
Forms of Ministry Among Baptists: Towards an Understanding of Spiritual Leadership. London: The Baptist Union of Great Britain, 1994.
Friedman, Edwin H. *Generation to Generation: Family Process in Church and Synagogue*. New York: Guildford, 1985.
Galeano, Eduardo. *Open Veins of Latin America: Five Centuries of the Pillage of a Continent*. Translated by Cedric Belfrage. London: Serpent's Tail, 2009.
Gardner, Trevor, and Richard Frost. *Faith in Exeter: The Story of the Palace Gate Project*. Exeter: Palace Gate Project, 1996.
Geertz, Clifford. *The Interpretation of Cultures*. New York: Basic Books, 1973.
The General Superintendents of the Baptist Union. *Guidelines for Churches Seeking Full-Time Ministers*. London: Baptist Union of Great Britain, 1990.
Giles, Richard. *Re-Pitching the Tent: Re-Ordering the Church Building for Worship and Mission in the New Millennium*. Norwich: Canterbury, 1996.
Gill, John. "The Mutual Duty of Pastor and People, Represented in Two Discourses, Preached at the Ordination of the Reverend George Braithwaite, MA, March Twenty Eighth, 1734 at the Meeting House, near Devonshire-Square." Little Britain: John Gill and Samuel Wilson, 1734.
Goodenough, Ursula. *The Sacred Depths of Nature*. Oxford: Oxford University Press, 1998.
Goodliff, Paul W. "Inclusive Representation Revisited." In *Challenging to Change: Dialogues with a Radical Baptist Theologian. Essays Presented to Dr Nigel G. Wright on His Sixtieth Birthday*, edited by Pieter J. Lalleman, 105–16. London: Spurgeon's College, 2009.
Gouldbourne, Ruth M. B. *Reinventing the Wheel: Women and Ministry in English Baptist Life*. Oxford: Whitley Publications, 1997.
———. "Voices." *Baptist Ministers' Journal* 268 (Oct. 1999) 6–9.
Gregersen, Niels Henrik. "Emergence: What Is at Stake for Religious Reflection." In *The Re-Emergence of Emergence*, edited by Philip Clayton and Paul Davies, 279–302. Oxford: Oxford University Press, 2006.
Grundy, Malcolm. *Understanding Congregations: A New Shape for the Local Church*. London: Mowbray, 1998.
Guest, Matthew, et al., eds. *Congregational Studies in the UK*. Aldershot: Ashgate, 2004.

Gustafson, James M. *Treasures in Earthen Vessels*. Louisville, KY: Westminster John Knox, 2009.
Halbwachs, Maurice. *On Collective Memory*. Edited and translated by Lewis A. Coser. Chicago: University of Chicago, 1992.
Hammersley, Martyn. "On Ethical Principles for Social Research." *International Journal of Social Research Methodology* 18.4 (2015) 433–49.
Harrison, F. M. W. "The Nottingham Baptists: Church Relations, Social Composition, Finance, Theology." *Baptist Quarterly* 26.4 (Oct. 1975) 169–90.
Harvey, David. *The Condition of Postmodernity*. Cambridge: Blackwell, 1990.
Hayden, Roger. "Baptists, Covenants and Confessions." In *Bound to Love: The Covenant Basis of Baptist Life and Mission*, by Keith Clements et al., 24–36. London: The Baptist Union, 1985.
———. *Continuity and Change: Evangelical Calvinism Among Eighteenth-Century Baptist Ministers Trained at Bristol Academy, 1690–1791*. Chipping Norton: Nigel Lynn and The Baptist Historical Society, 2006.
Haymes, Brian. "Integrity in Preaching." *Baptist Ministers Journal* 243 (July 2019) 5–17.
———. "Integrity in Preaching: The 22nd Lester C. Randall Preaching Fellowship Lecture." October 25, 2008. Bristol Baptist College Library special collections, FC1 (17e).
———. "Theology and Baptist Identity." In *Doing Theology in a Baptist Way*, edited by Paul S. Fiddes, 1–5. Oxford: Whitley Publications, 2000.
Haymes, Brian, et al. *On Being Church: Revisioning Baptist Identity*. Eugene, OR: Wipf & Stock, 2008.
Hedger, Graham. "The Challenge of an Ageing Population." *Future First* 10 (Aug. 2010).
Hill, David. *New Testament Prophecy*. London: Marshall, Morgan & Scott, 1979.
Holmes, Stephen R. "Knowing the Mind of Christ: Congregational Government and the Church Meeting." In *Questions of Identity: Studies in Honour of Brian Haymes*, edited by Anthony R. Cross and Ruth Gouldbourne, 172–88. Oxford: Regents Park College, 2011.
———. "Towards a Baptist Theology of Ordained Ministry." In *Baptist Sacramentalism*, edited by Anthony R. Cross and Philip E. Thompson, 247–62. Studies in Baptist History and Thought. Milton Keynes: Paternoster, 2003.
Hopewell, James F. *Congregation: Stories and Structures*. Edited by Barbara G. Wheeler. London: SCM, 1987.
"House of Commons Rebuilding." October 28, 1943. https://api.parliament.uk/historic-hansard/commons/1943/oct/28/house-of-commons-rebuilding.
Hughes, Philip Edgcumbe. *The Book of the Revelation: A Commentary*. Leicester: Inter-Varsity Press, 1990.
In This Place, at This Time. Report. North Western Baptist Association, 2014.
Inge, John. *A Christian Theology of Place*. Aldershot: Ashgate, 2003.
Inglis, K. S. *Churches and the Working Classes in Victorian England*. London: Routledge and Kegan Paul, 1963.
James, Isaac. *The History of the Dissenting Churches*. Vol. 1. Ca. 1777. Bristol Baptist College Library special collections, OS-G-93.
Jones, Keith G. "The Industrial Revolution: Effects upon the Baptist Community in Barnoldswick and the Resulting 'Split' in the Baptist Church." *Baptist Quarterly* 30.3 (July 1983) 125–39.

Josephus. *Jewish Antiquities, Books XV–XVII*. Translated by Ralph Marcus. Edited by Allen Wikgren. London: William Heinemann, 1963.

Kelper, Thomas S. "Angels of the Seven Churches." In *Dictionary of the Bible*, edited by James Hastings, 33–34. 2nd ed. Edinburgh: T&T Clark, 1963.

Kets de Vries, Manfred F. R. "Introduction: Exploding the Myth That Organizations and Executives Are Rational." In *Organizations on the Couch*, edited by Manfred F. R. Kets de Vries, 1–21. San Francisco: Jossey-Bass, 1991.

Kiddle, Martin. *The Revelation of St. John*. 7th ed. London: Hodder and Stoughton, 1963.

Kieckhefer, Richard. *Theology in Stone: Church Architecture from Byzantium to Berkeley*. Oxford: Oxford University Press, 2004.

Kovacs, Judith, and Christopher Rowland. *Revelation: The Apocalypse of Jesus Christ*. Blackwell Bible Commentaries. Oxford: Blackwell, 2004.

Lassetter, Vivienne, and Ernie Walley. *Journeying Through Conflict—Part of Life*. Didcot: Baptist Union of Great Britain, 2004.

Leas, Speed, and Paul Kittlaus. *Church Fights: Managing Conflict in the Local Church*. Philadelphia: Westminster, 1973.

Lebold, Ralph. "Decision Making." *Global Anabaptist Mennonite Encyclopedia Online*, accessed February 19, 2016. http://gameo.org/index.php?title=Decision-making.

Leonard, Bill J. "Being Baptist: Hospital Traditionalism." In *Why I Am a Baptist: Reflections on Being Baptist in the 21st Century*, edited by Cecil P. Staton Jr., 77–88. Macon, GA: Smyth & Helwys, 1999.

Lieu, Judith M. *Christian Identity in the Jewish and Graeco-Roman World*. Oxford: Oxford University Press, 2004.

Lincoln, Andrew T. "Liberation from the Powers: Supernatural Spirits or Societal Structures." In *The Bible in Human Society: Essays in Honour of John Rogerson*, edited by M. Daniel Carroll R. et al., 335–54. Sheffield: Sheffield Academic, 1995.

Lucie-Smith, Alexander. *Narrative Theology and Moral Theology*. Aldershot: Ashgate, 2007.

Lumpkin, William L., and Bill J. Leonard, eds. *Baptist Confessions of Faith*. 2nd rev. ed. Valley Forge, PA: Judson, 2011.

McGavran, Donald. *Understanding Church Growth*. Grand Rapids, MI: Eerdmans, 1978.

McIntosh, Alastair. "Engaging Walter Wink's Powers." In *Enigmas and Powers: Engaging the Work of Walter Wink for Classroom, Church, and World*, edited by D. Seiple and Frederick W. Weidmann, 101–12. Eugene, OR: Pickwick, 2008.

McSwain, Larry L., and William C. Treadwell Jr. *Conflict Ministry in the Church*. Nashville: Broadman, 1981.

The Meaning and Practice of Ordination Among Baptists: A Report Submitted to the Council of the Baptist Union of Great Britain and Ireland. London: Kingsgate, 1957.

Mennonite World Conference. "Guidelines for Making Decisions by Consensus." Accessed August 10, 2016. http://www.commonword.ca/FileDownload/13482/Consensus_Guidelines_ENG-1.pdf.

The Ministry Department of the Baptist Union of Great Britain. *Facing a Pastoral Vacancy: Advice for Churches During a Pastoral Vacancy*. Didcot: The Baptist Union of Great Britain, 2002.

Moon, Norman S. *Education for Ministry: Bristol Baptist College 1679–1979*. Bristol: Bristol Baptist College, 1979.

Morden, Peter J. *Offering Christ to the World: Andrew Fuller (1754–1815) and the Revival of Eighteenth-Century Particular Baptist Life*. Studies in Baptist History and Thought. Carlisle: Paternoster, 2003.

Moses, Robert Ewusie. *Practices of Power: Revisiting the Principalities and Powers in the Pauline Letters*. Minneapolis: Fortress, 2014.

Naylor, Peter. *Picking Up a Pin for the Lord: English Particular Baptists from 1688 to the Early Nineteenth Century*. London: Grace Publications Trust, 1992.

Newsom, Carol. *Songs of the Sabbath Sacrifice*. Harvard Semitic Studies. Atlanta: Scholars Press, 1985.

Niebuhr, H. R. *The Social Sources of Denominationalism*. 8th ed. Cleveland, OH: Word Publishing, 1957.

Norberg-Schulz, Christian. *Existence, Space and Architecture*. London: Studio Vista, 1971.

———. *Genius Loci: Towards a Phenomenology of Architecture*. London: Academy Editions, 1980.

———. *Intentions in Architecture*. Cambridge, MA: MIT, 1965.

Novick, Peter. *The Holocaust in American Life*. Boston: Houghton Mifflin, 1999.

Office for National Statistics. "Neighbourhood Statistics: Budleigh Ward. 2011 Census." Accessed June 14, 2016. No longer available online.

O'Reilly, Charles. "Corporations, Culture, and Commitment: Motivation and Social Control in Organizations." In *Psychological Dimensions of Organizational Behaviour*, edited by Barry M. Staw, 316–28. New York: Macmillan, 1995.

Owen, John. *The Works of John Owen D.D.* Vol. 13. Standard Library of British Divines. Edinburgh: Johnstone and Hunter, 1852.

Pannenberg, Wolfhart. *Toward a Theology of Nature: Essays on Science and Faith*. Edited by Ted Peters. Louisville, KY: Westminster John Knox, 1993.

Parker, Russ. *Healing Wounded History: Reconciling Peoples and Healing Places*. London: SPCK, 2012.

Patterns and Prayers for Christian Worship: A Guidebook for Worship Leaders. Oxford: Oxford University Press, 1991.

Payne, Ernest A. *The Baptist Union: A Short History*. London: Kingsgate, 1958.

———. *The Fellowship of Believers: Baptist Thought and Practice Yesterday and Today*. London: Kingsgate, 1944.

Payne, Ernest A., and Stephen F. Winward. *Orders and Prayers for Church Worship*. London: Kingsgate, 1960.

Philippson, Peter, and John Bernard Harris. *Gestalt: Working with Groups*. 2nd rev. ed. Manchester: The Manchester Gestalt Centre, 1992. Kindle.

Piper, A. R. *A Short History of Ebenezer Chapel 1843–1983 (compiled from the Minute Books)*. 1983. Bristol Baptist College Library special collections, PAM-BX-6490. D46.B9 Pip.

Quicke, Michael J. "Further Reflections on a Sacramental Understanding of Preaching." In *Questions of Identity: Studies in Honour of Brian Haymes*, edited by Anthony R. Cross and Ruth Gouldbourne, 18–33. Oxford: Centre for Baptist History and Heritage Studies, 2011.

Rackley, John. "The Acceptable Outsider." *Baptist Ministers' Journal* 304 (Oct. 2009) 3–11.

Ramsey, James B. *The Book of Revelation: An Exposition of the First Eleven Chapters Originally Published Under the Title 'the Spiritual Kingdom'*. Edinburgh: The Banner of Truth Trust, 1977.
Randall, Ian M. *The English Baptists of the Twentieth Century*. Didcot: The Baptist Historical Society, 2005.
Rhodes, A. J. *Newton Abbot: Its History and Development*. Newton Abbot: Mid-Devon and Newton Times, 1903.
Rusling, G. W. *Baptist Places of Worship*. London: The Baptist Union of Great Britain and Ireland, 1965.
Sack, Robert David. *Human Territoriality: Its Theory and History*. Cambridge: Cambridge University Press, 1986.
Samalavičius, Almantas. "'Spirit of Place' in Christian Norberg-Schulz's Phenomenology of Architecture." *Logos: A Journal of Religion, Philosophy, Comparative Cultural Studies and Art* 71 (2012) 119–26.
Savage, Sara, and Eolene Boyd-MacMillan. *The Human Face of the Church: A Social Psychology and Pastoral Resource for Pioneer and Traditional Ministry*. Norwich: Canterbury, 2007.
Schrock-Shenk, Carolyn, and Lawrence Ressler. *Making Peace with Conflict: Practical Skills for Conflict Transformation*. Scottdale, PA: Herald, 1999.
Schwartz, H., and S. Davis. "Matching Corporate Culture and Business Strategy." *Organizational Dynamics* 10.1 (1981) 30–48.
Seiple, D., and Frederick W. Weidmann, eds. *Enigmas and Powers: Engaging the Work of Walter Wink for Classroom, Church and World*. Eugene, OR: Pickwick, 2008.
Sellers, Ian. *Our Heritage: The Baptists of Yorkshire, Lancashire and Cheshire, 1647–1987*. Leeds: The Yorkshire Baptist Association and the Lancashire and Cheshire Baptist Association, 1987.
Shepherd, Peter. *The Making of a Modern Denomination: John Howard Shakespeare and the English Baptists, 1898–1924*. Studies in Baptist History and Thought. Oxford: Oxford University Press, 2002.
Shorter Oxford English Dictionary: On Historical Principles. Vol. 2, *N–Z*. Oxford: Oxford University Press, 2002.
Smith, Edward. *The Great Problem of the Times*. London: T. Woolmer, 1883.
Soja, Edward W. *Postmodern Geographies: The Reassertion of Space in Critical Social Theory*. London: Verso, 1989.
South West Baptist Association Records. Newton Abbot Baptist Church collection. Wonford Baptist Chapel, Exeter.
Steinke, Peter L. *Healthy Congregations: A Systems Approach*. Herndon, VA: The Alban Institute, 1996.
———. *How Your Church Family Works: Understanding Congregations as Emotional Systems*. Herndon, VA: The Alban Institute, 1993.
Stirling, D. M. *A History of Newton Abbot and Newton Bushel and Also Illustrations of the Antiquities, Topography, and Scenery of the Circumjacent Neighbourhood Including Teighnmouth, Torquay and Chudleigh*. Newton Abbot: W. F. Forord, 1830.
This Hope Baptist Church, Newton Abbot. "Home/Who Are We?" Accessed September 29, 2014. No longer available online..
Tole, Rachel. *Nothing Spiritual About Chaos: A Practical Guide for Baptist Church Secretaries and Administrators*. Didcot: Baptist Union of Great Britain, 2006.

Turner, Harold W. *From Temple to Meeting House: The Phenomenology and Theology of Places of Worship.* The Hague: Mouton Publishers, 1979.
UK Research and Innovation. "Framework for Research Ethics." Last updated August 17, 2021. https://www.ukri.org/councils/esrc/guidance-for-applicants/research-ethics-guidance/framework-for-research-ethics/our-core-principles/.
Underwood, A. C. *A History of the English Baptists.* London: The Baptist Union Publication Department, 1947.
United States Institute of Peace. "Former Senior Fellows 1990–1991." https://www.usip.org/grants-fellowships/jennings-randolph-senior-fellowship-program/former-jennings-randolph-senior-fello.
Walker, Michael. *Baptists at the Table.* Didcot: Baptist Historical Society, 1992.
Walton, Francis R. "The Messenger of God in Hecataeus of Abdera." *Harvard Theological Review* 48.4 (Oct. 1955) 255–57.
Ward, Matthew. *Pure Worship: The Early English Baptist Distinctive.* Eugene, OR: Pickwick, 2014.
Warren, Robert. *The Healthy Churches Handbook.* London: Church House Publishing, 2004.
Watts, Michael. *The Dissenters.* Oxford: Clarendon, 1978.
Weber, Max. *From Max Weber: Essays in Sociology.* Translated by H. H. Gerth and C. Wright Mills. New ed. London: Routledge, 1991.
West, W. M. S. *Baptist Principles.* 3rd ed. London: The Baptist Union of Great Britain and Ireland, 1975.
White, B. R. *Authority: A Baptist View.* London: Baptist Publications, 1976.
———. "Open and Closed Communion Among English and Welsh Baptists." *Baptist Quarterly* 24.7 (July 1972) 330–34.
White, Susan. "The Theology of Sacred Space." In *The Sense of the Sacramental: Movement and Measure in Art and Music, Place and Time,* edited by David Brown and Ann Loades, 31–43. London: SPCK, 1995.
Wikipedia. "Walter Wink." Accessed May 14, 2022. https://en.wikipedia.org/wiki/Walter_Wink.
Williams, Stuart Murray, and Sian Murray Williams. *Multi-Voiced Church.* Milton Keynes: Paternoster, 2012.
Willimon, William H. *Preaching About Conflict in the Local Church.* Philadelphia: Westminster, 1987.
Wilson, Linda. *Constrained by Zeal. Female Spirituality Amongst Nonconformists 1825–75.* Carlisle: Paternoster, 2000.
Wink, Walter. *Cracking the Gnostic Code: The Powers in Gnosticism.* The Society of Biblical Literature Monograph Series. Atlanta: Scholars Press, 1993.
———. *Engaging the Powers: Discernment and Resistance in a World of Domination.* Minneapolis: Fortress, 1992.
———. *Naming the Powers: The Language of Power in the New Testament.* Philadelphia: Fortress, 1984.
———. "Our Stories, Cosmic Stories and the Biblical Story." In *Sacred Stories: A Celebration of the Power of Stories to Transform and Heal,* edited by Charles Simpkinson and Anne Simpkinson, 209–22. San Francisco: HarperCollins, 1993.
———. *The Powers That Be: Theology for a New Millennium.* New York: Galilee Doubleday, 1998.

———. *Unmasking the Powers: The Invisible Forces That Determine Human Existence.* Philadelphia: Fortress, 1986.

———. *Violence and Nonviolence in South Africa: Jesus' Third Way.* Philadelphia: New Society, 1987.

———. *When the Powers Fall: Reconciliation in the Healing of Nations.* Minneapolis: Fortress, 1998.

Wise, David. "Multi-Ethnic Worship." *Ministry Today* 63 (Spring 2015) 23–31.

Wise, Graham. *The Baptist Church in Budleigh Salterton 1843–2018.* Ilkeston: Morleys, 2018.

Wood, J. R., and Samuel Chick. *A Manual of the Order and Administration of a Baptist Church.* London: Kingsgate, n.d.

Woodward, James. *Valuing Age: Pastoral Ministry with Older People.* New Library of Pastoral Care. London: SPCK, 2008.

Worrall, B. G. *The Making of the Modern Church: Christianity in England since 1800.* Rev. and updated ed. London: SPCK, 2001.

Wright, Nigel Goring. *Challenge to Change: A Radical Agenda for Baptists.* Eastbourne: Kingsway, 1991.

———. *Free Church, Free State: The Positive Baptist Vision.* Milton Keynes: Paternoster, 2005.

———. "Inclusive Representation: Towards a Doctrine of Christian Ministry." *Baptist Quarterly* 39.4 (Oct. 2001) 163–74.

———. *New Baptists, New Agenda.* Carlisle: Paternoster, 2002.

Wright, Tom. *Surprised by Hope.* London: SPCK, 2007.

Index

Page references followed by n
indicates footnotes.

"Acceptable Outsider, The" (Rackley), 124
Act of Toleration (1689), 48–49
age demographic, 86–91
ambience, 43–44, 57
ancient worldview, 18
angel(s)
    contested identities of, 24
    corporate, 7–9
    feminine/masculine portrayal of, 91
    humans addressing transcendent, 100
    as intermediaries, 30
    of nations, 8
    as visionary interpreters of Christ's will, 33–34
    of vocation, 11
angel of the church, general
    architecture and, 38–40
    becoming demonic, 66, 84, 90–91, 108–9, 154
    Biblical basis for, 218–19
    conflict and, 152–53
    congregations and, 128–29, 219, 225–28
    corporate spiritual identity and, 206–7
    demographics and, 97–99
    interiority and, 18–21
    Robert Warren's exercise to discover, 10–11
    stabilizing (gyroscopic) effect of, 35–36, 74, 124, 207–8, 219
    transformation of, 141, 219–25
angel of the church, identities of
    attributes forming, 5
    as collective entity, 4
    as colony of heaven, 34
    as congregation's alter ego, 26–27
    as Fravashi, 32–33
    as heavenly representative of earthly congregation, 31–32
    as human messenger, 24–25
    in Jewish intertestamental literature, 27–30
    as local church leader, 25–26
    as prophetic guild, 25
    representing earthly struggle, 31
    as visionary counterpart of community prophets, 33–34
angelos (messenger), 4, 35, 218
Angels and Principalities (Carr), 218
Angels at Qumran (Davidson), 29–30
anxiety, 58, 132–36, 208–9, 224–26. *See also* Newton Abbot Baptist Church
architecture
    ambience and, 43–44
    domus Dei and *domus ecclesiae*, 42–43
    effect of on congregations, 52–54
    as expression of confidence, 48–51
    four design types of, 42

INDEX

architecture *(continued)*
    influencing social functioning, 38–40
    nonconformist, 48–49
    phenomenology of, 40–43, 46–47
    postmodern perspective on, 47–48
    social geography and, 46–53
atemporal theism, 198–99
Aune, David, 24–27, 32–35, 218
authority, 101–9

Bacon, Fred, 108, 135, 192–93
Baptist Church in Budleigh Salterton 1843–2018, The (Wise), 15
Baptist denominational rubric
    acceptable outsiders, inviting, 163–64
    Baptists acting together, 162–63
    Christ as head and, 158–59
    differing opinions and, 159–60
    distinctive nature of, 157–58
    diverse opinions valued in, 160–62
Baptist Doctrine of the Church, The, 162–63
Baptist Order of Deaconesses, 92
Baptist Union of Great Britain
    Baptist churches leaving, 161–62
    Budleigh Salterton and, 77, 83–85
    first principle of, 101
    Home Mission Grants and, 75n55
    on importance of Scripture, 140n36
    relationship with Baptist congregations, 102n5
    Scottish and Welsh churches and, 72
Baptists
    artifacts and worship space, views on, 43
    association with other churches, 139, 146–47, 162–63, 165–67
    authority, understanding of, 101–2
    of Barnoldswick, 64–67
    in Britain and the United Kingdom, 111–12, 157–58
    church meetings and, 200–201
    early, 48–49, 70, 144–45, 162
    General, 109–10, 117, 144, 160, 162, 174, 176
    hymn singing, views on, 184–88
    liberty of, 190–91
    new members and, 92–93
    ordination, understanding of, 112–13
    Particular, 109–10, 117, 144, 160, 163, 176
    theological practice of, 178–79
    women, 92–96
Barker, W.A., 80–83
Beal, G. K., 31–32
Beasley-Murray, George, 32–33
Bebbington, David, 67, 92, 94–95
Bennett, Thomas, 64–66
Binfield, Clyde, 48–49
Blizzard, Charles, 52, 119
Book of Dreams (Qumran community), 30
Book of Revelation: Justice and Judgement, The (Fiorenza), 33
Boring, M. Eugene, 28
Bovey Tracey Baptist Church, 175–77, 202, 205n36
Boxall, Ian, 27, 31–32
Boyden Howes, Elizabeth, 20–21
Boyd-MacMillan, Eolene, 131–33, 141
A Brief History of the Baptist Church now meeting in South Street Chapel, Exeter, from the year 1656 (Bickers), 15
Brierley, Peter, 87–88, 89–90
Briggs, John, 184, 186
Briggs, Martin, 39–40, 48
Bristol Academy, 174–75
Brown, Jeremy, 209–10
Budleigh Salterton Baptist Church
    angel profile of, 226–27
    Baptist Union of Great Britain and, 77, 83–85
    Boy's Brigade program, 168–70, 191
    conflict presentation at, 133–34
    education programs at, 167–70
    finances of, 75–85
    generosity and ingenuity of, 81–86
    new appointments at, 78–83, 126–27, 181–82
    peaceful community of, 210
    records of, 12–13

INDEX

resignation at, 141–44
vocation at, 210–11
women in, 92–95
worship discussion at, 188–90
Burkett, Christopher, 211–12

Calvin, John, 114–15
Calvinistic theology, Newton Abbot and, 173–78
Charismatic Renewal Movement, 231
Christ
    addressing the angelic through, 100
    Baptist denominational rubric, role of in, 158–59
    desire to know the mind of, 9
    leadership model of, 121
    letters to the seven churches by, 24
    reflecting the mind of, 120
Christianismus Primitivus (Grantham), 185
Christianity as a lifestyle, 140
chronic anxiety, 132–33, 134–35
Church Administration (Bacon), 181
church leaders as angels, 25–26
church meetings, 107–9
church membership and transference, 203–6
Church of England, 48–49, 63–64, 144
churches
    current nature of, 5
    methodology of records use of, 15–16
    records of, 13, 193
    relation to topography of, 230
    vs. secular organizations, 8–9
    vocation of, 5–6. *see also* architecture
Churches and Churchgoers (Currie, Gilbert, Horsley), 70–71
Churchill, Winston, 38–39
Classical architecture, 42
collaboration, 137
collective memory, 195–97
Collins, Peter, 17
Colwell, John, 114–15
communal tradition of church construction, 43–44

communion, 144–45, 178
Complex architecture, 42
Condition of Postmodernity, The (Harvey), 47
confessions of faith, 117–18, 162
conflict
    beliefs and values, disagreement over, 144–52
    consensus and decision making and, 133–41
    God, role of will of in, 132
    interpersonal, 141–42
    nature of, 131–33
    nature of the angel revealed by, 152–53
    positive aspects of, 131–32
    restraint during, 141–44
    scapegoats and, 151
    types of, 130–31
congregational studies, 6–7, 16–17, 96–97, 132
congregations
    alter ego of, 26–27
    consensus at, 136–37
    corporate personality of, 11–12, 87, 204, 212
    cultural expectations of, 204–6
    demographics and, 70–73, 87–90
    divisions within, 104
    governance in, 127–28
    outsiders, appointing to, 124–27
    relationship to their building and, 52–53
    restricted freedom of, 122–24
    stagnation of, addressing, 220–21
    voting and, 135–36
consensus, 136–37, 143
Copeland, David, 186–87
corporate angels, 7–9
corporate spirit of an organization, 195, 201
Cosmic architecture, 42
Covenanted Persons list, 113
Cresswell, Julia, 32
Creswell, Tim, 44–46, 56
Crosby, Thomas, 184–85
Currie, Robert, 70–72, 73, 88, 90

245

Dakin, Arthur, 110–11
Davidson, Maxwell, 28, 29–30, 35, 218, 229
Davis, Stan, 203–4
de Chardin, Teilhard, 7
"Declaration of Principle" (Baptists Together), 101n3, 140n36, 158–59, 161
demographics
    age, 86–91
    church records and, 98–99
    economic class, 62–69
    education, 70
    gender, 91–96
    income, 74–86
    racial and ethnic background, 70–74
denominational rubrics
    Calvinistic theology of Newton Abbot Baptists and, 173–78
    education programs, 167–73
    nature of Baptist, 157–67
    theological reflection and, 178–79
    Wink on, 157–58
    worship practices and, 179–90
discipleship, Christian, 139–41
A Discourse Concerning Singing in the Publick Worship of God in the Gospel Church (Marlow), 186
Doctrine of the Church, The (Baptist Union of Great Britain), 118, 135–36
Doing Theology in a Baptist Way (Haymes), 178
Dominance of Evangelicalism, The (Bebbington), 92
domination system, 2
domus Dei, 41, 42–43, 58–60
domus ecclesiae, 42–43, 59
Dowley, T., 69–70

earth/heaven relationship, 18–21, 27, 32–33, 229
East Street Chapel, 49–53, 56–58, 140n37, 209, 223
Economic and Social Research Council (ESRC), 15–16
economic class, 62–69. *See also* income

education, 70, 167–73
"Effectiveness of Nonviolent Strategies for Social Change and the Biblical Roots of Nonviolent Philosophy, The" (Wink), 1
Egner, Malcolm, 13, 69–70
"Elderly in the Church, The" (Brierly), 87
Ellis, Robert, 121–22, 182–83
emergence, 197–201, 214
emotion, recording, 154–55
Engaging the Powers (Wink), 1–2, 18–20, 151, 206–7
Enlightenment period, 19
Enoch, book of, 28, 29–30
Enroth, Anne-Marit, 33
Epp, Menno, 132
eschatological theism, 200–201
ESRC (Economic and Social Research Council), 15–16
Essays in Sociology (Weber), 67–68
ethnicity and race, 70–74
ethos, institutional, 212–13
Evangelical Alliance, 158
Evangelicalism in Modern Britain (Bebbington), 67
Evans, Caleb, 174–75
evolving theistic naturalism, 198
Existence, Space and Architecture (Norberg-Schulz), 40
external constituencies, 70–71
extrinsic congregational studies, 6

Facing a Pastoral Vacancy (Ministry Department of the Baptist Union), 181
Fairbairn, Richard, 135, 138
Faith in Exeter: The Story of the Palace Gate Project (Frost), 15
Fee, Gordon, 27–28
Fiddes, Paul, 103n, 107–8, 136–37, 158–59, 161–62
Finamore, Stephen, 9–10, 102–3
Fiorenza, Elisabeth Schüssler, 33–34
flat religious naturalism, 197–98

Forms of Ministry Among Baptists (Baptist Union of Great Britain), 111
Fravashis, 32–33
Friedman, Edwin, 206, 214
From Temple to Meeting House: The Phenomenology and Theology of Places of Worship (Turner), 42–43
Frost, Richard, 15, 163–64
Future First (Hedger), 86
Future of Man, The (de Chardin), 7

Gabb, Arthur, 14, 144–52, 146n58, 159–60, 175
Gardner, Trevor, 15, 163–64
Gates, Edith, 95
Gathering for Worship (Blyth, Ellis), 43, 111
Geertz, Clifford, 212–13
gender, 91–96
General Baptists
  Bovey Tracey Baptist Church and, 176
  closed membership policy of, 176–77
  communion and, 144
  early confessions of faith from, 117
  evangelical expression of, 160
  local vs. wider ministry of, 109–10
  standard Confession of, 162–63
General Motors, 7–9, 195, 201–2
generosity, 85–86
genius loci (genius of the place), 40–42, 59
Genius Loci (Norberg-Schulz), 40
Gestalt, 21–22
Gilbert, Alan, 70–71
Giles, Richard, 48, 58
Gill, John, 179
Girard, René, 9–10, 151
Gnostics, 19
God
  atemporal theistic view of, 198–99
  eschatological theistic view of, 200–201
  evolving theistic naturalistic view of, 198
  inaccessibility of, 30
  role of will in conflict of, 132
  temporal theistic view of, 199–200
God, Order and Chaos (Finamore), 9
Goodliff, Paul, 111
gossip, breaking the cycle of, 224–25
Gouldbourne, Ruth, 94, 95–96, 139, 222
Grantham, Thomas, 185
Greenford Baptist Church, 72–74
Gregersen, Niels Henrik, 197–203
Guidelines for Churches Seeking Full-Time Ministers (General Superintendents of the Baptist Union), 181
Gustafson, James, 16–17

Halbwachs, Maurice, 195–96
Harvey, David, 45, 47–48, 53–54, 56, 58
Hayden, Roger, 108, 174–75
Haymes, Brian
  beginning ministry at South Street in Exeter, 163–64
  called to Newton Abbot as minister, 183
  on communal theological reflection, 178–79
  on discipleship, 139–40
  on ministry as a corporate activity, 116–17
  on preachers, 179–80
Healthy Churches Handbook, The (Warren), 10
"Hearing Formula in the Book of Revelation, The" (Enroth), 33
heaven, colony of, 34
heavenly temple, 28–29
Hedger, Graham, 86–87, 88–89, 90
Hedger, Violet, 95
historical geography, 45, 53–55
A History of Newton Abbot and Newton Bushel (Stirling), 14
Holmes, Stephen, 103, 108, 113–18, 192–93
Holocaust in American Life, The (Novick), 195–96

Holy Spirit, 185–86
Homily on Ephesians (Eusebius), 220
Hopewell, James, 15
Horsley, Lee, 70–71
House of Commons reconstruction, 38–39
How to Lead When You Don't Know Where You Are Going: Leading in a Liminal Season (Beaumont), 10
Hughes, Philip Edgcumbe, 25–26, 31
human messengers as angels, 24–25
hymn books, choosing, 187–88
hymn singing, 184–88

income, 74–86
Inge, John, 55
Inglis, K.S., 68
integral worldview, 20
Intentions in Architecture (Norberg-Schulz), 40
interiority, spiritual, 18–21
internal constituencies, 70–71
interpersonal conflict, 130–31, 141–42
intertestamental period, 218–19
intrapersonal conflict, 130–31
intrinsic congregational studies, 6
Israel, 30, 121

Jerusalem, 55
Jewish Antiquities (Josephus), 25
Jewish intertestamental literature, 27–30
John (Saint), 24, 25, 32, 219–20
Jones, Keith, 64–66, 97, 99
Josephus, 25
Journeying Through Conflict (Coffey), 132
Jubilees, book of, 28
judgment, angelic role in, 29
Jung, Carl, 20–21

Keach, Benjamin, 184–87
Kidd, Richard, 107, 158
Kiddle, Martin, 34

Kieckhefer, Richard, 39–40, 43–44, 51, 52, 56
Kilmington Baptist Church, 102
Kovacs, Judith, 31

leadership
    assisting in transformation, 99
    authoritarian, 122
    dominating quality of, 119–20
    language of, 121–22
    responding to demographic change, 72–74
    styles affected by socioeconomic class, 64–65
Lebold, Ralph, 137
Leonard, Bill, 157–58, 159
Lieu, Judith, 180
Living-Taylor, Maria, 95
London Confession (1644), 109, 117
Lord's Supper, 144–45, 177–78
Lucie-Smith, Alexander, 202, 205–6, 214–15

Making of the Modern Church, The (Worrall), 67
Making Peace with Conflict (Schrock-Shenk), 132
Marcus, Ralph, 25
Marlow, Isaac, 186–87
Marxism, 7
materialistic worldview, 19
McGavran, Donald, 62–63, 71
McSwain, Larry, 132
Meaning and Practice of Ordination Among Baptists, The (Clark), 112–13
Melinda (pastor), 4, 220–21, 222–25
Mennonites, 132, 137
middle class, 67–69
ministers
    calling to account of, 103–6
    influence of, 149–50
    newly appointed, 180–84
    restraint expectations of, 142, 143–44

stipends of, 76–77
women, 95–96
ministry
    Baptist understanding of, 103
    broadening the understanding of, 111–12
    as corporate activity, 116–17
    corporate nature of, 103, 118
    dependency and the practice of, 106–7
    local vs. wider roles of, 109–11
    ordination and, 112–15
    sacramental view of, 115–16
Morden, Peter, 174–75
Multi-Voiced Church (Murray Williams), 164
"Mutual Duty of Pastor and People, The" sermon (Gill), 179

Naming the Powers (Wink), 1–2, 218
Nature of the Assembly and the Council of the Baptist Union of Great Britain, The (Fiddes et al.), 103n8
Naylor, Peter, 144–45
neo-Pentecostalism, 231
New Connexion General Baptists, 160, 176
New Testament, 2, 10, 29
Newsom, Carol, 28–29, 35, 218, 229
Newton Abbot Baptist Church. *See also* anxiety; Baptist denominational rubric
    angel profile of, 225–26
    assistance request from, 164–67
    Calvinistic theology of, 173–78
    challenges of, 51–52, 103–6, 119–20, 137–38, 145–52
    closed vs. open membership at, 176–78
    collective memory among, 196–97
    communion and, 144–45
    hymn book choice at, 187–88
    lifestyle expectations from, 204–5
    meeting focus of, 170–72
    move to Highweek School, 50–51, 53, 119–20, 165–66

new minister appointment at, 182–84
    records of, 12, 13–14, 15, 205n36
    renting to an external organization, 172–73, 191
    vocation at, 208–10
Newton Abbot: Its History and Development (Rhode), 14
Niebuhr, Richard, 69, 71
nonconformists, 39–40, 48–49, 63–64. *See also* Baptists
Nonconformity in Exeter 1650–1875 (Brockett), 15
Norberg-Schulz, Christian, 40–42, 44, 59
Norman Moon, 174–75
normative principle, 172
Novick, Peter, 195–96

obituaries, 91
Old Testament, 28
On Being the Church (Haymes et al.), 116–17
oral history, value of, 229–30
Order and Administration of a Baptist Church, The (Chick, Wood), 181
Orders and Prayers for Church Worship (Payne, Winward), 43, 116, 231
ordination, 112–17
organizational (family) systems, 206–8
Orthodox Crede, 162–63
outsiders, acceptable, 124–27, 143–44, 163–64, 221–22

paedobaptists, 147–48
Pannenberg, Wolfhart, 200
Particular Baptists
    Bovey Tracey Baptist Church and, 176
    communion and, 144
    confessions of faith and, 163
    early confessions of faith from, 117
    evangelical expression of, 160
    local vs. wider ministry of, 109–10
    open membership policy of, 176–77

Patterns and Prayers for Christian Worship (Payne, Winward), 43, 116
Payne, Ernest, 9, 110–11, 160, 162, 231
peace and purity model for humanity, 132
Perls, Fredrick, 22
Pike, E.L., 123–24
Postmodern Geographies: The Reassertion of Space in Critical Social Theory (Soja), 54
power
    authoritarian leadership, 122
    of church members vs. ministry, 117–19
    congregational governance and, 126–28
    dominating leadership of, 119–20
    language of leadership and, 121–22
Powers That Be: Theology for a New Millennium. When The Powers Fall, The (Wink), 2–3
Powers trilogy (Wink), 1–2, 61–62
practical theology, 16–17
Practices of Power: Revisiting the Principalities and Powers in the Pauline Letters (Moses), 9
pragmatism, 173, 179, 181, 183, 192
preach with a view events, 180–84
preaching, 179–84
priesthood, heavenly, 29
prophetic guild as angels, 25
prophets, community, 33–34
Proudlock, Beth, 52, 119
purity and peace model for humanity, 132

Quicke, Michael, 107, 158, 181, 182–83
Qumran community, 25, 29–30, 31, 35, 218–19

race and ethnicity, 70–74
Rackley, John, 124–25
Randall, Ian, 231
recruitment of new members, 90–91

Re-Emergence of Emergence, The (Gregersen), 197
regulative principle, 172
Re-Pitching the Tent (Giles), 48
repudiation, 55
Revelation, book of
    angels mentioned throughout, 26
    images of believers and angels in, 31
    integral worldview and, 20
    Jewish apocalyptic tradition and, 28
    letters to the seven churches in, 3–4, 5, 18
    specificity of seven churches addressed in, 34
    term for angel of the church in, 24
    transformation of the transcendent angel in, 219–20
Rhodes, A. J., 14, 39, 49
Romantic architecture, 42
Rowland, Christopher, 31
Runcorn, David, xi, 99, 216, 229–30
Rusling, G. W., 48, 49

Sabbath Shirot, 28–29, 30, 35, 229
sacrament, ordination and, 113–15
sacramental tradition of church construction, 43–44
sacredness, relationship with history and location, 55
sacrifices, 29
Samalavicius, Almantas, 40–41
Savage, Sara, 131–33, 141
scapegoats, 151, 221, 224–25, 226
Schwartz, Howard, 203–4
Scriptures, 101, 140, 179–80
Second London Confession, 110
secularism, move towards, 7, 17
self-understanding
    collective memory, 195–97
    emergence, 197–201
    organizational (family) systems, 206–8
    transference, 201–6
    Walter Wink on, 194–95
Sellers, Ian, 77
Septuagint, 24, 28

Short Confession of Faith (Smyth), 117
"A Short History of the Baptist Cause in Newton Abbot" (Gabb), 14, 175
singing. *See* hymn singing
Slater, Clayton, 64–66
Smith, Edward, 68
Smyth, John, 117, 185
social geography, 45–46, 48–51
Soja, Edward, 45, 54–55, 58
Something to Declare: A Study of the Declaration of Principle (Baptist Union of Great Britain), 103n8, 107
Songs of the Sabbath Sacrifice (Newsom), 28
South Street Baptist Church (Exeter)
    angel profile of, 227–28
    condition of records of, 13
    extent of historical records of, 12
    published history of, 14, 15
    secession of, 123–24
    vocation of, 211
spirit, embedded, 201
spiritualistic worldview, 19
Steinke, Peter, 132–33, 134–35, 206–7, 214, 223
subcultures and vocation, 211–12
substantive conflict, 131
suburbs, migration to, 67

technology, 89–90
temporal theism, 199–200
Test and Corporation Acts, 63
theological reflection, communal, 178–79
theological worldview, 19–20
theology, practical, 16–17
Theology in Stone (Kieckhefer), 43–44
This Hope Baptist Church, 226
Thomson, Ronald, 135, 138
Tilby, Angela, 8–9
Toward a Theology of Nature: Essays on Science and Faith (Pannenberg), 200
transference, 201–6, 214
transparency, 104–6, 119–20

Turner, Harold, 41, 42–43, 46–47, 54, 59
"Twenty Truths About Twenties" (Brierley), 88

Unmasking the Powers (Wink), 2, 3, 37
Upton Vale Baptist Church, 165–66

Viking raid, church grudge from, 194, 195, 196, 212–14
Violence and Nonviolence in South Africa (Wink), 2–3
vocation
    angels of, 11
    at Budleigh Salterton, 210–11
    congregational governance and, 127–28
    demographic attributes and, 97
    denominational rubric and, 191
    identity and, 214–15
    at Newton Abbot, 56–57, 153–54, 208–10
    paralysis of, 122–24
    restricted fulfillment of, 167
    at South Street in Exeter, 211
    subcultures and, 211–12
    Walter Wink on, 208–9
"Voices" (Gouldbourne), 222
voting, 135–36, 142–43

Walker, Michael, 144–45
War Scroll, The (Qumran community), 31
Ward, Matthew, 184, 187
Warren, Robert, 10–11, 221
Weber, Max, 68–69
Western Association, 174–75
Western culture, 37
When the Powers Fall: Reconciliation in the Healing of Nations (Wink), 2
White, B.R., 102, 176–77
White, Susan, 55, 59
Willimon, William, 130–32, 141–42
Wilson, Linda, 91

Wink, Walter
  on demographic profiles, 61, 97–98, 224–25
  on denominational rubrics, 156–57, 160
  on embedded corporate spirit, 195, 201, 202–3
  on interpersonal relations, 122, 130, 151, 206–7, 221–24
  life of, 1, 20–21, 53–54, 217–18
  on link between earth and heaven, 27, 28–29, 35–36
  on self-understanding, 194–95, 213–14
  on theological belief and practice, 157–58
  theory of interiority, 18–21
  use of term "Gestalt," 21–22
  views on angel of the church, 3–7, 37, 66, 220, 231–32
  works of, 1–3, 9–10, 217

Wise, David, 72–74, 97, 99
Woodward, James, 87–88
Worrall, B. G., 63, 67–68
worship
  hymn singing and, 184–88
  paradox in, 179
  practicalities of, 188–90
  pragmatism in, 173, 179, 181, 183
  preaching and, 179–84
Wright, Nigel, 136–37
Wright, Tom
  on church meetings, 107–9
  "Inclusive Representation," 115
  integral worldview and, 20
  on leadership, 118, 121
  on ordination, 112–13, 114

Zoroastrianism, 32–33

www.ingramcontent.com/pod-product-compliance
Lightning Source LLC
Chambersburg PA
CBHW062009220426
43662CB00010B/1280